THE U-BOAT PERIL

THE
U-BOAT PERIL
A FIGHT FOR SURVIVAL

BOB WHINNEY

CASSELL&CO

Cassell Military Paperbacks

Cassell & Co.
Wellington House, 125 Strand
London WC2R 0BB

First published by Blandford Press 1986
This Cassell Military Paperbacks edition 1998
Reprinted 2000

British Library Cataloguing-in-Publication Data
A catalogue record for this book is available from the British Library

ISBN 0-304-35132-6

Line drawings and maps by
Paul Miller

Printed and bound in Great Britain by
Cox & Wyman Ltd., Reading, Berks.

CONTENTS

FOREWORD

This book contains the best description of anti-submarine warfare which I have ever read. It provides a fascinating picture of the battle against U-boats and makes the actual process of detection and attack comprehensible to the layman.

The author was an anti-submarine warfare specialist and was remarkably successful in sinking U-boats. He was very determined and seemed to be able to disregard senior officers' orders when he thought that he was right without due retribution. He was certainly not a 'Yes man'. The description of U-boat hunts brings out clearly the need for team work between all concerned – indeed the need for team work among a Ship's Company is well known.

The story starts at the Royal Naval College, Dartmouth, about which he has many criticisms – it is well worth reading for that alone. The picture he gives of Gun Room life between the wars is interesting, but the best part of the early book is about the Invergordon Mutiny of 1931 during which the writer was a sub lieutenant who got much involved and was able to see what was going on. He is sharp in his criticism of the Captain and Commander of the *Rodney*. As a result of clashes with authority, he was put 'under report' and he must be one of the very few officers who have suffered such a disaster and who later rose to captain's rank.

In 1936, he specialised in anti-submarine warfare and gives a vivid description of this vital branch which was so neglected by the Royal Navy. A few officers and scientists succeeded in introducing efficient anti-submarine systems with remarkably little encouragement from the rest of the Navy.

The war found him flotilla A/S officer on the China station but the story of his ship's career is a sad one and she had to be paid off. Sea service came soon in the famous HMS *Cossack*, where we served together. I can commend his account of the ship's doings and especially his character study of the Captain, the famous Philip Vian.

On return from a very unpleasant fifteen months at Freetown as A/S officer, where he found himself often in disagreement with his Admiral, he was given his great ambition – command of a destroyer, HMS *Wanderer* – and the tempo of the book accelerates. The process of completing a refit and welding a ship's company together is well described. Life was never dull. Yet again, the author did not agree with all the senior officers, some of whom he criticises, but he found a kindred spirit in Commodore 'Shrimp' Simpson at Londonderry with whom he got on very well and who helped him out of some scrapes. It was good to read the praise of the base at 'Derry, as it was also to find Captain Gilbert Roberts' Tactical School so well appreciated.

The *Wanderer* had a varied life, and his vivid account of passing through a hurricane in the Arctic circle is a particular pleasure to read. During the invasion of Normandy, the *Wanderer* was senior officer of one of the A/S invasion groups. Here again, he gives a particularly graphic account of sinking a U-boat in the Channel.

Bob Whinney showed that a true expert in the calling could produce results. Shortly after leaving the *Wanderer*, he went to the Admiralty to analyse A/S actions and was – rather late – promoted to commander.

Vice Admiral Sir Peter Gretton, KCB, DSO AND TWO BARS, OBE, DSC.

AUTHOR'S NOTE

Winston Churchill wrote 'the only thing that ever frightened me during the War was the U-boat peril ...'

In 1939 the Royal Navy was unready to meet this peril. The brunt of the long, hard, bitter Battle of the Atlantic was borne by that independent command, the Western Approaches.

In action, those in command of convoy escort vessels were not inhibited by unrealistic, peacetime training. They had also to rely on the support of their ship's companies, most of whom had come straight from civilian life ashore. One brilliant radar operator, for instance, was a peacetime grocer.

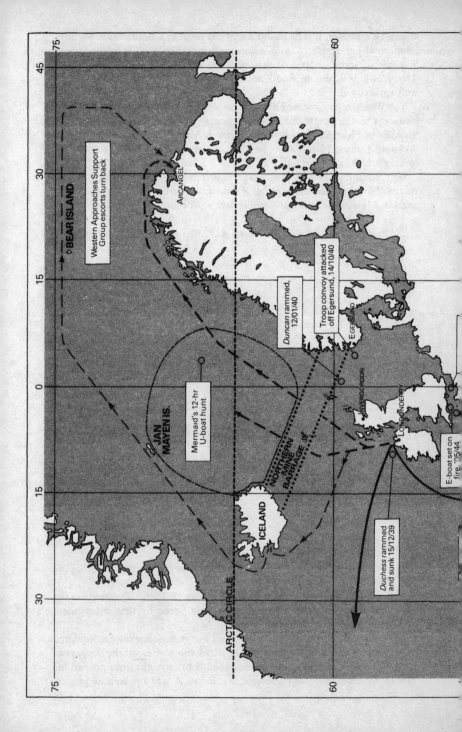

BEAR ISLAND

Western Approaches Support Group escorts turn back

ARCANGEL

Duncan rammed, 12/01/40

Troop convoy attacked off Egersund, 14/10/40

EGERSUND

INVERGORDON

Mermaid's 12-hr U-boat hunt

JAN MAYEN IS.

NORTHERN MINE BARRAGE

LONDONDERRY

ICELAND

ARCTIC CIRCLE

E-boat set on fire, 05/44

Duchess rammed and sunk 15/12/39

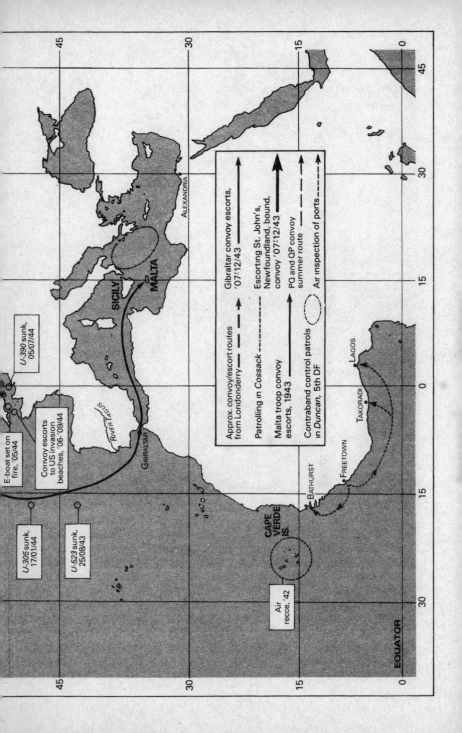

Approx. convoy/escort routes
from Londonderry ———

Gibraltar convoy escorts,
'07:12/43 ———

Patrolling in *Cossack* ---------

Escorting St. John's,
Newfoundland, bound,
convoy '07:12/43 ———

Malta troop convoy
escorts, 1943 ———

PQ and QP convoy
summer route ———

Contraband control patrols
in *Duncan*, 5th DF ⬭

Air inspection of ports - - -

U-390 sunk,
05/07/44

Convoy escorts to US invasion
beaches, '06-'09/44

E-boat set on
fire, 05/44

U-305 sunk,
17/01/44

U-523 sunk,
25/08/43

Air
recce, '42

SICILY

MALTA

ALEXANDRIA

GIBRALTAR

RIVER TAGUS

CAPE
VERDE
IS.

BATHURST

FREETOWN

LAGOS

TAKORADI

EQUATOR

1. NOT BY THE BOOK ALONE

Able Seaman Cartwright appeared, neat and smart in orthodox uniform. He stood discreetly back: not obsequious, this little man, but not prepared to be overlooked. He was there for a reason.

'Luncheon is served, sir,' he said.

There was the Officer of the Watch, holding on to the binnacle to steady himself against the roll of the ship, and myself wedged in the high chair in the centre of the bridge, the established throne of all destroyer COs – and Cartwright, obliged to hang on to a stanchion to keep his balance, waiting for his announcement to be given proper attention while the usual business went on. It was an amiably comic but entirely incongruous piece of routine to expect on the open, unprotected bridge of an escort destroyer in rough winter weather in the North Atlantic.

Reports were coming through to the Officer of the Watch – men changing over watches and 'tricks' – stints, usually an hour for helmsmen as for lookouts in the bridge wings, and a four-hour Watch for radar operators and guns' crews. But Cartwright waited.

The invariable smell came up from below, the same smell in every small ship in those days, rather like a sickly sort of beef stew with overstrong carrots and onions, not at all helpful to those feeling queasy. The true ingredients of the smell were more probably from the boiler room exhaust fans, cigarette smoke and wet clothing from the mess decks – and from the galley, the ever-stewing tea and whatever the cook on duty had going for the next meal. But Cartwright wanted an answer about the Captain's meal.

Cartwright was always dressed in the strictest uniform practicable, no woolly hats, no balaclavas for him, not even sea-boots unless the weather was really wet; just harbour uniform, sometimes with a duffle coat, always with his sailor's cap firmly and squarely on his head. Whether this funny, outspoken little Cockney thought his act was a joke or whether he saw himself as a post-war butler, I never decided. Sometimes he styled himself the Captain's Yeoman, sometimes as Captain's Attendant, sometimes even as the Valet. Anyway, there was a remarkable consistency about the act, whether we were hanging on against the roll of the ship or ducking the spray from a head sea; whether it was the Arctic or, more rarely, the Mediterranean, whether I was having a meal in peace in my sea cabin or a sandwich during a flap on the bridge.

He was getting impatient. 'Beg pardon, sir. Luncheon is getting cold. We are on a nice piece of hashed bully today.'

The ship *Wanderer*, built as a Fleet destroyer and launched way back in May 1919, was one of four ships normally employed on convoy escort work but at that time was working in a support group, a formation normally used to back up the escort of a convoy which was under threat of attack by U-boats. The Americans called these formations Hunter-Killer groups with an optimism which was not always justified. On this occasion, we were, unusually, carrying out a patrol intended to intercept an enemy blockade runner. The chances of action looked very remote and, if anything did occur, there would be plenty of warning by way of a long-range radar contact – or so I thought. Furthermore, the ship was not, so far as I could estimate, on any route likely to be taken by a U-boat on its way to or from war patrol.

'Going down to my sea cabin now,' I said to the Officer of the Watch, thin, pale, intense Sub Lieutenant Kidd, 'I've got a stinking cold and won't come up to the bridge till later.'

'Nothing likely to happen, sir?'

'No. But there's a gale warning. If the wind freshens much more, let me know.'

After lunch, I read a thriller, was soon asleep and dreaming very pleasantly of the past, miles from the sea and ships. Then, on the bridge directly overhead, the scraping noises of faster-moving boots, muffled reports on the bridge voicepipes and brief, unusual instructions.

'Captain, sir,' from Kidd, calling down the voicepipe, 'asdic contact bearing 060 degrees, range 1200 yards.'

Fully awake now, I could hear the asdic bridge loud-speaker from my bunk. 'Sounds to me like fish from here,' I said.

'No, sir,' – firmly – 'it's not only fish. There's another echo there as well.'

I got up to the bridge quickly. The small fry on the surface indicated the presence of fish shoals all too clearly. There were fish in plenty all right. Listening carefully to the loud-speaker, the wailing 'ping' of the asdic beam going out every three seconds, the fish echoes were audible – but there was something else.

At the back of the bridge, and on the same level, was the asdic cabinet, a low, wood-built compartment painted grey, in which three men could sit cramped at a bench facing their anti-submarine instruments. This was Kidd's province. He and the asdic team had trained very hard since the beginning of the commission; and he was the Anti-Submarine Control Officer. His right-hand man was Leading Seaman Cocks, the Higher Submarine Detector, who had joined the Royal Naval Volunteer Reserve before the war and was, like Kidd himself, from infinite practice, an excellent operator.

'Send for Cocks,' I said to Kidd, 'and go into the asdic cabinet yourself. Let me know what you think of it. I'll look after the ship for a few minutes.'

'Cocks is here now. Definitely something there, sir, but operating conditions are very chancy.'

'Come out and take over the ship. I'll come into the cabinet myself.'

In the cabinet could be seen the chemical range recorder on which revolved the iodised paper which recorded a visual display of each pulse of asdic transmission. This appeared as a long, thin, black horizontal line when the asdic conditions were good; but these were not good conditions. They were very bad. Some transmissions were not going out because the ship was pitching and banging in aerated water. The audible ping was stifled and the visual recorder lines showed faint and indistinct. Some went out properly but contacted only fish and the echo back was blurred. But about every fifth – sometimes tenth – transmission would go out and show both the fish and, from the same transmission, a firm, black echo mark, concurrently giving a crisp metallic noise in the headphones. This meant that the beam had hit something solid. It could well be a U-boat; just possibly it was a whale. I was nearly sure what I thought.

'What do you think, Cocks?'

'U-boat, sir. But hard to hold in contact.'

'Kidd, agree?'

Yes, he did.

Then, turning to the Leading Signalman on watch and waving a hand at a frigate on the horizon: 'Call up the senior officer and make "Am investigating submarine contact."'

The shutters of the ten-inch signal projector in the wings of the bridge clattered as the signal went out and the First Lieutenant, hearing there was something up, appeared.

'Number One, it's a U-boat all right, and it's going to be a very chancy one,' I said. 'We'd better go to action stations. Get some ready-use ammo up, then close the magazines. All watertight doors to remain closed. Nothing to be opened without your personal permission. Tell the Chief to tell his braves in the engine room and boiler rooms.'

And then, to the Officer of the Watch: 'Reduce speed to eight knots. We don't want to do a *Hurricane*.'

It was only a matter of a few days before this that HMS *Hurricane*, the Senior Officer's ship of our group at that time, had unexpectedly come upon two U-boats. *Wanderer* was in harbour undergoing repairs but *Hurricane* was, the story went, doing twenty knots and one U-boat fired a short-range, defensive torpedo, code-named the Gnat. This weapon was designed to home on to the propellers of any attacking ship whenever that ship was doing more than eight knots and less than twenty-five. With her propellers blown off, *Hurricane* was entirely vulnerable. The U-boat then sank her with a straight-running torpedo.

The orders were clear enough; in such a situation, escort ships were to attack with the ahead bomb-throwing mortar, the Hedgehog. I disliked this weapon and distrusted it. The ammunition used on a previous occasion had been most unreliable. Yet, we should disregard neither the order to use the weapon nor the order to proceed at slow speed in the presence of a U-boat. And anyway, attacking at slow speed with depth-charges would result in the charges detonating too close to the ship, which would cause *Wanderer* serious damage. I called up the Action Plot (the Ops Room) directly below the bridge.

'Anything from the asdic cabinet to give course and speed for the target yet?'

'Yes, sir. Not a good plot but estimate the course is 105 degrees, speed two knots.'

'Asdic cabinet. We can't hang around in these conditions. Going in to attack with Hedgehog. Speed eight knots.'

Asdic: 'Lost contact – contact regained – bad quenching.'

This meant the asdic beam was being masked, attenuated, by the aeration of the rough water. Calm self-control; no good talking sharply to anyone. They were very good operators, working under difficult conditions.

'Kidd, fire the Hedgehog, even if you think the attack's not accurate.'

Asdic: 'Bearing 120 degrees. Range 1,000 yards.'

'Well done.'

Asdic: 'Quenching again – keep losing it – bearing 130 degrees. Range 800 yards – lost contact – got it again – range 500 yards – 400 – 300.' Kidd: 'Stand by – Fire.'

The Hedgehog bombs sailed into the air to splash spectacularly into the sea in an oval pattern ahead of the ship. Then we waited seconds. Will there be the explosion caused by one or more bombs hitting? Will there be the far bigger explosion of the remainder of the bombs counter-mining as they should?

Asdic: 'Possible underwater explosion.'

'What do you mean "possible underwater explosion"?'

'Well, sir, one bomb might have gone off but there was bad quenching. Hard to be sure. Not the whole pattern, though.'

Bloody useless weapon. Theory was no damn good.

The Senior Officer's ship had now arrived on the scene and obtained a contact.

'She's not in contact with the same contact as ours,' reported the Plot.

From the Officer of the Watch: 'Senior Officer's ship attacked and says it was fish.'

'Well, that makes sure there aren't two U-boats.'

This was where Bower, the Navigator plotting the positions of surface ships from radar information and the underwater contacts from the asdics, came in.

'Plot. Pass to the Senior Officer the range and bearing of the contact from him and tell him the course he should steer for it.'

Again, he attacked some other contact – probably fish. No advice from *Wanderer* could put him right.

We had been at it from about 1.30 pm. About 4 pm, with the wind increasing, came the report from the Yeoman of Signals: 'Signal from the Senior Officer, sir. "There is no U-boat there. Leave the area and proceed in execution of previous orders."'

He was telling us to go back to the anti-blockade runner patrol, soon due to end anyway. By now I knew beyond doubt that we were in contact with a U-boat. Despite the difficult conditions, despite the worsening weather and the oncoming darkness, it seemed there was a fifty-fifty chance of sinking this U-boat. I did not know this Senior Officer or anything about him – my regular Senior Officer had just had his ship, *Hurricane*, sunk under him. There had been no discussion about this instruction to leave the area, just a direct order from a ship which, despite our help, had been unable to pick up the good, if difficult contact. Argument was, under such circumstances, fatuous. Outright unequivocal refusal of the order seemed to be the right course.

'Reply,' I said to the leading signalman 'No. I will remain and attack U-boat.'

The Senior Officer's ship and the two other ships then abandoned their anti-blockade patrol and proceeded to Londonderry, leaving us to it. This was nothing to worry about. It was difficult enough on our own.

The gale had now developed. It was blowing Force eight and the sea was rising. There were, thank goodness, no more fish echoes but the asdic operating conditions were now so difficult that the prospects of doing a sufficiently accurate attack on the U-boat were receding. We might even lose contact permanently, and then I was going to look pretty silly! Also, with the rising sea, it was now dangerous for men to go from forward to aft and vice versa; the 'iron deck' – the long totally exposed area amidships – was washing down dangerously when the ship was on most courses. Men could easily be swept over the side. At the best, some men were getting soaked needlessly at their action stations. I called a brief conference in the Plot.

'Kidd, it's no good trying to operate the asdics heading into the sea. There's too much quenching. And it's no good operating when the target's on the beam because we're rolling too much. We'll try to attack going down sea.'

Turning to the First Lieutenant, I said: 'Number One, tell the guns' crews to take shelter but not to go below. Post sentries of reliable Petty Officers at either end of the iron deck to see that no one goes forward or aft except when the ship is on a safe course. The Hedgehog's crew is to take shelter, too, until we are on a firing course and it's safe for them to nip on to the forecastle. The depth charge crews are to take shelter. With the sea astern, we might get pooped going at such a slow speed and I don't want anyone washed over the side.'

Then in we went to make a Hedgehog attack at eight knots. Slowly, the ranges came down, 1,200 yards, 1,000 yards ...

From myself: 'Officer of the Watch, course 045.'

'Aye, aye sir, 045.'

Myself again down the wheel-house voicepipe: 'Watch your course Cox'n. I know it's tricky.'

'Can't keep exactly accurate course, Sir, in this sea. Could we go a bit faster?', from the Coxwain at the wheel.

'No, Coxwain, we cannot. Do your best.'

'Range 600 – 500 – lost contact,' from the asdics.

'Kidd, fire by estimate.'

'Stand by,' from Kidd. 'Fire.'

And then we wait. There was no report of an underwater explosion.

'She's gone deep,' said Kidd: calm, no exasperation, I noted.

Now, it was pitch dark and the sea had increased. I was feeling quite unusually exhausted and for the only time in the war asked for a drink on the bridge, a weak whisky and soda. There remained only one option, to work up-sea of the U-boat and come back to attack again with the sea astern, because down-sea was the only direction in which the asdic beam could operate effectively. Furthermore, in order to be able to steer a steady course and avoid the danger of being pooped, it meant an increase to fifteen knots, and that ruled out the Hedgehog mortar which could only be fired at slow speeds. The chances of the U-boat getting off a Gnat torpedo in that weather and of a Gnat homing on to our propellers at the higher and dangerous speed, I persuaded myself, were lessened. At the faster speed we should be obliged to do a depth charge attack; but, again, as the U-boat was deep, we should be doing the last sixty seconds or so of the attack blind, or rather deaf, with the asdic beam going over the top of the target, so the best chances lay in firing the maximum number of depth charges, rather than the orthodox pattern of ten.

'Plot, give me the course to get 1,500 yards up sea of the target,' I said. And then, to Kidd, 'We shall be going in at fifteen knots, down sea, to fire a depth charge barrage. Charges set deep.'

I repeated this instruction by telephone to Mr Franklin, in charge of the depth charges aft, adding, 'Do your best to get twenty charges off and to reload the throwers as we have done before, but without too much risk of losing a man overboard.'

The Plot got the ship into position and, once more, an attack was started; this time at fifteen knots. The ship was pitching slightly, rolling only a little.

'That's excellent, Coxwain. Keep it going.'

'Yes, Sir, she's nice and steady at this speed.'

'Range 1,000 yards – 800 – 600 – contact fading – lost contact,' from the asdics.

We must wait long seconds for the order to fire, to start the barrage – the barrage of depth charges.

'Fire,' from Kidd, and he pressed the Fire buzzer. Again, we must wait while the charges sink – a seemingly endless half minute this time – but at least no man overboard! Then, in the darkness, the heavy, shuddering thumping explosions started.

I let the ship run on the same course. It gave the best chance of regaining contact with the target.

'Contact regained, bearing 275, it's ...'

'Breaking-up noises,' interrupted Kidd.

'Yes,' from Cocks, 'breaking-up noises.'

'Certain?' I said, 'Bloody clever if you're right.'

'Yes, sir. Quite. Come and listen on the headphones.'

Sure enough, on the asdic cabinet headphones there were the small explosions, the creaking and grinding of metal. Not pleasant, perhaps, but it was what we had spent six very tense, tiring hours trying to do. We searched the area for survivors or any wreckage but found nothing. If anyone had managed to surface from the submarine at that depth, they would not have been able to live long in the full gale and very rough sea which was by then running.

'Well done,' I said to the asdic cabinet and, to Frost, the Officer of the Watch, 'Pity we have nothing to show for it.'

My immediate feeling was one of profound relief. It was all over. There was no more to be done. I had not enjoyed any of it much and in the last somewhat hazardous, very difficult attack I was apprehensive. We were breaking the rules by steaming at a dangerous speed, namely fifteen knots, which might attract the Gnat homing torpedo from a known U-boat. We were breaking the rules by attacking with depth charges while the orders were that the Hedgehog mortar should be used. There was a danger of losing a man overboard, especially from the depth charge crew in such foul weather and while using an unorthodox barrage attack. But worst of all was the threat of failure. That would land me profoundly in the soup for failing to carry out the Senior Officer's orders: no U-boat: no mitigating circumstances.

As to the ship's company, they were tired, they were cold and many of them were wet through. Most had been kept inactive at, or near, their action stations for some six hours, partly in case they should be needed but, also, to ensure that no one could get on the mess decks and open any watertight doors (the flooding and near-loss of *Duncan* while I was serving aboard her a few years before still remained vivid). There was some personal satisfaction that we had apparently sunk a U-boat but who was going to believe that? There was nothing to show for it! It was only quite certain that none of us, whatever we thought, considered the fact that a number of Germans who had wives, children and sweethearts had been slain. Our concern was for our own families and friends ashore. There was, in those days, not without good reason, much anxiety about air raids during blitzes and worry about the insufficiency of food. For my part, there was Jimmy, my wife, who lived in Dorset and had certain problems. My mother too – bombed out of her London flat and moved to another off Sloane Street was a constant worry. And there was Joan, a friend from her childhood, living at the top of a block of Kensington flats and driving a Red Cross ambulance throughout the London blitzes.

When they had recovered, were warm and fed and had talked to the asdic ratings on the mess decks, the Ship's Company were cocky enough. They reckoned that they had definitely sunk another U-boat and they were delighted. I, on the other hand, had misgivings. If the Senior Officer reported me and, particularly if it were concluded that there was no proof of a U-boat's presence, I could be in serious trouble. That could mean having my command taken away and an end to prospects of further promotion. After some thought, I decided to put in the routine report of attacking a submarine contact, making no mention of disobeying the Senior Officer's orders, no specific mention of breaking the rules by attacking at a dangerous speed and no stress of the fact that the Senior Officer's ship had never attacked the U-boat but only fish shoals. Then it was a matter of waiting.

The first thing that happened was that *Wanderer* was moved to another escort group. This seemed, at the time, ominous. The next thing was that the Admiralty, on receiving my report, 'through the usual channels', pronounced that a U-boat had been 'probably slightly damaged'. This assessment was, I was convinced, nonsense; but it did mean that the Admiralty confirmed that there was a U-boat there. That justified my having told the Senior Officer that, in the face of his orders to the contrary, I was remaining to attack. At a guess, what actually happened was that the Senior Officer later concluded that he was wrong, under the circumstances, to leave *Wanderer* alone and unsupported and so he kept quiet about it. But, continuing to guess, the Commodore, Western Approaches heard the whole story on the grapevine and decided to do nothing about it, unless it was brought, officially, to his notice, and that was not untypical of that shrewd boss of the Londonderry Escort Force. Thus, no one was bowled out breaking any rules. There was no infringement of the Eleventh Commandment and, a few days later, it was confirmed by the Admiralty that the U-boat had been sunk.

Much later still, I learned that the enemy submarine sunk was *U-305*, a Type VIIC, one of the mass-produced U-boats, which some days previously had sunk the frigate HMS *Tweed* and might have survived to sink more of our war and merchant ships. Kapitänleutnant Bahr, holder of the Iron Cross 1st and 2nd Class, had been awarded the Deutsche Kreuz in Gold only two days before his death.

Looking back, after the action, two things struck me. The first was that it was another of those series of events which showed how close team work between all officers and all men was essential to success, and in a way never envisaged before the war. The second thing that struck me, especially in the final attack, was the parallel with riding in a point-to-point race. Once committed, it was exciting, rousing – alarming as when the horse is doing it all and the rider hopes he will not make a mistake, come unstuck and fall off – perhaps through sheer exhaustion.

2. INTO THE GUNROOM

In the days before World War Two, the Royal Naval College Dartmouth produced nearly all those officers who would later be qualified to command HM ships at sea. They joined as small boys of thirteen and a half years of age, in uniform, as young officers and gentlemen. They had naval pensioner servants, who called them 'Sir', who made their beds, cleaned their shoes, sent the laundry to the wash. Conversely, they were in for four years' sojourn of being chased around in an atmosphere of rigid (and in my day, uninspired) discipline which towards the latter months left many of them bloody-minded.

They came, these young gentlemen, from fee-paying schools and were the sons of gentry, of professional men and, in some cases, of the aristocracy. Very probably Queen Victoria boosted recruiting for Dartmouth when she put the royal children into sailor suits, an example followed by humbler parents whose thoughts thence led to the navy as a career for their sons. In any event, the competition, the passing of an entrance exam, an interview and, of course, a medical were severe: forty-eight were taken out of some two hundred applicants in my case. I passed in about twelfth but had the advantage of a prep school where the alternative to working hard was a rare, effective, never-resented walloping on the backside.

Dartmouth was in effect a public school run by a Captain, Royal Navy, with a Naval staff and a headmaster with a civilian teaching staff. The fees were reduced for the sons of serving officers. This had a particular attraction for my family as my father was then serving as a major in the Oxford and Bucks Light Infantry. A dashing fellow my father, a first class cricketer, he was disapproved of by his straight-laced father, a wealthy City of London business-man who commanded a battalion of volunteers and lived in minor state north of Regents Park and who had had a mysterious German mother and was (improbably?) said to have been the illegitimate son of a duke (the Duke of Wellington to those who back outsiders).

To avoid simplicity, my father – no intellectual – married the bright and beautiful daughter of an idle Irish landowner, a master of foxhounds, who thought seriously only of horses. My parents had little in common except for the desire to spend money immediately – if not before – they could lay hands on it. They were legally separated.

Back to Dartmouth: The Naval College was a vast, shiny, spotless place with highly polished floors throughout and the front of the buildings, seen from the outside, was impressive and elegant, built in red brick with white facings – again spotless with no sign of weathering permitted.

When we new cadets first arrived we fell under the charge of a young man called Casement, our Term Cadet Captain, that was to say, senior prefect. Wasting no time, Casement told us we would be called the Greynvile Term and would remain so for the whole of our time until we left. Then he told us of a serious fact of life called 'guff'. It was, we were told with severity, guff to speak to anyone in a Term senior unless they spoke first. Then, each Term had its own Gun Room, or common room, and no cadet might enter the Gun Room of any other Term. In addition, it was forbidden to walk past the Gun Room of any Term senior to one's own – one had to double without speaking. Infringement of the guff rules meant three cuts with the cane. Then there were guff rules attached to dress: no hands in pockets, for instance; not difficult as there were no pockets in our monkey jackets (the double-breasted uniform working coat), nor in the white flannel trousers we wore in working hours, nor in the blue trousers we wore after tea.

In the evening, the junior college, followed by the senior college, attended prayers on the quarter deck, which was the assembly hall, and *sanctum sanctorum* of the college. Immediately afterwards, the Terms were doubled away and we had three minutes from reaching our dormitories to being in bed with our clothes folded and displayed in the top of and on the horizontal lid of our sea chests in an entirely precise manner. In the middle of the three minutes, a bell went – clang – and, with it, the order 'Say your prayers'. We all flopped to our knees at our bedsides, prayed silently or not at all, then – clang again – we stopped praying (or not) and got on with laying our clothes and getting into bed. A shirt folded with a button undone or a sock facing the wrong way, and the Cadet Captain made a tick in his notebook. Three ticks against anyone's name meant three cuts with the cane. Every night, after lights out, the defaulters were called from their beds in alphabetical order and, one by one, to the noisy swish of the cane, dealt with. No one, except, of course the victim, took this too seriously. In the college swimming bath, it was a matter of general interest to see which cadets had red and blue backsides. The pretty wife of one of the very senior officers used to come to watch the junior cadets bathing – bruises and all!

Serious offences, such as being found in possession of cigarettes or photographs of ladies without all their clothes on were awarded 'official cuts'. The offender was then held down over a box-horse in the gym while a Petty Officer performed the execution of six cuts.

There were ludicrous paradoxes about such treatment, severe even compared with the public schools of that day. We were supposed to be officers! The Petty Officers and pensioners always called us boys 'sir'! As a lesser paradox, the lower half of our sea chests was never looked at. I was, unlike most, never caught out over the layout of clothes, yet was a very untidy boy and remained a very untidy man. Those few, say twenty-five per cent, who were successful and either became Cadet Captains or played rugger for the first XV – or both – might not agree with me but I thought the system was badly at fault in that, as we reached the top of the college, we had no more responsibility than the day we joined. This compared very unfavourably with the Royal Military College at Sandhurst. Again, I criticised the teaching of the technical subjects, such as seamanship, navigation and engineering. It was uninspiring and uninspired. Against this, the civilian schoolmasters taught well and included some appealing characters; most of us who knew them would never forget them.

What was really wrong with Dartmouth then? Well, my answer is cynical. The jobs of captain in command of the college and of his second-in-command, the commander, were 'promotion jobs'; and, in those days, the incumbent in a promotion job had only to do the same as his predecessor had done and he could hardly fail to be promoted. Further, these same captains and commanders had, while at Dartmouth or in HMS *Britannia* which had preceded it, usually themselves been Cadet Captains. What was good enough for them ... The requirement was to keep the sausage machine going. The one danger to the 'management' was a case of buggery. For obvious reasons, buggery was taken very seriously in the Navy and a case could well get to the ears of the Commander-in-Chief, Plymouth! In my time, I do not think there were any such cases, but the preventative rules were so strict that I even had to seek permission to speak to my younger brother! Very critical of Dartmouth, I cannot pretend that I was among the more successful cadets of my Term, although I played squash for the college and had minor boxing successes. I was lazy and had several bouts of sickness which, inevitably, for a time affected my work. Well after I had left the college, officers of a high calibre who came to serve there made some worthwhile and stimulating changes.

One good memory of the RNC was, however, of the Term Officer who looked after us when we first joined. Lieutenant Commander David Simson was a bachelor. A Scottish trial rugger cap, he was a cheerful, red-haired driver but friendly and kindly, a man to inspire great liking. After leaving Dartmouth as a Term Officer, Simson was promoted to commander and then to captain. In the early days of World War Two, he took his destroyer into Boulogne to help evacuate the army, then in retreat prior to Dunkirk. It was a hot day and the ship was lying alongside a jetty firing at German tanks up the road. Simson, not untypically, and despite the advice of his officers, was on the bridge, coat off, in his white shirtsleeves; he was an easy target for the German sniper who got him. In different ways, some of us modelled ourselves on David Simson. The pity was that he looked after us when we arrived, as opposed to when we were finishing at Dartmouth.

Right at the end of my time at the college, when the zest for the navy should have been at its peak, I and certainly other Greynviles were thoroughly fed up. I tried to get my father to have me removed but that was no good. It would have meant paying an indemnity, so I tried to transfer to the Royal Marines; no good again.

However, there were others whom the Royal Naval College suited less. Among the better-known misfits was Guy Burgess of the ill-fated spying firm of Burgess, Maclean and Partners. He was, too, for a time at my prep school, Eastmans, a little boy of no account though a good swimmer. According to my friends, at the beginning of one term at Dartmouth, Burgess just did not reappear. He had been withdrawn and gone to Eton, thence to Cambridge and the Foreign Office. The rest of his story is only too well known.

Another such from my own Term who was quietly oozed out as unsuitable managed to get into the Royal Military College Sandhurst – and even received some preferment there; thereafter he joined a reputable Scottish regiment. Within a remarkably short time he was imprisoned in the Tower of London prior to trial by court martial and conviction for elementary spying. As the result of his flouncing around the battlements in a kilt for the benefit of press photographers, he became known as 'the Prisoner in the Tower'. His name was Baillie-Stuart.

Not long before leaving the college we were told that the lowest form of life at sea was a 'snotty', the nickname for a midshipman, and that a cadet was thus even lower in the scale of humanity. But it was a thrill to us six cadets running up the port gangway ladder in best dress – round jacket (bum-freezer) and dirk – to join the battleship *Resolution* at Malta. 'Come aboard to join, sir': that was the standard report we all had to make to the Officer of the Watch.

It took little time to confirm that we newly joined cadets were a truly low form of life. We were soon in trouble: it was all too frequently six very painful cuts with the cane from the sub lieutenant who ruled the Gun Room. To start with, life was constant confusion, fear and bewilderment.

For the cadet, the offences in the main resulted from a genuine lack of understanding. But, to these offences had to be added those for which a midshipman might 'cop it', such as missing a boat back to his ship when returning from shore leave, or forgetting to call a Ward Room officer for his Watch. I remember one case of a senior midshipman aged twenty-one getting six cuts for exceeding his wine bill of fifteen shillings a month. That there was a degree of sadism in some ships was beyond doubt. On the other hand, those were the days in which the young were treated rough. The Law Courts would prescribe the birch for the young, the cat o' nine tails and, of course, capital punishment for anyone over the age of seventeen. The law and discipline were effectively imposed by fear. Times have changed.

At that time, 1926–1929, and not for the only time, the Navy was having an economy drive. In order to save fuel, sea time was reduced so we usually worked to a harbour routine. Midshipmen and cadets alike. It was strenuous. At 6.30 am, a Petty Officer, Physical Training Instructor, exercised us all on the quarter deck for half an hour, in among the sailors who were scrubbing decks, or a Petty Officer Gunner's Mate would take us for rifle drill on the forecastle. And then came a four-course breakfast.

At 9 am came Divisions, the daily parade on the quarter deck with prayers, and that was followed up by technical instruction in gunnery, torpedo, navigation or, fortunately as appears later, ship construction, including pumping and flooding of compartments. Also, it should be said, periodically we had lectures from the Assistant Fleet Wireless Officer,

Lieutenant Lord Louis Mountbatten. All I could remember was his quip that genius was ninety per cent perspiration and ten per cent inspiration and some juggling with gin bottles to illustrate a technical point which I never understood. Lunch was another vast meal and then we went back to instruction. After tea, again not negligible, there were ship duties: Midshipman of the Watch, or understudy, which was every third day. For some, there was charge of a picket boat, a duty which came to those concerned every other day. Any of the young gentlemen, as we were sometimes called, not required for duty (provided their leave had not been stopped) could go ashore! Like most others, I played games or went for a long run on my days off.

The really active bullying of the younger members of the Gun Room was on the verge of disappearing then, but, I thought, a very definite atmosphere of fear existed among all the older and senior Ward Room officers in the ship; a fear of responsibility, of doing the wrong thing and of making a mistake. This arose from the 'Geddes Axe' of 1921, an economy measure which caused a number of lieutenants and lieutenant commanders to be discharged from the navy without warning. The consequences of the Geddes Axe affected most ships of the Fleet to varying extents for some years to come. It was not unknown, when the need arose, for the more senior officers to shift blame downwards so that it landed on some unhappy Midshipman.

Life in the *Reso'*, as she was called, was not particularly pleasant but became more so with the knowledge and understanding of how to handle situations as they arose. At the end of 1926, the ship went home to pay off. We all left her and, on 1 January 1927, proudly put up our white Midshipman's lapel patches. We were also given some leave. I went off to Germany, near Wiesbaden, to join my father and to have more excellent shooting. He told me that not long before, he had met and made particular friends with Captain Jack Tovey, Royal Navy, while they were doing the Naval Senior Officers' War Course together. Tovey, who became Admiral of the Fleet Lord Tovey and finished his career as Commander-in-Chief, The Nore, reappears later in my story.

Early in 1927, nearly all of us from *Resolution*'s Gun Room transferred to another battleship of the same class, HMS *Royal Sovereign*, which ship, through the surprising wit of a civil servant, had been given the motto *Pro gloria quid* (the golden sovereign of that day being known as a quid). Captain W.M. James had been appointed in command; then a red faced, stocky man with receding curly hair, he was known as 'Bubbles' because, as a little boy, he had sat as a model for the artist Millais' picture which was subsequently used as the advertisement for Pears' soap. Bubbles had an initially deceptive manner: often an expression of pained surprise and vagueness. In fact, he was very much switched on, had an excellent practical brain and was a Captain for whom officers and men worked well, happily and without fear. There was a romantic touch to the life of 'Bubbles' in that he had married the daughter of Millais.

In those days of national economy, the conservation of oil and less sea time there was a weekly harbour exercise known as General Drill, universally loathed by all participants. Amid the invariable confusion, Bubbles would walk round to watch and, in his detached way, would offer occasional advice – no shouting, no swearing from him. With him around, the results were always better.

In fact, I did not always do too well with Bubbles. Once, when playing racquets to make up a four, I hit him slap in the back of his not too slim neck with the small, white and hard, wood-cored ball. Painful it must have been; I was not asked to play again.

Nearly all my time, for choice, I ran a picket boat on the day-on day-off basis, harder work than being Midshipman of the Watch and thus not sought after by all; but I had a long and very happy co-operation with the coxwain of my boat, Petty Officer Holmes. So long as the boat was manned quickly when wanted, looked smart and smashed nothing, no one worried us.

My picket boat had a dramatic time when, in June 1927, the ship was lying off Port Said as guardship and the battle cruiser *Renown* came through the Suez Canal with HRH the Duke and Duchess of York (later the King and Queen) on board. I had to take their cousins Commander the Marquess of Milford Haven and then his brother Lieutenant Lord Louis Mountbatten off to *Renown* as she went through. The Duchess (now the Queen Mother) was sitting on the wooden rail and nearly overbalanced. Following in my boat astern of the battle cruiser, for a moment I thought my chance had come!

Interesting in the light of today's navy, when a picket boat went in to fetch officers from ashore it always had to leave at a specified time and the Midshipman in charge had to ask the senior officer in the boat for permission to leave. The 'senior officer' in this and in other similar cases was the senior Executive Officer. Thus, there might be commanders of the Engineer or Paymaster Branches in the boat but, if there were, say, a lieutenant or even a senior midshipman of the Executive Branch present, it would be he who would give the order for the boat to leave.

For a rather smug, very keen young man with a keep-fit complex, a midshipman's time in the Mediterranean, mostly spent at Malta, was very enjoyable, especially that part in the *Royal Sovereign*. There was every kind of game to play and the Gunnery Officer, Lieutenant Commander P.L. Vian — a quiet, efficient and (you will later be surprised to read) then a kindly if serious officer – taught me to hit a polo ball. Incidentally, six of the ten Australian midshipmen that we had in *Royal Sovereign* plus one 'Pommie' – the author – made up the battleship's water polo team.

Polo and gunnery were very much the 'in' subjects of the day. The Commander in Chief, Admiral Sir Roger Keyes, an officer of great dash who had made his name in the raid on Zeebrugge in World War One, considered polo good training for war and, to set an example, played himself. Thus, all officers with any pretence to riding and the cash to spare played polo. After two years in the job, the C in C was relieved by Admiral Sir Frederick Field who was not a polo player. He was a conjurer, a member

of the Magic Circle, no less. At the time of the change-over, an advertisement appeared in the local Malta paper which read: 'Any officer willing to exchange a reliable box of conjuring tricks for two polo ponies, apply to Lieut. Comdr. Blank'.

Promotionitis was definitely a universal and distressing complaint, and small wonder. Two out of three lieutenant commanders were being superannuated aged about 38, never to be promoted and to be chucked out at 45 with a, then, very small pension. Lieutenant Commander Blank could afford to be funny. He had had it.

In the early days of 1929, my time as a midshipman was drawing to an end. I had been an assiduous, very conscientious young man whose 'flimsies' – synopsis of confidential reports – were well above average; who had kept clear of all trouble since cadet's time and who was essentially ambitious. My target then was to become a four-stripe captain, to command a destroyer flotilla, then a battleship and to retire as a rear admiral. In those days, everyone was given a step-up in rank on retirement, so that a captain became a rear admiral – but without the step-up in pension! Only after a guest night and much wine, did I silently consider the chances of climbing higher.

A first and very important step was to get awarded a first class certificate in the seamanship exam which came at the end of a midshipman's time. We were told in advance that the examining Board of a captain and two commanders were only going to give one first class among the five of us – and I was determined to get it. When it was announced that another midshipman had, by the smallest margin, beaten me to it, I did not believe it – and, furthermore, was right. The wrong system had been used to add up the marks, for the marks for technical subjects, not related to seamanship, had been chucked in. The officer in charge of midshipmen admitted it and asked me not to make a fuss. If I did, he said no one might get a 'first'. Foolishly, angrily, I backed down. Petty? Trifling? No. Certainly not. A 'One' in Seamanship really counted.

After the exam, all of us shipped, with great pride, a single gold stripe instead of our white lapel patches and, after leave, off we went to the Royal Naval College, Greenwich, 'the most stately procession of buildings we possess'.

The course at Greenwich was intended to polish and finish our education. It was an interesting syllabus but we could have benefited from greater personal supervision and personal contact with the professors who taught us. As it was, the general approach was to treat it solely as a rollicking form of emancipation, with a car costing ten pounds and an evening tail coat.

Having served three years abroad, I started to make new friends outside naval circles – friends who directly and indirectly affected my professional and personal outlook for some years to come. They included Joan, then a fourteen-year-old schoolgirl, whose mother and mine were friends and whose father and mine had played cricket together.

3. RODNEY – THE OUTBREAK OF MUTINY

Each of us, Sub Lieutenants aged about twenty-one, in a dark plain clothes suit, white starched collar, black shoes and bowler hat, reported to the Second Sea Lord's Office in the Admiralty building to ask for an appointment to a sea-going ship as soon as our technical courses were completed. The need was to get to sea to qualify for a Watchkeeping Certificate to establish ability to take charge of the Watch on the bridge of a ship at sea. This was the essential preliminary to getting promoted to lieutenant. What I had in mind was an appointment to a cruiser on the East Indies Station where there was a comparatively small fleet; more important, where I hoped to get cheap, if not free, polo from my uncle who was Starter to the Calcutta Race Club. I expected to be interviewed by a Lieutenant Commander or, at best – no, at worst – a Commander.

But I was ushered into the office of the Assistant to the Second Sea Lord, Captain Jack Tovey, my father's old friend, a stocky little man with sharp, firm, lively features in the severe, formal plain clothes all officers wore in London.

'Where would you like to go?' he asked pleasantly from his deck.

'To the East Indies, please Sir,' I said.

Sternly and looking astonished: 'Why?'

'To get experience in a cruiser and,' I foolishly added, 'because of the polo, Sir.'

Quite sharply Tovey said: 'You will go to *Rodney* where the Captain, Captain Cunningham, is a personal friend of mine.'

This was to prove remarkably bad news.

Rodney and *Nelson*, to which latter ship my brother was not long after sent as a cadet and then midshipman, were the biggest and latest ships in the navy. They were hideous to look at; perhaps the ugliest ships the navy ever had. They were very heavily armed with three triple sixteen-inch gun turrets and sixteen inch was the biggest gun there had ever been. These gun turrets were all forward. The intention was that there should have been more of these heavy guns at the after end of the ship but the Washington Treaty imposed limits on the ship's construction which caused the after end of the ship to be lopped off. There was no grace, no spectacular appeal, no line about these vast battleships. They looked, in silhouette, like gigantic old boots – rather inelegant ones.

Appointments to *Rodney* and *Nelson* were regarded as 'good jobs' (of

which more later) on the apparent basis that officers serving in them would be in the public eye, a shibboleth of that day. It was not hard to see that this would apply to the senior officers, but the young commissioned officer needed to go to a small ship. In a destroyer (and destroyers were small ships then), he would have the responsibility for the ship's navigation or the gunnery or the torpedo control as well, perhaps, as the pay for the Ship's Company, the food, or – vile task – the paper work and (worst of all) the Confidential Books. Most important by far, he would have to keep watch on the bridge alone, including in bad weather. The main job, as the (one and only) Executive Sub Lieutenant in *Rodney*, was to run the Gun Room, the midshipmen and cadets in the subordinate officers' mess and to maintain discipline according to a code which would seem, in the light of today, unacceptably harsh.

With the Commander, my main task was to make sure that all the midshipmen played games and played them successfully. I, too, had to play, to ensure that the Gun Room rugby XV always won their matches. I also had to run the ship's cross-country team and be ready to use a hockey stick (but never a polo stick). Keeping fit and playing games were fine for a young man but they were not enough and life soon palled.

To escape, to try to get down to some real professional work, to get among friends and messmates of my own age – and also because there was a genuine appeal about it – I volunteered for flying duties. One morning I was summoned to appear at 9 am in frock coat and sword on the quarter deck before the Captain. This meant trouble. I wondered what I had done.

'Why did you join the Navy, boy?' asked the Captain.

To this hackneyed standard question there was an equally fatuous hackneyed standard answer; unsure whether it would be appropriate to laugh, I decided against it.

'To go to sea, Sir,' I said, wondering what next.

'Well, don't join the Fleet Air Arm. Take your name out. That's all.'

That was the end of that. I was dismissed. Ten years later, as Commander-in-Chief of the Mediterranean Fleet in war, Cunningham, later to become Admiral of the Fleet Lord Cunningham of Hyndhope, was greatly indebted to the Fleet Air Arm for their outstanding services, as he was to be again when he became First Sea Lord.

I suspected my father was actually responsible for putting me in balk like this and that he went to Tovey to say that I was so appalling a car driver that, in an aeroplane, I would be lethal and that Tovey had passed this on to my Captain, Cunningham. If so, those were poor decisions. The Fleet Air Arm was surely the right place for a keen and ambitious young officer who was not likely to make his mark as an intellectual.

Several months after I joined the ship, *Rodney*'s two-and-a-half year commission ended and a new crew joined. Cunningham left and was promoted to rear admiral. The Commander, Bob Burnett, whom I was to meet later when he commanded a Russian convoy in the war, similarly left to be promoted captain. Most of the other officers also left the ship. To my disgust, I was left behind with most of the midshipmen and cadets.

The new commission brought startling change. The new Captain came from the Plans Division of the Admiralty and he brought with him his Commander from the same place. They were both very different from their hearty, robust predecessors and it was their lot to deal with the 1931 Invergordon Mutiny: *Rodney* was one of the worst ships.

Most of the big ships of the Fleet had arrived at Invergordon on Friday, 12 September and, amidst various rumours and press reports, the Captain had had the lower deck cleared and had read aloud to the whole Ship's Company a formally-worded Admiralty Letter, couched in very general terms, about the financial state of the country and the need for governmental economy. What the men wanted to know was what cuts in pay were coming. This the letter did not say. The men were confused.

Then, on 14 September, the night before the outbreak, I was the Officer of the Watch of the ship, lying at anchor, when the libertymen came back from visiting the canteen ashore. There was no alcohol for the men on board in those days, except for the daily rum issue, so they often pitched into the beer ashore. A large number of men had landed that day and we heard that there had been some rowdiness at an informal meeting in the canteen and that the shore patrol had had to intervene to maintain order. The men were singing in the boats coming off to the ships but there was nothing too unusual about that and they were quiet when the boats arrived alongside the ship. At 4 am the next morning, I had to take over again as Officer of the Morning Watch and was having a cup of cocoa in the quartermaster's lobby, a small compartment off the quarter deck, while taking over from my predecessor. He told me about the weather forecast, about the ship's boats which were in the water, about the men who were absent without leave.

'The Commander says you are to tell him if there is any trouble in getting the Hands to turn out in the morning,' he added.

'What,' I asked, 'why should there be? There never is.'

'How the hell do I know?' he replied. 'He didn't say why but you know there was trouble in the canteen last night and that the Captain cleared lower deck yesterday about the coming pay cuts. Perhaps it's something to do with that.'

This chap, a lieutenant (and the equivalent of an Army Captain) was sound, responsible enough. Had the Commander gone off his rocker like the Commander of *Royal Sovereign* of my midshipman's days? I only knew him as an officer far senior to me who was almost suspiciously serious and academic.

When the bugle call reveille sounded at 5.40 am, the normal procedure was for the Boatswain's Mate, the Corporal of the Gangway and some of the Regulating Staff – the ship's police – to go round the mess decks to get the men out of their hammocks. The Officer of the Watch never went down to the mess decks, no officer ever did if he could avoid it, except during formal routine 'rounds'. It would have been an invasion of the men's privacy. With misgivings, on that morning I felt obliged to do so and, waiting five minutes after the bugle and taking the Corporal of the Watch, down I went. The men were not turning out but I never expected them to do so at once. However, when the Corporal of the Watch gave them an order and seeing the Officer of the Watch was there, they obeyed immediately. This I reported to the Commander who seemed surprised and told me to try again. So I went to a different part of the mess decks, and found that the men, when ordered to do so, reluctantly obeyed.

At 6 am, the bugle was sounded for 'Hands Fall In'. I read an account inferring that there were seventy-five junior ratings present for this muster. The fact was that there were the usual number of officers, some of the Petty Officers, a few marines – and no sailors at all. I suggested to the Commander that I, as Officer of the Watch, should go down to the mess decks with a Petty Officer and chase the men up. Being junior, it would not matter so much if the men did not obey me; but, no, he would not have it.

Imagine this against the background on which the Navy ran, on firm, strict rigid routines – routines in which a solitary man who was late falling in would be in trouble – routines in which if several men from the same part of the ship were late there would be recriminations to follow. And on this occasion, there were not several men adrift; there were several hundred!

On *Rodney*'s forecastle that early morning, like the other officers I was horrified and deeply shocked. Of course, we knew there were to be cuts in naval pay; the Captain had cleared lower deck the previous day to warn us all, to give a pep talk in sadly erudite terms. It thus became very clear very quickly that the men had two sources of information, namely their Captain and the organisers of the mutiny. It was also clear that the men were persuaded that the Captain and officers could not, or would not put things right. And, furthermore, they were persuaded that mutinous collective action was in their best interests.

The story goes that, immediately after 'Hands Fall In' that morning, the Marine subaltern, a respected officer of nearly thirty, went straight down to the Marine Barracks, as they called their mess deck, sat down at one of the mess tables and said in his quiet, authoritative voice:

'Come round me.' Slowly, they did this and when he had an adequate audience, he stood up and said: 'I would like to remind you that you are all sworn men and, if you are not present at the next muster of the Hands, I will see you are shot.'

The Marine subaltern was named Hardy, later General Sir Campbell Hardy, GCB, DSO and two Bars. Thereafter, it appeared that all the marines attended all musters.

For me, there were two immediate problems. The first was what to do about the ship's routine during the rest of my Watch, and the answer was easy as the next item was to pipe the 'Hands to Breakfast'. The second was to guess what the mutineers would do next, but, in the meantime, the Midshipman of the Watch reported that the officers' bathrooms had hot water and their breakfasts were being prepared in quite the usual manner. My Marine wardroom attendant even brought me shaving water.

Early that Tuesday forenoon, we learned that the whole Fleet present at Invergordon was infected. Some ships which should have gone to sea for exercises had not done so; binoculars and telescopes confirmed that no men were working on the upper decks of any of the ships in company. It was only possible to see and hear groups of men assembled on the forecastles of ships, including *Rodney*'s, who would periodically cheer. The normal organised three cheers from a body of men can come over as an emotive, heartening concord, but these cheers-cum-jeers from an ill-humoured rabble had an equally threatening discord. Some accounts of the mutiny later said these cheers were a means of communication between ships. This is improbable and it was far more likely that they were part of a pre-arranged plan among the organisers to maintain the momentum of the mutiny throughout the Fleet.

It was despite these displays that the ceremonies of hoisting Colours in the morning and lowering them at sunset were observed with respect and the sixteen-inch gun magazine safety regulations were adhered to with a sentry, smartly dressed on duty at the official keyboard. As Officers of the Watch, we, in turn, wore our frock coats and sword belts and carried telescopes, as was customary. As was also customary, the quarter deck staff of a Petty Officer Quartermaster, Leading Seaman Boatswain's Mate, Royal Marine Corporal of the Gangway and Sideboys – young ratings who ran messages – all appeared on Watch, punctually and smartly dressed. Although I do not recollect having been given any instructions on the subject, the procedure I followed when Officer of the Watch, and I think all others used something like it too, was to express wishes rather than giving orders so that no rating could be put in the position of disobeying an order. Thus it worked that, if a boat was required to go inshore to fetch the mail or provisions, there would be no trouble. But, if it were for some other purpose which the boat's crew thought disadvantageous to the mutineers, then the crew would not man the boat. The Engineer Officers and the Supply Officers must have been permitted by the mutineers to function in the same way. It took some skill to run the domestic sides of a vast ship but the mutineers, using their officers as necessary, did it.

The uncertainty was maintained by rumour and lack of information. At one time there was a buzz that the officers were to be 'arrested' and shut up in their cabins, though this would not have been in the mutineers' interests as the officers were helping them to run the ship! Then, one of the senior lieutenants, a sound, balanced chap in his late twenties, told me he had heard that there was a possibility of the Fleet being fired on by Army shore guns. Surely, that could not be so; ships would be damaged; officers might be killed and wounded and so would any ratings who were loyal. In addition, it would be possible that the mutineers could man our guns and return the fire. The idea seemed utterly crazy and yet, in years to come, I read in one published account that consideration was given, at quite high level, to 'the Fleet being bombarded by heavy howitzers'.[1] For reasons which come later, there must have been a confused interpretation of fact somewhere.

As to the Captain and Commander, there was no indication that they

1 Eira, Alan. *Invergordon Mutiny*, Routledge and Kegan Paul, London

knew what to expect. However, as soon as he had enough official information on the pay cuts, the Captain, Bellairs, cleared lower deck again, ordering all officers and men to assemble on the forecastle. Normally, on such occasions, everyone would be formally fallen in. On this and subsequent occasions, they were told to gather round while he spoke to them from the top of a sixteen-inch gun turret. He, the Captain, had a gentle, soft voice so that what he said came over with no force – but worse, once again he tended to talk well above the heads of his audience. But for the 'troops', the men, one simple factor was confirmed, namely that the Leading Seaman, the Able Seaman and, especially the Ordinary Seaman, often a married man, was to have his pay reduced by twenty-five per cent. He and his family could not live on this. The Captain had not said he was going to do anything other than investigate the individual cases of men who stated complaints 'through customary Service channels'. That meant a man had to appear formally before, in turn, his Divisional Petty Officer, his Divisional Officer, then the Commander and finally the Captain.

Even at the best of times, 'Stating a Complaint' was unpopular. In these circumstances, the junior rating was afraid that, by bringing his name forward, he might be earmarked as a mutineer. Moreover, he knew he would probably be doing so in an atmosphere which was not sympathetic. The Divisional Petty Officer did not want to seem to be on the same side as the men making trouble. The Divisional Officer would be anxious lest he be thought to have any form of compassion for those who had allowed their grievances to form the cause of mutiny.

From the line they took, the Captain and the Commander still thought that by using the established procedures – or something like them – the men would respond to a reasoned appeal; the organisers of the mutiny thought otherwise. Both the Captain and the Commander cleared lower deck separately and, up to a point, the mutineers' policy of being respectful to their officers continued. Progressively, however, the men became more disrespectful. Some were not properly dressed in uniform; some smoked while their Captain addressed them; some jeered or just walked away; some did not attend at all. Then the Captain tried clearing lower deck and telling the officers not to attend. The reasoning of this was hard to follow as it gave an impression that the officers and men were not 'on the same side'. This was true to some extent but it was probably a mistake to draw attention to it.

At this point, with the behaviour of some ratings openly discourteous – even contemptuous of their Captain – an outbreak of violence was possible and I decided, as the junior and youngest commissioned officer on board, to beard the Commander myself. The little Commander was in his cabin, seated at a large roll-top desk doing paper work, with the right side of his head visible through the open sliding door. I knocked.

'Yes, what is it?'

'May I speak to you, Sir?'

'Yes, what do you want, Sub?'

'You and the Captain, Sir, have spoken to the Ship's Company and I think I should say, Sir, that they do not quite understand.'

31

Turning in his chair towards me: 'What do you mean?' This was getting difficult.

'Well, Sir, I think the men really want to understand about their cuts in pay and to know what is going to be done about them.' Pause – then, sharply: 'Thank you, that will do.'

Years later as a Commander myself, I thought that this was bold if not verging on the impertinent, but that I would have found out exactly what had driven a normally rather shy, inarticulate young man to be so outspoken.

How did it come about that a large part of the greatest and most prestigious navy in the world found itself in this shameful impasse? In the first place, the Admiralty was a civil Ministry under a political Minister, the First Lord of the Admiralty, who had a Board of Sea Lords, Admirals. Complying with Government policy of economy, a system of reduction in naval pay was evolved and passed by the Board. Through the most remarkable error of judgement, the pay cuts imposed on junior ratings were not only harsh, but unrealistic. Some families of junior ratings would have starved. The Admiralty compounded their error by making a muddle over the way the bad news reached the men in the Fleet so that reports in the press and rumours – neither necessarily accurate – reached the men before they were told the position formally, on board their ships.

When the Fleet had sailed from Home Ports, the Commander-in-Chief, Admiral Sir Michael Hodges, was sick so, on arrival at Invergordon, the command fell to Rear Admiral Tomkinson, the Flag Officer, Battle Cruisers. He, the two other Rear Admirals in the Fleet, the seven Captains of the capital ships (the battle cruisers and battleships) and the Captains from the four cruisers knew there had been beery, unruly meetings in the ratings' canteen ashore and that cuts in pay were discussed. On Monday, the night before the outbreak, some Captains of ships were dining with Admiral Tomkinson and it would seem that only then, for the first time, they sensed there might be serious trouble. As a precaution, to avoid anything like refusal of duty, the orders for some ships to sail for exercises next day were cancelled. I have never read that the Captains of ships expected a definite refusal of duty; if so, why did *Rodney*'s Commander give me the order for the men to fall-in for work at 6 am on the following fatal Tuesday morning if he thought it was likely to be disobeyed?

Now, consider it at the level of the mutineers – the real hard-core, the organisers. Who were they? Well, it was said that they were Able Seamen with a few Leading Seamen chucked in; but many of the Petty Officers must have been at least sympathisers. There was, inevitably, a central organising committee with sub-committees in each ship and a good system of inter-ship communications. From what I saw, especially of the unanimity and general conformity between ships while the trouble lasted, I cannot believe the whole affair arose from three noisy, beery meetings in the canteen ashore on the evenings preceding the outbreak. In the background, there was surely an organisation so strong, so emotionally stimulating that the men trusted it and not their Captains and officers.

Take the Captains in command; they suddenly found they were no longer in charge of their own ships; an anonymous group of ratings had taken over. Could any officer in command imagine anything worse, more overwhelmingly shocking and humiliating than to find his men would no longer trust, much less obey him?

It is over fifty years ago now and so easy to speculate what, say David Simson, my Term Officer at Dartmouth, would have done had he had command of those ships at Invergordon. He would have probably cleared lower deck (not a thing that any Captain did often) at the very, very first sniff of threatening trouble. He would have promised personally and immediately to examine every possible cause and case of hardship and he would have been trusted by his men to do so. He would have avoided any use of the established system whereby men had to 'State a Complaint', as it was well known that such cases tended to be considered troublesome, so much so that frivolous complaints were punishable. He would have told the men he would keep them informed about what he was doing on their behalf. After that, he would have ordered his Commander to read aloud to those assembled an extract from the *Articles of War*. This was a very formidable document. When it was read, officers and men stood to attention and removed their caps. The document listed various crimes and gave the extreme penalty for each. Mutiny came high up the list and the penalty was 'death or such other punishment as is hereinafter mentioned'.

What I have written is mainly eye-witness stuff – or based on it. Sometimes, as in the preceding paragraph, it is speculation, but it is based upon the experience of later commanding a destroyer, then being the Executive Officer of a cruiser, and later still as a Captain in command. Finally, I have chewed it over as an OAP. Sometimes, to keep things in context, I have relied on information from books.

As an example of the latter, I read, after all was over, that the mutineers had an ultimate plan: if they failed to get satisfaction by other means, they would seize the ships' boats, and land and march on London, using any available transport as they went. The story was that, in such event, Army units had been detailed to fire on them. This probably accounts for the startling rumour referred to earlier.

In the early evening of the second day of the mutiny, the Ships' Company was told that all ships of the Fleet would be sailed to their home ports and that the Admiralty would review the cuts in pay. The immediate question was whether the men would agree to weigh anchor, to man the engine rooms and boiler rooms and provide the various duty men in Watches to get the ship back to Devonport. One account says – 'Rodney's Ship's Company readily agreed'. This is incorrect. The matter was put to the vote and only carried by a small margin. The scene when weighing anchor was that of a disorderly rabble with officers, Petty Officers and midshipmen doing the manual work while there were a number of men watching and getting in the way.

Shore leave was immediately given after arrival. In those days, the libertymen all went ashore in uniform and were marched in a body to the

Dockyard gate. For some days after we got back to Devonport, *Rodney*'s libertymen were marched to the gate by a circuitous route so as to avoid passing other ships – especially the destroyers. They were shaming days for us. Other ships did not want to know us.

When it came to the question of disciplinary action, it slowly percolated through that there would be no formal action taken against anyone. Unofficially, though, I heard that four *Rodney* ratings were sent to do a special 'disciplinary course' in the Royal Naval Barracks. By chance, I happened to see them one nice warm day in 'full marching order', wearing oilskins, doubling round the parade ground with their rifles painfully at the slope, bruising their shoulders as they ran! They did not look at all happy. After the 'course' the men were discharged SNLR – services no longer required. Later, I read that the number of men discharged SNLR from *Rodney* was much higher than the four about whom I knew at the time. All this was, of course, unofficial punishment. Under the unhappy circumstances, no orthodox measures would have met the case. The unorthodox measures did not, however, stop there.

Many books were written analysing the Invergordon disaster though none previously, so far as I know, by an officer who was actually present. Most books lash Rear Admiral Tomkinson with blame. In the absence, sick, of the Commander-in-Chief, Tomkinson was certainly in command of the Fleet; the Fleet mutinied under his command and the very word mutiny had a deeply established, evil and shaming ring. Tomkinson did not, however, cause the trouble. The trouble was caused by gross, unbelievable blundering at the Admiralty. Then, when the mutiny broke out – and there was never any doubt from the first that it was mutiny – the Admiralty gave Tomkinson no firm, definite support at all.

Different accounts may vary inversely with the amount of applied penmanship and whitewash. But while the Admiralty provided the ample wrongs for discontent, the men in each ship would not rely on their Captains to right these wrongs through the 'normal Service channels'. They accepted instead, as stronger and more effective, the mutinous leadership of a plainly very powerful organisation of junior ratings.[2] Maybe – and this is a personal 'bee' – too many officers were afraid, after the 1922 Geddes Axe, of doing or saying the wrong thing. Maybe there were not enough David Simsons about, robust men like Captain A. B. Cunningham, of infinite physical and moral courage. It could have been that some Captains did, however vaguely, sense coming trouble and did not like to tell their Admiral. It is only possible to say with conviction that the changes in relations between officers and men, which started immediately after the mutiny, were beneficently expedited by the war which was to follow.

2. Astutely whitewashed written reports probably distorted exactly what did or could have happened at Invergordon One Captain, for example, is understood to have maintained (in writing) that men always stood to attention when spoken to by him This can be taken two ways In those days, Almighty God was treated with awe by all – and a four stripe Captain in command was only marginally less so Thus, if the Captain spoke to one man he would perforce stand rigidly to attention. But the same situation did *not* apply when the same Captain spoke to his whole Ship's Company at Invergordon.

As an early consequence of the mutiny, the Atlantic Fleet, to be dissociated from its recent past, was renamed 'The Home Fleet' and sailed under its new Commander-in-Chief, Admiral Sir John Kelly – this time to Rosyth. 'Joe' Kelly was a large, imposing, spectacular man with a very red face, a long nose and dewlaps which hung over the top of his high, starched butterfly collar – a man of powerful presence indeed. The Fleet at Rosyth was much the same as it had been at Invergordon. *Nelson* was the Flagship, *Rodney, Malaya* and *Warspite* the battleships and *Hood* and *Repulse* the battle cruisers, then there were cruisers and destroyers.

On arrival, Admiral Kelly visited the ships to address the Ships' Companies. The occasion was entirely formal, in marked contrast to the way most, if not all, Ships' Companies had been addressed at Invergordon. In a resonant voice, very firm but not harsh, with a great sense of the histrionic, the C-in-C explained how the King, George V, had sent for him and how deeply upset the King, who had himself served some years in the Navy, was to learn of the mutiny – although the actual word 'mutiny' was never used by Admiral Kelly at all. He went on to say that, in looking for a new C-in-C, the King had gone through all the Service Certificates (the official papers of ratings) of all those Admirals available for the job until he came to that of one named Kelly who, he noticed, had been in trouble himself. It was for that reason that the King thought him to be the right man for the job.

It was a magnificent act, very emotional, very shrewdly worded. In effect, he said that all of us, officers and men, had disgraced ourselves in the eyes of the King, the country and the world. The actual wording he used was such as to stir the audience to shame and contrition, lumps in the throat, even a few damp eyes I saw – but he also struck an ultimate 'Never, never anything like this again; now get on with your work' note.

Rodney's commission dragged on dismally. The ship was sent to Portsmouth, rather than her home port, Devonport, to refit. This was heartily disliked by the sailors, many of whom had their homes in the West Country around Devonport.

At last, in January 1932, the ship's complement of officers and men was reduced; I begged to be allowed to go and was sent on leave with a 'flimsy' which did not indicate an adverse Confidential Report.

Eventually, after some weeks, I wrote for a job and was summoned to the Admiralty to be confronted by a grim-faced Commander.

'Can I have a job at sea, please Sir, I've been unemployed for some weeks now,' I said.

'Your case will need consideration,' he replied, 'there has been an adverse report on you.' What on earth could he mean? No one had ever complained to me and it was, anyway, weeks since I had done any work at all.

'Who reported adversely on me and what have I done, Sir?' I asked.

'I am sorry, I cannot tell you that, but you are to be placed under special report. If special reports on you are adverse, you will be discharged from the Navy. If you receive two satisfactory reports, you will not be.'

Entirely astonished, very badly shaken indeed and much steamed up: 'I would like a trial by Court Martial,' I said. 'At least there would be a Charge and I would know what I am supposed to have done Sir.'

There was a pause.

'No. That is impossible. You are under consideration for being discharged as unsuitable and would do best to make no more trouble.'

Later, I learned that the normal procedure before an officer could be placed in the Quarterly Report, as it was called, was that he first had to be warned formally by his Captain; then, the officer had to be given an adverse confidential report if he had not improved and he had to be told this. None of that had happened; yet Bellairs, my Captain in *Rodney* was a man whom I trusted as one unlikely to break such rules.

It thus looked like an unofficial penalty as the outcome of what someone senior to me had said of my behaviour during the mutiny. That there were such recriminations among the more senior officers was not in doubt. The only misdeeds that could be ascribed to me were telling the Commander that the Lower Deck – the men – could not understand when addressed by the Captain and himself and, possibly *indirectly* expressing sympathy with the plight of the junior ratings. Perhaps it is relevant that the Security Service (MI5) and the Special Branch were said to have carried out secret enquiries; perhaps evidence was given to my detriment. It was a point of interest that, although Officer of the Watch when the mutiny broke out, I was never called as a witness before an enquiry. The reason for this could have depended on whoever nominated the witnesses!

More leave came after this very unpleasant interview; then followed an appointment to HMS *Iron Duke* of the Battle of Jutland fame. She was the gunnery-firing training ship and lay off Portland, going out to sea several times a week with gunnery classes, mainly so that they could let off the six-inch guns of which I was given charge of a battery. There was plenty of work, plenty of responsibility and, in the minimum time, six months, I was in the clear again from an official point of view. Spare time I used up in boxing and was surprised to be asked to box for the navy. Sometimes, on a Saturday, I had a day with the South Dorset and Cattistock or the Portman Foxhounds.

It had been a hell of a thing, this Quarterly Report – frightening and mortifying. In later years I met other victims, all of them shaken. A few – but not all – could be labelled unsuited to be naval officers or, more unkindly, just wet.

I left *Iron Duke* with a favourable report to join HMS *Suffolk*, a cruiser going out to join the China Station. It had been refreshing to serve in this ship under Captain King and Commander Figgins. They were straight spoken and to be trusted.

It took some years, gradually, to live down this unnerving Quarterly Report session. The blow to self-confidence and the feeling that it was passed on via the grape vine – that I had been 'in the report' for a reason which had never been stated, was a constant, if decreasing strain.

And the moral of this is, one should not follow one's own convictions, regardless. But I never learned this, even after Invergordon.

4. WATCHKEEPER

Service in the Atlantic Fleet (renamed the Home Fleet after the Invergordon mutiny) and in the Mediterranean Fleet had been tense. The biggest single contributor to the tension in both these main Fleets had been the top brass; at least, that is how many contemporaries and I had seen it.

Oppressive zeal was dormant in the Far East. Relaxation, of one sort or another, was never too far to find. The weather was agreeable, apart from an occasional typhoon. Also, the top brass was not too thick on the ground or, rather, the water.

So far as professional training to fight the enemy went, it fell into about three groups. First, strategy and tactics were based on the last war, what else? Major Fleet exercises would be based on the 'Red Fleet' – nothing political about this – versus the 'Blue Fleet' and then on the assumption that the contest would be a gunnery slogging match. Secondly and logically, weapon training was mainly devoted to the importance of the main armament firing. The firing of the big guns always caused an inordinate fuss. In a big ship, there would be numerous midshipmen with stop watches and record forms (I was always one of the Gunnery Officer's – Lieutenant Commander Vian's – recorders in *Royal Sovereign* as a midshipman). There was much briefing; great preparations were taken to avoid damage from gun-blast; hatches were battened down and scuttles (portholes to those outside the navy) with deadlights were levered tight. Then, against a background of screwed up tension and bad temper, there would be delays in opening fire. The tug towing the target would be out of position, or the range would be fouled by some fishing boat getting in the way or, if it were an anti-aircraft firing, the aircraft towing the sleeve target would be late. Eventually, the fire-gong ordering the guns to open fire would go 'ting-ting'. There would be an immense crash, much smoke, a clatter of what had not been properly secured and always a tinkle of broken glass. When it was all over, days of grim and usually ill-humoured analysis followed.

Torpedo firings were different. Destroyer flotillas might do dummy attacks in which no torpedoes were fired at all. Alternatively, there could be a heavily stage-managed affair in which one or more torpedoes were actually run and, when that happened, they would at once be pursued in case they sank, in which case there would be Court of Enquiry and someone would be in trouble. In the war which was to come, I know of at least one salvo of torpedoes which was fired with the wrong deflections – aim off – set on the sights! Lack of practice? Yes, of course.

Depth charges *could* also be fired; all destroyers and most cruisers carried them but there was not much point in firing them. They shook the ship and could perhaps cause damage. Anti-submarine tactics were given little or no thought.

Now comes the third component of preparing to take on the enemy, namely physical fitness. Our Captain in *Suffolk* on the China Station was a physical training specialist and so was his second-in-command, the Commander. Games and all forms of such organised activity, especially the Fleet Regatta and, to a lesser extent, the cross-country races, football and so on, were of much importance in assessing how good a ship – and thus her officers – might be. Captain Errol Manners had selected his officers with this in mind. We had, in the Ward Room, among others an international rugger player and an international hockey player. Reasonably sure that the Captain knew of my past Quarterly Report background, I decided to colour the image athletically and so captained the ship's running team (thank goodness for old age and no more running); played for the Navy at rugger (the captain of the team was a friend of mine); boxed in the Fleet championships and rode a good deal and with success in the pony races.

When HMS *Kent* went home to refit, the Flag of the Commander-in-Chief Admiral Sir Frederick Dreyer, was transferred to *Suffolk*. Carrying the Flag of an Admiral was always a nuisance to us lesser lights. From midshipman's days, I remembered the constant cry at nights 'Don't wake the Admiral'. There were some six foot four of this one; very formidable he was, slightly stooped, rather slow-moving and sometimes very acid.

Carrying the Flag had its dividend. It took us to Japan where we attended the funeral of the Japanese Admiral Togo who had so crushingly defeated the Russians at the Battle of Tsushima in 1905. It took us to Bali, to Borneo, to Java and the Celebes Islands where the water was so clear that the ship's anchor could easily be seen on the bottom and where one night I caught a shark. We got it in – 10 feet 6 inches of it – without waking the Admiral but made a bloody mess on the quarter deck slaying it. Next day, the Commander was not pleased!

The quarter deck was the scene for *Suffolk*'s really big melodrama as the China Fleet's Flagship and, paradoxically, it came when the ship was six hundred miles from the sea, up the Yangtse River, lying off Hangkow. The Admiral had brought off a political coup of great importance. The Young Marshal, a Chinese warlord (one among many of that day with private armies) and a man of consequence, had agreed to visit the ship in order to call on the British Naval Commander-in-Chief. The teak deck had been scrubbed with holystone that morning, all brass brightwork was gleaming. The enamel paint on the eight-inch gun turret had been polished with beeswax and the awning was hauled taught and flat so that even the tallest marine in the Guard of Honour could not put his bayonet through it when presenting arms.

The Royal Marine Guard and Band, in full dress, were paraded on the quarter deck and everything shone to the polished tips of the marine's helmets. Remembering that on the last formal occasion the effect had been spoiled by a couple of the ship's cats copulating at the C-in-C's feet, I had mild misgivings but dismissed them as irrational. The Admiral, the Captain, the Commander and myself, the Officer of the Watch, were all ceremonially dressed in cocked hats, frock coats with gold-tasselled epaulettes. The Admiral and the Captain were walking up and down, swords clanking, waiting for the C-in-C's barge – the special green motor boat – to return to the ship with the Chinese General. Suddenly, in a menacing boom, the Admiral said:

'The bugler boy has no gloves on.' The Captain looked at the Royal Marine bugler and said sharply:

'Commander, why has the bugler not got his gloves on?'

'Officer of the Watch,' said the Commander to me, 'where are the bugler's gloves?'

I turned to the Corporal of the Watch who said something very offensive to the bugler, who looked at his hands and found they were naked. A moment of stultified horror followed; every other marine had his white gloves on but not the bugler and there was nothing that could possibly be done about it. The C-in-C's barge was at the bottom of the gangway ladder.

'Sound the Attention,' said the Admiral, by way of starting the ceremony.

'Sound the Alert,' said the Captain, quickly correcting him, and the order passed down the line till it reached the unhappy bugler. He brought his bugle up with a flourish and nothing happened. Some really vicious invective was directed at the poor boy but still nothing happened. Then, quite suddenly, very red in his face with a tremendous blast, cheeks extended, he blew his gloves, rolled up in a white ball, out of the end of his bugle. They flopped to the deck at the feet of the Young Marshal like an exhausted dove of peace!

It was within days of the ship's eventual return home that, as the result of the Italian Dictator Mussolini's invasion of Abyssinia, the Reserve Fleet was mobilised for use in the Mediterranean. For reasons both personal and professional, and with the prospect of action against the Italian Fleet, I went to the Second Sea Lord's Office to ask for a job in a destroyer in the Med and was told to report forthwith to the Royal Naval Barracks, Devonport, prior to passage out.

'We were expecting you, Sir', said the Hall Porter at the Barracks. He made no mention of the fifty or so other officers who were so suddenly sprung on him.

What men those Hall Porters were – in Naval establishment or in London Club – welcoming, entirely knowledgeable, the servant in control, a friend when one got to know him and never one to get the wrong side of.

I was to serve as First Lieutenant of *Wolsey*, one of the old 'V' and 'W' class destroyers built at the end of and just after the end of World War One and brought forward out of the Reserve Fleet at Malta. The lieutenant commander in command of *Wolsey* was a passed over officer. He looked perhaps more amiable than he was and had a reputation for drinking gin!

Very soon after we had commissioned with a full crew, the ship was put into the 19th Flotilla and the Captain (D) in command said he wished to come on board, informally, to walk round and see the men at Divisions.

'Fall those men out,' he said when he arrived on board, dressed in a frock coat, perhaps deliberately to put us in the wrong. Then: 'Bring me the Ward Room Wine books,' he added.

A precise record was kept in all HM ships of all drink consumed by officers each month; a total of £5 a head for each, with a limit of not more than three whole tots of spirits a day, was permitted. Captain P. L. Vian, whom I had not seen since *Royal Sovereign* days, was the Captain (D). He left the ship glowering.

'Oh, you're here, are you?' he said to me, looking slightly less aggressive as he went over the side into his boat.·

My then Captain was not the sort of man Vian liked; he was a pudgy and diffident lieutenant commander – but with what an outlook! Some twenty-five years after joining Dartmouth as a boy, he, like so many others (some very keen and able) had no prospects but to soldier on to the age of forty-five and then be put out 'on the beach' with a pension, then very small, and with limited chances of a worthwhile civilian job.

In the event *Wolsey* was detached almost immediately from the 19th Flotilla to act as 'bloodboat' to follow *Courageous,* our biggest aircraft carrier, when aircraft were flying on or off, so that we could pick up pilots who had ditched. When these flying operations first started from Alexandria, there were reports of submarine periscopes – Italians snooping on our ships. Rear Admiral Ramsay, flying his Flag in *Courageous,* saw fit to order aircraft to drop live depth charges for practice nearby; and the periscope sightings then ceased.

Alexandria was exceedingly hot, so much so that in harbour work started at 5.15 am and ceased for the day about 1 pm. One morning, at about 6.30, I was skipping for exercise on the upper deck when I noticed a neat looking man in a khaki shirt approaching, rowing a neat looking skiff. Through a stream of sweat I saw him stop and rest on his oars and cast an absorbing, even critical eye on the ship.

'Can I help you?' I asked.

'No, thanks,' he said. 'I am just taking a little exercise, too, and having a look round. I'm R.A. (D).' This meant he was Rear Admiral in command of the destroyers.

'I'm very sorry, Sir, I'll fetch the Captain.'

But, no, he waived the idea and rowed away to look at some of his other ships. This was Somerville, later Admiral of the Fleet Sir James, who was to be one of Britain's greatest fighting seamen of all time when the war came – also to be the father-in-law of my cousin Elisabeth.

Then, just as things were starting to stabilise and look promising, orders arrived for me to go home to specialise in anti-submarine duties. This was infuriating. I was, quite by chance, the youngest First Lieutenant in any destroyer. All efforts to get out of the A/S course unfortunately failed.

Going through Malta on the way home, I was summoned by the Staff Officer Intelligence. 'It is really quite handy you going home now,' he said. 'I've booked you home from Sicily overland.'

'The Itis won't like that much Sir.'

'No. Maybe not, but here's the train's route. Here are the naval ports you will pass through. And here are the silhouettes and details of the Iti battleships and cruisers you may see. Mug it all up – no notes. And no notes of what you see or where you see it. Put in a written report to Naval Intelligence when you arrive in London.'

The Italians provided a tail but the tail proved very useful. He came into my carriage every time the train was about to pass anything of interest, pulled the blind down and, out of politeness, then left the carriage. This made it all to easy. It was not difficult to produce a comprehensive report. It was my first introduction to the Intelligence world!

It was then the end of 1935, a time of increasing international tension. Germany, under the absolute control of the National Socialists, and Japan had denounced all armament control and thus the control over the building of warships. In the years to follow, the Chancellor of Austria was murdered (1938) and Austria fell into the hands of the Nazis; the King of Italy was proclaimed Emperor of Abyssinia; the Rome-Berlin Axis was set up; the Balkans were in turmoil and Japan was mopping up as much of China as she could contend with. All this set the scene for much that was to follow.

As with all other Executive, or Seaman, Branch specialist courses at that time, the theory component of the anti-submarine course started at the Royal Naval College, Greenwich. If one had to go back to school, there was surely no comparable place for relative comfort and for an interesting, beautiful and spicy background.

The site and environment of the Royal Naval College are riddled with history, going back to early times. In the Middle Ages, Henry VIII was born in the old Royal Palace and, after his marriage to Catherine of Aragon, several of his matrimonial escapades took place thereabouts.

There was a notable difference returning to Greenwich, as I did a second time for the A/S Course and was to do a third and fourth time much later. On each occasion, the appearance of the people differed. The second time, the local people – the men, women and children of that mainly slummy area – looked so very much fitter, no longer so pale and thin and bloody-minded. The third and fourth times, well after the war, they looked quite as healthy and as happy and prosperous as anywhere; Greenwich had ceased to be a slum.

The theoretical work on this course was painful and tedious from civilian teachers. It was uphill work for them. They had our sympathy, all of them except Professor Searle, a lanky, red-haired, slow-speaking man who had our admiration. He said little, seemed to make little effort and yet was the most effective teacher, listened to perhaps because of his background. By repute, he had been a World War One cypher-breaking expert and, when a really difficult cypher cropped up, it was said that the professor would be locked up in a room with the unbroken cypher and bottle of whisky and that he always finished both concurrently and quite fast. While teaching at Greenwich, he was rumoured to be running a profitable night-club in London.

These few months were enjoyable. My mother had a flat in London so I often saw her, as well as my father from time to time. Joan, too, had a flat in London. With the real and imagined adverse effects of being in the Quarterly Report slowly wearing off and with the likelihood of war increasing, a different side of life loomed.

That the A/S Branch was the Cinderella among the Specialists of the Executive Branch was beyond dispute. The Gunnery Branch was accepted as the elite, within the elite. Battles at sea were won by guns and these battles were mainly a matter of major fleet actions, slogging matches; such actions brought the Gunnery officers into the public eye. This angle was not entirely accepted by the Signals specialists (Mountbatten included) but they were too blue-blooded and self-satisfied to say so. Nonetheless, they did have a special tie of equal stripes; grey for the colour of the ships and blue for the colour of their blood. The Torpedo Officers, in contrast, gave the impression of utter lethargy although their Branch did produce some very fine senior officers. The Navigators did not, on the whole, do this; perhaps they were unduly quiet. Rather out on a limb was the Fleet Air Arm, too light-hearted to enter into any such competition; the Submarine Branch thought itself above it all – and, in my opinion was quite right. It was realistically professional in a manner like no other part of the Navy.

From Greenwich, we five lieutenants moved down to Portland to start the practical side of our Training. The Anti-Submarine School had a ship's name like all the other shore establishments, and HMS *Osprey* came as a depressing shock to us. It was a series of dilapidated World War One wooden huts. A first impression was appalling; the senior staff of lieutenant commanders were outcasts, sad chaps who seemed to have given up hope and taken to beer and gin.

This impression was wrong. Some of them were most able and keen, but they were outcasts, and mainly superannuated. In no way could the Anti-Submarine School compare with the well-established, smart schools of Gunnery, Torpedo and Navigation at Portsmouth. No use being depressed about it. There being no accommodation for us in the wooden huts, John Mosse, Gordon John Luther and I hired a caravan, imported a barrel of cider and a barrel of sherry and (for a short time) aided by my primitive concertina and some of the young ladies of Dorset, there was revelry each evening.

Brick buildings went up, however, and we were obliged to move into civilisation to prepare for the important sea-going and practical exam. This we took seriously and I passed well and became qualified to deal with the tactical and practical use of asdics – so-called from the initials of the Allied Submarine Detection Investigation Committee, set up in the latter days of World War One.

As it is to feature with some consequence later on, here is the rough outline of how anti-submarine weaponry of that day worked. The Americans preferred to call the asdic 'sonar' and this term is more commonly used today. By whatever name, it transmitted an underwater *sound* beam. As a point in passing, for those unfamiliar with it, this underwater beam was not then, nor later, radar. The beam was actuated – pushed out – by an oscillator, later called a transducer, under American influence again, perhaps. The oscillator was a heavy disc, around two feet in diameter, containing built-up layers of quartz crystal. The quartz layers had the property that if high voltage, low amperage current of a frequency to match the thickness of the layers was applied, the layers of quartz would vibrate. This would cause a physical sound wave which took the form of a cigar-shaped pulse or transmission. When it hit anything under water, it bounced back as an echo. The oscillator, which could be directed to point at a target, lived inside a dome under the ship's bottom which an electric motor would raise inside the hull or lower to protrude from the hull for operation.

The electronic power to work the oscillator came from an adapted wireless set. The transmitted beam, usually about 15 k/c, and any resulting echo were made audible to the human ear electronically. At the same time, both beam and echo were displayed on an iodised rotating paper roll. This measured the time between transmission and echo and, the speed of sound through water being known, thus gave the range, that is, the distance of the echo from the ship in yards. The range recorder, as it was called, was great magic in those days, and was also an automatic transmitter. It only remained to have a simple motor to train the oscillator in azimuth to enable the operator to sweep with the asdic beam and thus pinpoint the source of the echo.

Elementary, you say? Just a matter of sweeping till you get an echo off a submarine, then driving the ship to attack it with a load of depth charges? Well, no, it was not quite like that. In those days, the electronics and the control instruments failed all too often – curses, embarrassment and red faces! Breakdown apart, results would depend on 'asdic conditions'. If, for instance, it were rough, the ship might be rolling or pitching badly so that there was aerated water around the dome and this would prevent the beam from going out. If there were variations in the temperature or salinity of the water, the beam could be bent upwards or downwards. Then, of course, the beam could echo off solid objects like other surface ships, wrecks and rocks and less solid objects like fish shoals, ship wakes and tide rips. All such echoes were classified as 'non-subs', and not important; when the target *was* a submarine, it was not going to wait, tamely, to be swatted.

It was a matter for the ship's A/S Control Officer and the senior operator to sort all this out and identify the echoes received. When contact had been made with a genuine submarine, the first indication might be 'Doppler effect', when the pitch of the echo, if the submarine were approaching, would be higher than the pitch of the transmission, and, conversely, if it were retiring, the pitch of the echo would be lower. (The same principle applies to an express train passing through a railway station – there is a

THE ASDIC RANGE RECORDER

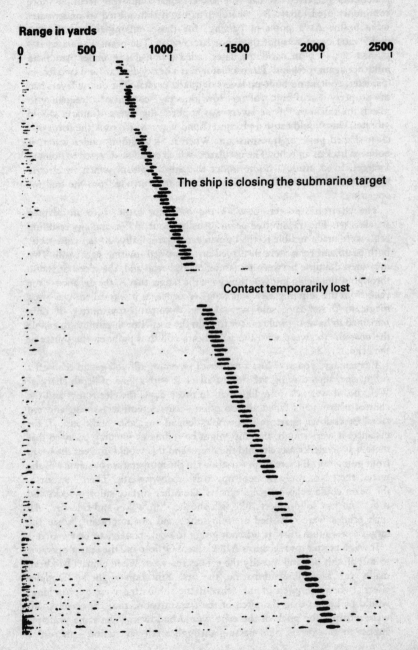

Range in yards

0   500   1000   1500   2000   2500

The ship is closing the submarine target

Contact temporarily lost

higher note when it is approaching and a lower one when it is retreating.) A second indication that the submarine was genuine could, time permitting, come from the plot in the chart house below the bridge, giving the course and speed of the target. That was, of course, if the submarine was not stopped on the bottom! Whether you find this simple or confusing, please believe that it was a process needing very much practice, application, essential team-work and often patience as well.

The weapon was, of course, the depth charge, 300 lb of high explosive which could be set to detonate at various depths according to the estimated depth of the submarine. Thirteen yards was the lethal range of the depth charge; there was not much margin for error. Then, and in the war years to come, it was a game which had to be played, at least to some extent, by ear.

It was the job of the qualified A/S officer to teach the more senior operators, the A/S control officer in asdic-fitted ships and to advise senior and commanding officers on the formation of their ships for the best protection of big ships or convoys needing anti-submarine screening.

Those few months spent at the A/S School at Portland, trying to take all this in, were again happy. With no more than Naval pay, it was possible to hire a horse and go out with the local foxhounds, the Cattistock, the South Dorset, Blackmore Vale or Portman, once a fortnight or so and to shoot whenever asked as well as to play rugger and squash. It was also possible, once a month, to go to London. Often, hard to believe now, we went to dine and dance at the Savoy – always a tail coat and white tie when taking a young lady out in those days. As a counter weight, it meant no pub-crawling, no smoking in the week – just an undesirable amount of nightly homework.

Professionally, as well, our time of training was satisfying. The early signs that the go-ahead leadership of Captain Madden (later Admiral Sir Alec) was getting the Branch on the map were apparent. The Branch was lucky too with some of its more junior but serious and efficient non-boozers (but not teetotallers) like 'Egg' Burnett and John Grant, both of whom were to become Rear Admirals.

Lo and behold, we were even getting brick-built buildings both to live in and for the display of asdic equipment. In one, there was the ironmongery, and in another there was the mechanism whereby anti-submarine manoeuvres

The asdic range recorder automatically actuated each transmission of the sound beam. At the same time it caused a stylus to travel across a slowly rotating roll of impregnated paper and to give a visual presentation of each transmission and of any object (such as a submarine) which the sound beam might strike and thus cause an echo. A range scale gave the distance of the echo and the slowly rotating roll of paper thus gave a range plot of the echo. If the asdic (or sonar) conditions were not good, if the ship were rolling or pitching badly and if there were fish shoals to give false echoes – often blurred and widespread – the range plot would be adversely affected.

This is an excellent range plot. The target stands out clearly. The asdic conditions are very good. The ship is not rolling or pitching, and there are no fish about. The ship is closing the contact (the first contact shown is at the bottom of the page).

could be simulated. Someone somewhere had seen the light in sending a man like Alec Madden to the Anti-Submarine School at that time.

Almost immediately after passing the examination and qualifying, an appointment came for me to be the Assistant Anti-Submarine Officer, 5th Destroyer Flotilla. At once, half the Flotilla (four ships) were sent off to patrol the North coast of Spain to protect British interests during the Spanish Civil War. HMS *Echo*, to which ship I was appointed, was the senior ship and was based in St Jean de Luz. No war there: refugees and press men, diplomats from the British Embassy evacuated from Madrid to Hendaye, as well as a sprinkling of spies and pretty girls would, when possible, congregate at the Bar Basque each evening to drink champagne cocktails.

The unrest which led up to the Spanish Civil War built up from the early 1930s and, initially, it was a simple matter of the 'have-nots' rebelling against the 'haves'. Without question, the outstanding characteristic of the Civil War was the harsh, unlimited brutality shown by Spaniard against Spaniard – not the calculated torture of the Nazis so much as the brutal taking of life including women and children under inhuman conditions.

It was not until early 1936, when the Spanish King had already gone, that the worst happened. The Army (of the political right) was not doing too well and the Spanish Foreign Legion and Moroccan troops under General Franco were called upon. The political right adopted the name of Falange and assumed a policy that was Fascist – single party control, like that of Mussolini in Italy and Hitler in Germany, though Franco was not anti-church. Franco appealed to Mussolini who, flushed with success after his invasion of Ethiopia, sent warships, aircraft, pilots and soldiers. An appeal to Hitler was equally successful. It was soon after that that Russia gave aid to the Republican Party; also to help the left, the much publicised International Brigades of Communists and Socialists were formed. In their ranks were at least two men who had been mutineers at Invergordon. One of them, ex-Able Seaman Fred Copeman, commanded a company. There was, incidentally, a unit of the International Brigade named to commemorate the sympathy of Clement Attlee, Britain's post-war Socialist Prime Minister: Major Attlee's Brigade.

Visiting the Spanish ports, one met both sides; at Santander, Franco's, and at Bilbao, the Reds. Too often it was a sombre business: Spanish friends one had seen on the last visit had disappeared to prison or been shot. *Echo* did, in fact, bring one quite large consignment of nuns out from Bilbao on one occasion together with Jessica, one of the famous Mitford sisters. A pretty little girl, she had run away with Esmond Romilly, a small ginger-haired youth with dirty shoes, a nephew of Winston Churchill. Somehow, the British Consul had managed to winkle these two out. When the ship got back to St Jean de Luz, they ran away again and got married.

Echo came back to England for the inspection of the Fleet at Portland by King Edward VIII at the end of November 1936. We had on board for training a party of Royal Fleet Reserve fishermen from the Outer Hebrides. Hairy in every way, they had been put in my charge.

'What is your name?' said the King to the first man as he walked down their ranks.

'Mackay,' said the man – no 'Sir'.

'What's your name?' said the King to the second man.

'Mackay.'

The King then missed out a few and, again:

'What's your name?'

'Mackay.'

'What's this?' said the King, irritably, 'they can't all be called Mackay.'

'They are really, Sir, they nearly all come from the same clan.'

We had champagne ready but the King, tired and strained, asked for a cup of tea. He would not even go down to the Ward Room. We had gone to much trouble; every ship did it for a Royal visit but the King could not compete. It was only a few days before he abdicated – a sad occasion.

My old friend and Term-mate from Dartmouth days, Ivan Sarell, was the Flotilla Gunnery Officer at that time and it fell to him to organise the 5th Flotilla contingent lining the route for the Coronation of the new King, George VI. I was put in charge of one platoon in the Mall. After a thoroughly uncomfortable part of a night – in Olympia, together with some of the Army, who always so readily accept discomfort – we set off at an extremely early hour to be in position by 6.30 am.

Most of us bought our full dress especially for this occasion – cocked hat, high-necked swallow-tailed double-breasted coat with gold collar and cuffs and gold tasselled epaulettes, gold-striped trousers and very highly polished half-Wellington boots. For me, an anxious moment came when a processing Royal Horse Artillery battery got held up opposite my platoon and one of the horses was so ill-trained as to stale. Slowly, the stream swept across the road towards my boots. To move or not to move? In the event, by a very narrow margin, it missed.

Soon after the Coronation came the Fleet Review at Spithead. Very, very spectacular: lines and lines of grey hulls – battleships, battle-cruisers, aircraft carriers, cruisers, destroyers, minesweepers and submarines from all civilised nations.

After the Review, there was to be a ball ashore, and the foreign guests were invited to dine in various HM Ships beforehand. We, in *Echo*, had some German naval officers who made repeated and gauchely forceful requests to see the anti-submarine instruments. They were eventually taken up the bridge where they made an attempt to remove the instrument covers which had all been painted that afternoon with slow-drying sticky enamel; not an accident, just a dirty trick.

The end of my appointment to *Echo* meant the return to serve on the staff of the Anti-Submarine School – with some clearly-formed ideas. The A/S – the 'ping' – exercises were given relatively far too little consideration in the Fleet. There were three reasons. First, gunnery and (also-ran) torpedo exercises were, by custom, accorded more priority. Secondly, 'ping' exercises called for a 'tame' submarine as a target and one of these was not easy to come by; the submarines gained nothing thereby and had their own training to do. Thirdly, however, those A/S exercises were usually dull and sometimes quite ineffective as well.

The reasons for this were, in turn, that no attempt was made to stage the exercises in waters where the asdic conditions were known to be good: 'bad conditions' were almost useless for training the operator. Then, the asdic equipment was not at all reliable. Finally, poor results in an exercise, unlike what would happen with a gunnery shoot, brought no hideous recriminations. They could be shrugged off. It was in such an atmosphere that many operators and officers lacked confidence and were all too often harrassed on the job.

The A/S Branch was a new one. It was isolated at Portland, away from the other Gunnery, Torpedo and Signal Schools at Portsmouth. Such factors had all contributed towards making the Branch a Cinderella. Furthermore, they promoted what, to a comparatively junior officer, seemed to be a marked sense of inferiority. Senior ratings – and some officers – spent too much time hiding behind their screw-drivers and behind the 'ping box' (the asdic set), about which little was known – or often cared – in the Fleet.

With this in mind, Gordon Luther and I asked to be sent to the Gunnery School, HMS *Excellent*, to qualify in field training – square bashing – and then to institute it in the syllabuses of all ratings qualifying for Submarine Detector. Captain Madden approved it all: the introduction of guards of honour, armed sentries and the accompanying 'bull'. It was far from popular but it did smarten the place up. Great stuff, this square bashing. The man in the squad is on a spot and cannot play for time. Then, the member of the squad called out to take temporary charge has to think ahead and to exercise control. Unpopular – yes, but when it is all over, a fine boost for the ego.

In addition to the parade ground, I was teaching both at sea and ashore in the class rooms, where my limited understanding of technical matters was actually a help. Concurrently, I was put in charge of the building in which the 'Ironmongery' was on display. This meant being present to say my piece to all visiting VIPs. Winston Churchill, then not in office at all, came down to the A/S School in the early summer of 1938.

When he arrived, the Captain turned to the great man: 'Sir, this is Lieutenant Whinney, who will explain the underwater equipment to you.'

'Winnie' looked quite sharply at the Captain. 'What, Captain, did you say this officer's name was?'

Madden repeated my name. Churchill gave me a quizzical look and asked me some brief, simple but very practical questions. Later, at lunch in the Ward Room, I was placed near him, actually next to him I think. The 'hot' (we had no 'choice') was something slushy, probably stew. Mr Churchill, mouth right down to working level, made a noisy two-handed attack on it. There was nothing elegant about his table manners but did he have any elegance apart from his turn of phrase?

In June 1938, HM King George VI, accompanied by Commander HRH The Duke of Kent with Captain Lord Louis Mountbatten in attendance,

The battleship HMS *Royal Sovereign*, Malta, 1928. The 'Tiddly Quid' was one of some eight such ships in the mighty Mediterranean Fleet.

The Quarterdeck. Everyone stepping on the quarterdeck saluted it. It was the scene of all ceremonial, discipline, official entertainment and parties.

HMS *Royal Sovereign*'s picket boat. It was a midshipman's proud charge. If he smashed the boat or a gangway – and the author never did – it was six with the cane or a fortnight's leave stopped.

Battleship firing 15-inch broadside, 1928. There was a vast fuss beforehand; then a nerve-racking delay in opening fire. The series of thunderous crashes preceded the tinkling of broken glass. Thereafter came days of acrimonious analysis.

Admiral James, one-time Captain of HMS
Royal Sovereign. Millais' portrait of 'Bubbles'
James was the original advertisement for
Pears Soap; Bubbles married the artist's
daughter. (IWM)

Fairey Flycatcher over Malta in 1928. Early
vintage Fleet Air Arm – taken by the writer
with a Box Brownie camera.

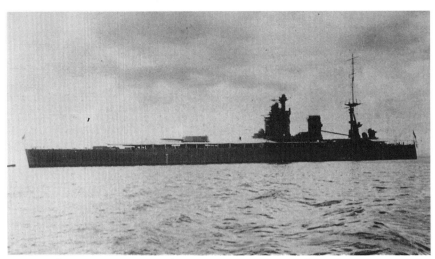

HMS *Rodney* at anchor, 1931. One of the worst ships in the Invergordon Mutiny, years later she helped destroy the formidable German ship *Bismarck*.

HMS *Rodney*: 16-inch guns, 1931. A formidable sight they were. Each shell weighed over a ton.

HMS *Valentine, circa* 1931. The author did destroyer training service in her prior to later service in *Wolsey* and *Wanderer*. All three were 'V and W' class destroyers. The first 'V' class laid down and the second launched, she was also the longest-lived of all the 'V' and 'W' class, for, although an early loss in World War Two, her hull survived until 1953. Compare her with *Wanderer* after conversion.

HMS *Suffolk* and Chinese Junk. The eight-inch cruisers were well suited to the Far East. The sails of many Chinese Junks then (1934) could consist of holes with old sacks round them.

A winner at Hong Kong races in 1934. The animal was in no hurry to stop.

King Edward VIII inspected the Fleet just before abdicating, 12 November 1936. Almost three years later *Royal Oak* was sunk in Scapa Flow, at anchor, by *U-47*, with 833 lives lost. (Popperfoto)

King George VI arriving at Portland to visit the Anti-Submarine School in June 1938. The King came for an informal visit soon after that of Winston Churchill. The writer, as a lieutenant, had to explain the 'ironmongery'. (Graham Herbert)

HMS *Cossack*, 1940. This 'Tribal' class destroyer achieved great fame by freeing British seamen POWs from the German ship *Altmark*. Later, she pursued *Bismarck* but was finally sunk by a U-boat.

Captain P.L. Vian on the bridge. Brilliant, quick and calm in action, but there was seldom a smile on the face of the tiger. (IWM)

Admiral Sir John Tovey, later Admiral of the Fleet Lord Tovey C-in-C Home Fleet when *Bismarck* was sunk. He was an old friend of my father's. (IWM)

Bismarck – a 15-inch broadside photographed from *Prinz Eugen* as the battleship engaged HMS *Hood*. The great German battleship, already hit by aircraft torpedoes, was attacked by destroyers, finally to be sunk by the Home Fleet. (Popperfoto)

Bismarck sunk. The survivors appeared as little black dots in a rough sea. (Keystone Press Agency Ltd)

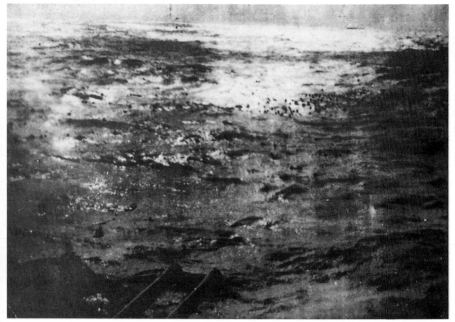

Survivors from *Bismarck*. The cruiser *Dorsetshire* and the destroyer *Maori* recovered
115 out of the two thousand or so. (IWM)

Admiral Willis, the C–in–C South Atlantic. He was a puritan; perhaps ill; perhaps·tired; but eternally grim in Freetown. (Keystone Press Agency)

Rear Admiral Pegram, followed Willis in command in Freetown, an inspiring, driving, cheerful, popular leader. As Admiral Sir Frank, he was Controller of the Navy, sadly to die, it was said from overwork. (IWM)

Beyond the range of Coastal Command in the early war years, the predator U-boat hunted surfaced in all weathers.

Harbour Defence Motor Launch. In the dire days of escort shortage, these 72-foot HDMLs, with make-shift upperdeck diesel tanks, were invaluable for West African coastal convoy escort duty. (IWM)

HMS *Wanderer* at anchor, camouflaged and showing her pennant number I.74. Flag L and I were reserved for escort destroyers.

HMS *Wanderer* converted to an escort destroyer. Designed for fleet work twenty-five years earlier, these sturdy old hulls, with modern A/S equipment stood up well to the job. The German Secret Service is believed to have taken this photograph in the Straits of Gibraltar on 15 August 1943 to show the H/F D/F mast.

HMS *Wanderer*, fuelling at sea trials. The oiler gave the ship to be fuelled a hemp rope and an oil hose. The hemp rope was for station-keeping and to prevent the oil hose getting broken. Too much strain and the oil hose broke. Then, no-one laughed. (Admiralty, Bath)

HMS *Wanderer* undertaking embarkation at sea trials in 1943. She was launched in 1919 as a 'Modified W' class fleet destroyer and was converted for convoy escort work in World War Two. She is trying new methods here. (Admiralty, Bath)

Wanderer ship's company. There were 193 of us crammed into primitive accommodation designed for 154. The Admiralty approved a 'Hard Lying' allowance.

also came to visit the A/S School. The King, who had of course served in the Navy himself, accepted the standard explanations and asked me few questions. The direct interest of the Monarch at this level and at this time was significant as was that of Winston Churchill.

In the autumn of 1938, I heard that the Captain intended to send me off to be the Anti-Submarine Officer of the destroyer flotilla on the China Station. At long last, anxious days over, I was clear of the direct and indirect effects of the Quarterly Report. The appointment was a good one and professionally, it came propitiously. On 30 September 1938, the Prime Minister, Neville Chamberlain, had obtained his so-called 'Peace with Honour' Agreement for the Anglo-German Friendship, which temporarily relaxed the tension. To me, it looked like two years away on the China Station or war with Germany, or both. The change in circumstances disrupted my personal plans: very sadly, the long and so close friendship with Joan became overstrained and events prevented it being put right.

It then happened that my departure for China was postponed. With little work to do, I decided to fill in the time by training for, and riding successfully in the naval races at the Blackmore Vale Hunt and the Cattistock point-to-point meetings. Time passed the more quickly because the Captain, Alec Madden and his wife, both very musical, organised a theatrical revue. Without the option, I started as the understudy to the leading male part but was progressively demoted as useless to left-hand man of the rear rank of the chorus. As a money raiser for charity, *Hands to Dance and Skylark* was a success. Off the stage, some members of the cast took the Skylark element too literally – at least three divorces and other marital upsets resulted.

5. VOICES IN THE DARK

This time, the China Station was more serious. Japan's invasion of the coastal areas of China had progressed and there were a number of incidents in which HM Ships and British merchant ships were involved. Hong Kong, though, was full of bright light. The 'Number One' Hotel, i.e. the best – known as 'The Grips' because that was the limit of activity permitted on the dance floor – was doing great business.

However, tensions existed in the Colony and not the least was that the Governor's lady had recently carried out a vigorous, though ill-supported campaign against the Colony's brothels. Many of the girls took avoiding action by moving to the nearby Portuguese Island of Macao. Not to be so easily seen off, the lady pursued them (metaphorically, of course) and the Portuguese were forced in self-defence to counter-attack by awarding the lady the Order of Chastity (Third Class). Where girls had good local logistic support and opted to stay in Hong Kong, advertisements appeared in the local press offering help to those interested in 'Playful Kittens' or, presumably for the more mature, 'Well-trained Pussy Cats'. To the satisfaction of many, the lady's campaign was a failure.

Not very long after I joined HMS *Duncan*, leader of the 5th Destroyer Flotilla, as the Flotilla Anti-Submarine Officer, the ship was sent to Shanghai. The Shanghai Club, the Country Club, the French Club and most of the wide-ranging amenities of the Settlement were going strong. The Japanese were just outside the boundary and among the European business men there was an air of apprehension, fear of the day when this then very prosperous centre of World trade, this sophisticated city upon which their livelihood depended, would be seized by the invaders. Nonetheless, at that time, there was no problem for me to cross the Japanese boundary to get to the polo ground. A British insurance company policy, an imposing-looking document covered with seals, held upside down was readily accepted by the Japanese frontier guards in place of the more commonplace official pass.

The headlines of the latest copy of *The Times* we had on board still referred to cricket, but it came as no great surprise when the signal came giving the code word meaning: 'Commence hostilities against Germany'. So languid and dull did this little message seem that it took time to absorb its significance. In fact, neither then nor for some weeks to come did any of us in that ship have a realistic idea of what might be coming, though I remember some anxiety lest London might be bombed!

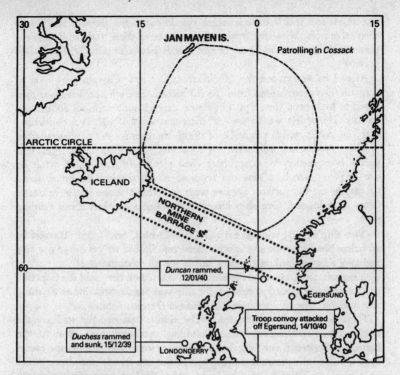

Map 2. Two Winters 1939–41
Winter 1939–40 brought two rammings, one personally experienced, but winter
1940–41 brought a very successful action off Egersund by 'Tribals' and 4th DF
escorts and patrols in the North Sea, North Atlantic and (broken ring) the Arctic.

My Captain's immediate reaction to the hostilities signal was to send me,
as Officer of the Guard, to a Japanese battleship carrying an Admiral's flag
and to an Italian sloop, to tell them to leave Shanghai at once. The Officer of
the Guard from any warship was the formal representative of his
Commanding Officer. The boat in which he travelled flew a Commanding
Officer's pennant in the bows as well as the national ensign at the stern and
he was entitled to be piped over the side. Some nations blew bugles at the
Officer of the Guard, the French and the Italians making especially
unseemly and nerve-racking noises. My Captain had absolutely no
authority to give orders to these foreign ships. Their countries were not at
war with Great Britain and Shanghai was an international port. The Italian
sloop received me with courtesy and left harbour at once. The Japanese
were discourteous; they kept me waiting on deck; their ship did, however,
leave harbour within an hour or so. *Duncan* followed after a decent interval.

Back in Hong Kong and later in Singapore, after the flotilla had been
ordered to sail for the Mediterranean, there were increased degrees of

uneasiness and fear lest the Japanese should come into the war and invade their territories. We – that is we sailors – expected them to do so. It was not pleasant clearing out and leaving our friends ashore to what was so plainly coming.

After *Duncan* reached the Mediterranean, a new Captain took over as Captain (D), a gentleman from the Admiralty. The whole flotilla was then based in Malta and the ships, in groups, carried out a series of contraband patrols. The object was to prevent merchant ships of whatever nationality carrying goods which might be of use to the enemy. A few neutral ships were stopped and some were even boarded, but to no effect, perhaps, partly, because they were never searched adequately. One night, while on one of these patrols, a look-out reported seeing through his binoculars a submarine on the surface. *Duncan* went to action stations and gave chase. Guns were loaded. Our ship was doing 17 knots and just about keeping pace.

'This ship's going too fast for a German U-boat, Sir,' I said. 'It could be an Italian but we're not at war with them yet. Should we get out to one side and take a better look at the ship before we do anything else?'

'Yes, very well, but keep the armament trained on her,' said the Captain.

Retrospectively hard to believe, the ship was not a submarine or anything like one, but one of our latest Blue-Funnel merchant ships!

These patrols did not last long. The flotilla was ordered to leave the Mediterranean and return home, providing anti-submarine escort for the battleship *Barham* from Gibraltar to home waters. Anti-submarine escort duty involved the destroyers being spread out in a fan-shaped screen rather over a mile ahead of the ship being screened. We had done a little of this in peace-time exercises by day when it was not too difficult but the flotilla had certainly never done it by night. With all ships entirely darkened, the problem at night – before the advent of radar – was to estimate distances. I had suggested to my Captain that all ships in the flotilla should be advised, when in doubt, to take occasional snap asdic ranges of the ship being screened and of adjacent destroyers. He would not have it, on the basis that distances could be estimated by eyes and that if the asdics were not constantly on submarine search, the ship being screened might be endangered.

Off the west coast of Ireland, we had a particularly dark night and the time came when *Barham* and, of course the destroyers screening her, had to alter course towards the Clyde. The alteration was to be made by what was known as a Red Pennant Turn. In simple terms, it meant that when the battleship altered course the fan-shaped screen of destroyers would have to move so as to be ahead of her on her new course. What was in doubt, however, was *when* they should move. Should they move before the battleship altered course so as to be in position when she did alter – or should they wait until she altered and then move over? With this ambiguity, the destroyers usually started to move gradually in advance of the battleship's alteration of course.

It happened that at the critical time on that night, I was on watch in the flotilla leader as the Principal Control Officer with a very reliable officer as Officer of the Watch. At the vital moment, I went to the back of the bridge to watch the other ships of the screen through binoculars, especially those ships on the outside of the turn. Suddenly, in the middle of the manoeuvre *Barham* switched on her navigation lights. Then she switched on a searchlight. In the searchlight's beam was, apparently, a submarine. The assumption was that the battleship had rammed a U-boat. At first, no signal was made to say what had happened. Then came a signal from *Barham* telling us to pick up survivors. The Captain was, of course, on the bridge by this time so I, as First Lieutenant, went down to lower a boat to pick up survivors from a U-boat – or so I thought. As the boat was being lowered there were several loud explosions. There must be a second U-boat which had fired torpedoes and hit *Barham*. As an immediate reaction, I thought we should release a life-saving raft for the survivors for the time being, and seek and attack this supposed second U-boat.

Back on the bridge, however, I saw through binoculars what seemed at first to be a fire on the rammed vessel. Then, with horror, I realised that it was the red anti-fouling on the bottom of a destroyer and that the imagined conning tower was, in fact, the asdic dome. It became clear that what earlier were thought to be torpedoes from a second U-boat were the depth-charges of the capsized destroyer which had been primed and had fallen out of their stowage racks and reached the depth at which they were set to explode.

The unhappy ship was, we learned, *Duchess*, the ship on the outside wing. She must have turned late, underestimating the distance, cut too fine across the bows of *Barham*, been rammed and capsized. To the best of my belief, neither my Captain nor any other officer on our bridge was aware of the truth earlier than I was.

Casualties were very heavy. The Commanding Officer, Lieutenant Commander Robin White, an up-and-coming chap and one very well liked, was among those lost. He should have been on the bridge; as it was, the sliding door of his sea cabin, just below the bridge, jammed. He could not escape. A number of men in the water were killed by the ship's own depth charges bringing to light another ambiguity in orders: whether depth charges should or should not be primed to fire before an attack on an enemy submarine commenced. One moral might be said to be that there was a painfully clear need for practice of such obvious manoeuvres by darkened ships in peace time.

The findings of the Court of Enquiry were, of course, secret, but to me, this wretched event very firmly established the outstanding importance of clarity, of immediately passing information, and of never assuming that others concerned knew the score. Very soon after this disaster, two other ships from the Flotilla were lost. The circumstances were quite different but *Duncan*'s company were very upset and shaken. My Captain wanted to hold a memorial service in our home port, Chatham. No, I said, definitely please no: we had had more than a belly-full of woe in the Flotilla. He finally agreed.

In the short period of leave which followed the ship's arrival at Chatham, at Christmas, by Bishop's Licence, I married Nora. Known to her family and friends as Jimmy, she was the very pretty girl from the days of the *Osprey* theatricals. My parents, who normally never agreed on anything at all, were united in their disapproval.

Early in the new year, 1940, the 5th Destroyer Flotilla, or what was left of it, broke up as a unit and *Duncan* thus ceased to be a flotilla leader. The four-stripe captain was replaced by a commander in his first command and I was kept as First Lieutenant. The ship's first trip under the new Commanding Officer in January 1940 was to be as Senior Officer of the escort of one of those trade convoys which ran between Methil, on the Firth of Forth, and Bergen, on the West coast of Norway.

Those were the days of the Phoney War – *Sitzkrieg* to the Germans – and if the civilian population of Britain was not otherwise affected, they had started to endure severe food and petrol shortages; there was also the black-out on all houses, street lamps and traffic and the threat of invasion by sea and air was taken very seriously. It has been stated[1] that, had the invasion been launched and if other methods of defence failed in repelling it, the intention was for the British to use mustard gas against the German beach-heads.

At sea, however, the months of the Phoney War were active. SS *Athenia* was sunk by a U-boat on the first day of the war. Ten days later, HMS *Courageous* was sunk and losses of merchant vessels by surface raider, submarine and mine followed. Then, in mid-October, came the sinking of HMS *Royal Oak* by Oberleutnant Guenther Prien in *U-47*. The battleship, which lost some eight hundred officers and men, was lying anchored in Scapa Flow behind defences thought to be entirely secure when Prien made his approach, attack and escape – manoeuvres which were, by any standards, outstandingly skilful and audacious.

This was only a bitter foretaste: the U-boat offensive had not yet really been developed. The Germans actually started the war with a total of only 57 U-boats. The offensive against our shipping was at the outset primarily based on attack by dispersed surface ships, including the pocket-battleship *Graf Spee*. This ship had sunk nine British merchant ships, transferring at least some of the prisoners to the armed merchant ship raider *Altmark*, before she was brought to battle by a force of four cruisers.

In a gunnery action, the pocket-battleship, faster, more heavily armed and said to have been equipped with radar, unlike our ships, was so badly damaged that she was obliged to seek temporary shelter in neutral waters. Later, on the orders of her Captain, Landsdorf, *Graf Spee* was scuttled off Montevideo. As already stated, the unofficial elite of the Royal Navy were the gunnery officers, and as on this occasion, their high standing was reflected in their successes in hitting the enemy.

To complete the picture at sea, British submarines had scored successes against German naval forces and there had been skirmishes between our heavier forces and those of the Germans, while our minelayers were busy

1 *Rise and Fall of the Third Reich*, by William Shirer, page 785.

putting down the Northern Barrage between Iceland, the Faroes and the Outer Hebrides and our minesweepers were clearing channels around our coasts. Merchant ships had come under attack, not only from mines but also from U-boats and from the air.

If, on land, there was a comparative state of stalemate, it was a somewhat threatening stalemate and the threat definitely included invasion of Britain by both sea and air on a front stretching from the Straits of Dover to Lyme Bay. The civilians had little to be cheerful about and yet those whom I met on leave seemed to live in the happy belief that in a few months all would be over and we should have won the war. In fact, at that time in January 1940, the prospects for the Germans winning looked better.

Early in the month, we sailed from Methil for Bergen with the new Captain in charge of the convoy escort. The weather was foul, very cold with a strong head wind, a short, rough sea and snow showers, weather fairly typical of the North Sea in winter. It is fair to say that at that time there was a more or less established tactical policy for meeting an attack on a convoy by enemy surface forces. It was simple: the destroyers would attack the enemy with torpedoes and gunfire; but there was no such clear policy to contend with an attack on the convoy by U-boat. This was neither practised, nor even seriously considered in peace time. For this particular convoy, the escorts were allotted positions round the convoy to look out for and counter enemy surface ships and aircraft.

As was usual from the start of the war, and as a valuable relic of World War One and subsequent peace time exercises, the Ship's Company was at Cruising Stations, with half the men closed up at the armament and the other half off watch. During the night, the sea and the head wind increased so much that the merchant ships, slow at the best of times, could make little headway. To prevent *Duncan* getting too far ahead of them, to lose ground so to speak, the Officer of Watch decided, with the Captain's permission, to turn one or more circles occasionally! In one of these circles, the ship was caught in a heavy snow shower with the visibility almost nil. Suddenly, up the voicepipe from 'X' Gun, the 4.7-inch gun at the after end of the ship, there came a report: 'Please, Sir, voices in the dark.'

The Officer of the Watch had no time to find out what this astonishing and apparently irresponsible report might mean. There came a heavy, shuddering thump amidships, violently shaking the whole ship. The engine room-boiler room bulkhead, a particularly vulnerable spot, had been hit. At first, it was thought the ship had been torpedoed. I was sleeping forward in the sick-bay that night, and I dashed out in stockinged feet and fell straight on my backside on the snow-covered deck – never again to take off my boots when turning in at night at sea till the war ended! I tried to estimate the angle at which a torpedo might have been fired so that some other ship might get the U-boat. After a slight delay, the Captain made it clear that we had been rammed.

The voices in the dark had come from a Norwegian merchant ship which was out of position. I went to the engine room and the boiler room to make sure that there was no one trapped below and then reported this. The

Captain then ordered the placing of the collision mat, a peace time remedy designed to deal with all holes that might be caused when ships were hit by the enemy's shells or in minor collision. This mat was a rug-like object with lines attached to all four corners. The twenty-foot hole in the ship's side was plainly far, far too big for the collision mat to be of the slightest use and some minutes were lost in persuading the Captain that this was so. It remained to make sure that all watertight doors, hatches and outlets to the sea were quickly closed. An outlet drain normally above the water line, in the Ward Room (officers' mess), was found to be choked open with wet newspapers so that the compartment was progressively flooding.

Volunteers were needed to go down into the unlit compartment – all electric power was, of course, off. This was going to be a dangerous and difficult job and I was pleasantly surprised when two men – two of the ship's 'black sheep' – volunteered. The morale of the ship was not after all so bad, I began to think. Leaving the scene to inspect other parts of the ship where water might be coming in, I took a torch and eventually went aft, below again to look at the progress. There, in the dark were the two men, both horizontal, rolling happily unconscious – very drunk on the flooded deck, and surrounded by bottles. They had had the lot from the Ward Room wine cupboard: beer, whisky, port, sherry, brandy – all of it. Hoisted on to the upper deck, they recovered sufficiently to fight, until the Torpedo Coxwain, the senior rating on board a destroyer, rendered both harmless with a convenient wooden mallet and then had them lashed up in strait-jackets. He, above all others, was excellent throughout. He had a third case, a young rating who became uncontrollably hysterical, similarly treated.

The ship did not sink. She settled with six inches of freeboard on one side and eighteen inches on the other and, with the upper deck awash, was towed slowly by another destroyer to Invergordon. All the ship's store rooms were, of course, flooded or inaccessible during the long, cold tow and we existed on tea, ship's biscuits and, for lack of anything else available, cold tinned Irish stew. Even the seagulls tired of what we threw away.

When *Duncan* berthed on the wooden pier at Invergordon, there were a number of civilian fire engines awaiting us. With speed and efficiency, they had their pumps working and kept the ship afloat until a salvage firm had put a wooden patch, about twenty-five feet along, over the hole in the ship's side. In the meantime, the destroyer leader *Exmouth* came alongside to help remove the ammunition and thus lighten the ship. Next came a minesweeper to help carry on the good work. Both these ships then went to sea and were lost, *Exmouth* with all hands.

It had been too much for the ship's company. They were jumpy and lacking in confidence to a degree that I had never seen in a ship's company before and have not seen since. This ship had had a poor start to the commission; there had been too many changes among the officers, the Ward Room was not a happy one and there was neither a good feeling throughout the ship nor had there been good accord between officers and men in some branches. It was agreed that the ship should be towed south to

Grangemouth to refit and be paid off.

By this time, February 1940, the German auxiliary ship and raider *Altmark*, with three hundred prisoners of war from *Graf Spee*, had reached Norwegian waters on her way back to Germany. From a force of ships in the North Sea, HMS *Cossack* was instructed, through the orders of Mr Winston Churchill, then First Lord of the Admiralty, to intercept her and free the prisoners. *Altmark* was in neutral waters escorted by two Norwegian motor torpedo boats. The Norwegians, perhaps because they did not know the truth, insisted that there were no British prisoners on board *Altmark*. The Admiralty informed Captain Vian in *Cossack* that there were. In the meantime, and during negotiations, *Altmark* turned inshore and entered Josing Fjord.

Vian followed and *Altmark*, a very much larger vessel, came astern and attempted to ram *Cossack*. By deft ship-handling and determined work of the boarding party, the three hundred prisoners of war were re-embarked in *Cossack* and, with very limited casualties on both sides, *Cossack* headed for the open sea and Leith in Scotland. It was a dramatic as well as a highly skilful operation.

It has been maintained[2] that the protests of the Norwegian Government about the incursion into neutral waters by *Cossack* clinched Hitler's intention to invade Norway and beat the British to it. In this, he had his way: the Germans got there first and they successfully seized control of Norway, while the British Expeditionary Force was obliged to withdraw. From a naval point of view, it was another matter. In a complex campaign, the German losses in warships were very heavy.

It is not for one who is not a naval historian, who was not there anyway, to comment in detail on the First and Second Battles of Narvik and associated actions, other than to say they were primarily close-range, hard, bloody battles fought by gun and to a lesser degree torpedo fire. The First Battle is notable for the fact that Captain Warburton-Lee in *Hardy*, with other destroyers in company, was faced, it seemed, with vague if not vacillating orders and proceeded up the fjord at first light. In the very successful action off Narvik, *Hardy* was lost and Warburton-Lee was awarded a posthumous Victoria Cross – the first of the war. One result of the heavy losses and damage suffered by the German ships from our own surface ships and submarines in this campaign was that it emphasised that Hitler had no fleet adequate for the invasion of Britain, though it is not certain if he then realised it!

The stirring accounts of the outstanding action against *Graf Spee* and the *Altmark* episode, as well as those of the Norwegian Campaign, contrast sharply, you may think, with those mishaps described earlier in this chapter. Yes, of course they do. But 'being in the presence of the enemy' is remarkably inspiring – which is not to say that fear is absent! Then, Commanding Officers of HM Ships knew that a high standard of manoeuvring and gunnery was expected and they gave it. Conversely, the unexpected and what had never been practised or considered in peace time,

2 *Op cit*, page 679

did not come so easy – at least it did not during my time in *Duncan*!

As was usual for specialist officers, at the end of my sea appointment in HMS *Duncan*, back I went to the Anti-Submarine School, HMS *Osprey*, at Portland. There, Captain William-Powlett ('Wallop' we called him though not to his face!) told me to start a system for training destroyers, sloops and corvettes for war against U-boats. It was not easy. I told the captain the standard was abysmally low but that the Commanding Officers did not altogether like being told by an officer, often junior to them, how to put things right. I submitted such training should all be put on a much higher level. It was indeed put on to a far higher level under a most lively Vice-Admiral, retired and serving as a Commodore: 'Monkey' Stephenson (Vice Admiral Sir Gilbert). An outstanding personal character, he and his small staff ran a most effective training programme for ships about to serve in the Western Approaches as escorts.

In the meantime, there had been a buzz in *Osprey* that two jobs were to be filled at sea as Flotilla A/S Officers: one was in Captain Lord Louis Mountbatten's Destroyer Flotilla, the other in Captain Vian's. Knowing that Captain Mountbatten was an outstanding technician, I thought it prudent to avoid serving under him: he would know far more about the theory than me! Fortunately, 'Egg' Burnett, very brainy, ultimately a Rear Admiral, got the job. It was some months later that William Powlett then sent for me. 'Captain Vian wants a new A/S Officer in the 4th Flotilla,' he informed me. 'They are 'Tribal' class destroyers. It's a good job but you need not go if you don't want to.'

'Whatever is this?' I thought, 'Has Vian turned cannibal?' but I answered unequivocally. 'Yes, Sir, I should like the job very much. I've known Captain Vian for some years – since I was a Midshipman.' (Vian had even taught me to hit a polo ball those many years before, though that information did not seem worth volunteering.)

Meantime, in the dramatic and disastrous late spring of 1940, Hitler's armies had marched unopposed through Holland and Belgium, and the French Maginot Line of fortresses, assessed by some as impregnable, had fallen. Our Army in Europe was in full retreat – a retreat which, because of inexplicable military thinking by Hitler, was not immediately followed up by the German Army. By an utterly determined series of operations from Dunkirk, from the French ports in the Channel, and the west and south coasts of France, some half million British and Allied troops were brought back to England. This evacuation was a complex and miraculous affair in which every kind of available vessel was involved, including private yachts and other small vessels. It was, as stated earlier, the operation in which Captain David Simson, my Term Officer at Dartmouth, was killed.

Militarily, we had suffered a massive, perilous defeat. Hitler had taken Europe, including, of course, the French ports and airfields. We were left with the remains of a broken, unarmed army, but I saw some of the soldiers returning; they came from a beaten, yet not a cowed army.

Having failed to exploit our army's defeat on the Continent, Hitler again failed by not staging his invasion of Britain. One reason for this was that he lacked the necessary warships. Yet another reason may have been that he seriously thought that Britain might sue for peace! Churchill's famous broadcast speech on 4 June 1940 should have put him right on that matter: 'We shall go on to the end, we shall fight on the seas, we shall fight on the beaches, in the fields, in the streets, we shall never surrender.'

My impression is that at that stage the real bitterness of war had not set in. The people of Britain were angry at the shortage of food, the black-out and the general inconvenience; and they were frightened by the threats of invasion and serious bombing; also, they were, inevitably, confused. But not for a moment did it occur to anyone, come what may, that we should not win the war – and win it alone.

6. BISMARCK

When I joined his ship, *Cossack*, at Southampton and reported to him, the Captain was in his bath. He had got very skinny, I thought. He took one look at me and said: 'Thank God you're not fat. That's all for now.'

Vian had always been spare. He was tallish and fair with heavy bushy eyebrows; in fact, the slate-coloured eyes were surrounded by fair hair. Unusual this was, but, it was said, the girls over a number of years had liked it. His face never showed much expression – perhaps the hair hid it. PLV was a man who lived on his nerves – and very resilient they must have been and, especially after the *Altmark* episode and the Second Battle of Narvik, he was not imbued with any sense of inferiority. As compared with other ships I had known in those early days of the war, *Cossack*, leader of the 4th Destroyer Flotilla, was a very efficient ship; she had good officers and the Captain was trusted by his officers and men alike as one who would pursue the enemy hard and effectively but would never take a risk rashly or by accident. He was not, though, a gentle gentleman!

As part of the Home Fleet, the ship, when not undergoing refit or repairs, was based on Scapa Flow, a bleak, dismal, God-forsaken place. It was made the worse because one could so easily see the sad battleship *Royal Oak*, only masts, a funnel and superstructure showing above the water, lying sunk on an even keel, a reminder of the power of the U-boat. Scapa had its appeals only for the walks ashore across the heather and because there were to all intents and purposes no air raids to keep one awake at night in harbour.

For us, it was more often than not a matter of escorting fast convoys – on one occasion a cruiser carrying bullion to the United States – and of giving anti-submarine protection to the bigger ships when they put to sea, plus an occasional foray as a flotilla into the North Sea. Once, when on the bridge, I sighted what appeared to be a U-boat's conning tower – it showed only for a matter of seconds.

I reported it to the captain, got an asdic contact, he said I could fire one depth charge but that he would not hang around longer. This was quite useless, of course. There was the need to shape up to the contact and drop a full pattern of depth charges on it – just for a start. Vian was by specialisation a gunnery officer and, like a number of others at that particular time of the war, was not so interested in asdics!

Throughout the late summer and early autumn of 1940, one of the Flotilla's potential commitments was to contend with the possibility of

Hitler's Operation SEALION, the planned invasion of Britain. In fact, despite the enemy warship losses in the Norway campaigns, it was not until mid-September 1940, after the Royal Air Force's bombing of the German invasion vessels and, additionally, after the German air force's considerable losses in the Battle of Britain, that the order was given by Hitler for the indefinite postponement of the invasion.

My suggestion to the Captain at the time was that if Operation SEALION were to come off, we should try to avoid action with warships escorting invasion convoys, and attack the convoys from the rear while steaming slowly in line ahead up the columns of convoys, firing as we went. Thus, any retaliatory fire from the enemy would be quite likely to hit their own side. I think Captain Vian accepted this and it became broad Fleet policy. Of course, we never had to try it out.

In October, there was one short, spectacular action which was typical of Vian. An intelligence report came through of a German troop-carrying convoy off the Norwegian coast. *Cossack* was ordered to proceed with three other 'Tribal' destroyers, at high speed to intercept. Vian selected a point of encounter for midnight off Egero Light and issued his simple orders to the destroyers in company. He would lead them in line ahead (the RAF, for some reason, call the same thing line astern) to attack the enemy. Just before midnight Egero Light was sighted. The silhouette of the enemy convoy and escorts could be seen against the flashing beam of the lighthouse. Vian's plan was to get in to point-blank range.

The enemy made the challenge on a small lamp: two letters flashed. To gain a few seconds the Captain ordered the Chief Yeoman of Signals to flash those same two letters back. The enemy then promptly opened fire and the 4th Flotilla replied. At such close range there was no fancy fire-control. It was what was known as 'quarters firing'; this meant that guns were locally controlled. For the occasion I was put in charge of the two foremost twin 4.7-in gun turrets and banged away, for preference at the troop ships – not so easy to see because of the blinding flashes of our own guns and the cordite smoke. At that short range, however, there was not much missing the target and with our own ships in line ahead, it was safe to assume that anything seen on either side was enemy.

The night was lit up by a firework display made up by burning enemy ships, gun flashes and tracer fire from the smaller guns of the ships on both sides. Precise identification of the target was not always easy. At one juncture, I reported to the bridge the approach of E-boats; there appeared to be the wash of fast-moving craft coming straight for the ship. Ordered by the Captain, I at once opened fire only to cease fire just as quickly. What at first had looked like a wash turned out to be, when seen closer, a string of life-saving rafts, with bright lights attached, from one of the sunken German troopships.

PLV was at his best: no cursing, no swearing and, according to my wrist watch, eleven minutes from the moment of opening fire (Vian, in his book *Action this Day*, says fifteen minutes) the enemy convoy and its escorts were badly hit, on fire or sunk by gunfire and torpedo. *Cossack* had been hit once aft with one man slightly wounded. After a brief search for escaping enemy ships, our ships disengaged and were doing thirty knots for Rosyth.

And what was it like, this baptism of fire in a surface action? Unnerving? No. It was exhilarating to us all. Despite the darkness, I had only to indicate the targets and the guns' crews were on and had opened fire. If *Cossack* was being fired on, the gun flashes were the brighter and thus provided an indication for return of fire. We should not get hurt and the fire of the enemy made it the more inspiring to hit back quickly and accurately.

For twelve very, very exhausting hours of daylight on the return trip across the North Sea, we were bombed with an intensive vengeance: high level and dive-bombing. Once again, I was in charge of the two forward turrets. Attacks were coming in from all angles – especially up-sun – and everyone on deck did his best to keep the bridge informed of impending attack while those of us in charge of guns opened fire at anything threatening without awaiting orders.

As often as not it was possible to see the bombs dropped from high level and observe their fall. Where necessary, the avoiding action taken by destroyers was to alter course, often towards the descending bombs so that they would go over the far side of the ship. Dealing with the dive-bombers was different: the ideal was to wait until the German Stuka was committed to his dive and then to alter the ship's course towards its attack. This was intended to make the angle of dive impossibly steep so that the aircraft's pilot was either forced to pull out of his dive, finding his bombs were going to miss over – or, if he did not think quick enough, find himself plunging fatally into the sea.

'Why did you hit me, Sir?' said a young seaman on B Gun Deck, turning suddenly towards me, rubbing his back.

'You can keep that,' I said, picking up a lump of metal from a very nearby bomb, 'and show it to your grandchildren!' It had come from a bomb which no one saw coming and which landed nearby with the usual nasty grey splash. One of the serious shortcomings of those 'Tribal' Class destroyers when under air attack was that their 4.7-inch guns would not elevate above forty degrees. However, surprisingly little damage was done to the ships; but then, they came from a very efficient flotilla with very experienced Commanding Officers in each ship. Some fighter cover did appear but not until we were nearly home. So often when the Fleet was being attacked, fighter cover was not available. The pity was that we were never told the reason; presumably all available aircraft were needed for tasks of higher priority. There would have been much less bad feeling if the reason had been adequately promulgated.

As a contrast to this action, one day soon after, the Captain told me that he had been bidden to a meeting by R.A.(D), the Rear Admiral commanding the Home Fleet destroyers and that he was taking me. The meeting was to discuss a night action which had taken place between five destroyers under the command of Captain Lord Louis Mountbatten and three German destroyers (said at the time, I think, to be four) in the Channel. Official history may differ, but my recollection was that Captain

Mountbatten said that he had received a report giving the position, course and speed of the German force and had told his navigating officer to set a course to come upon the enemy. He decided to depart from the entirely orthodox and customary formation with the senior officer's ship leading into battle. Instead, he put his force into a staggered line of bearing, with his own ship in the middle. He gave preliminary instructions for Master Ship Control[1], which meant that all ships' gunfire would be controlled by the senior ship, his own.

The initial contact with the enemy was perfect and (still no radar then) HM Ships came up astern and got in undetected to 1,500 yards – three quarters of a nautical mile! At this close range, Mountbatten had given the order to open fire but it seemed that, somehow, the range passed to the guns was not 1,500 but 15,000 – seven and a half miles! The enemy destroyers were alerted by gun flashes and shells whistling overhead. The German ships followed the standard procedure, all turned together and fired their torpedoes – with devastating success. Captain Mountbatten's ship was hit twice and had both bow and stern blown off; other ships were hit and the enemy retired partially, if not wholly unscathed. There was a story that while awaiting rescue, the Captain sat in his sea cabin in the remains of his ship calmly reading a novel!

When Captain Lord Louis had delivered his account of the action to the meeting, the Admiral turned to Vian who was the senior Captain present, saying: 'Would you like to ask any questions or make any comment?'

'No, Sir,' said Vian.

The Admiral then got the views of the other Captains (D) present, came back to Vian and said more formally: 'Vian, what would you like to say?'

'Nothing, Sir,' was the reply.

The third time round, the Admiral said stiffly and firmly:'Captain Vian, I would like to hear what you have to say.'

'I have nothing to say, Sir,' said Vian; and he got up and left the meeting with me, of course, following.

It was not untypical of the man to whom simplicity and clarity meant everything, tolerance very little and to whom good manners depended on how he was feeling. But it was he, Vian, who remained successful in action – or, as he put it in his book *Action this Day* – lucky. Captain Mountbatten, on the other hand – with a series of glorious disasters – remained unlucky in action and always seemed to have a rough time. It is of passing interest, perhaps, that his DSO was not, as was then usually the case, awarded for a specific action or service. In the 1941 New Year's Honours List, the citation read: 'For outstanding zeal, patience and cheerfulness and never failing to set an example of wholehearted devotion to duty without which the high tradition of the Royal Navy could not have been upheld.'

Further cases of Vian's intolerance were not few to find. One of the duties of destroyers in the Home Fleet at that time was to provide anti-submarine screens for the big ships, the battle-cruisers and aircraft carriers which were

1. The writer has never seen written confirmation of this

often covering the minelayers against attack by heavier German forces. The minelayers were then laying the Northern Barrage of minefields running between Iceland, the Faroes and the Outer Hebrides. The weather was permanently rough and cold – not good for the temper.

On one occasion, the senior officer's ship was making a long signal detailing policy to be followed by the ships under his temporary command during the night. He was also a Captain but marginally senior to Vian who did not, it seemed, much care for him. This was not surprising; the particular Captain's nickname, at my level, was 'Charlie Turmoil'. I had once met Charlie Turmoil in a brief visit to the Admiralty. He had a telephone in each hand and was, it seemed, speaking into each on different subjects, dictating a signal on a third subject and keeping a queue of people waiting to see him. Vian's comment on him that day at sea was: 'Any bloody fool can make things complicated. It takes a little more to make them simple.'

Fireworks on the bridge were no novelty. On another occasion, *Cossack* and other destroyers under the Captain's orders had to form an anti-submarine screen for one or more big ships.

'Select a screen formation from the book,' said the Captain.

I was working it out when he said: 'Hurry up. If you can't make up your mind, we'll have this one. Is that all right? Yes, it is, we will have it.'

From myself: 'No, Sir, I do not think that one will do.' Pause.

'Why?'

I explained that the distances were wrong and that the screen which he had selected was not appropriate. Quite suddenly, he switched round: 'Get off the bridge at once,' he said, 'and never come back.'

I went down to the chart house directly below the bridge. He immediately sent for me again.

'What screen was it you recommended? We will have that one. I am sorry, I was wrong.' Then, feeling that perhaps he had overdone it, he added quietly: 'And don't you ever speak to me like that again.' This made me laugh – later, when clear of the Captain, of course. At the time I was not so sure.

In the year I served in *Cossack*, six of the twelve officers were sacked – one because the Captain said, without much justification, that he smelt! It was certainly never dull in that ship.

There were other encounters with the Captain on the bridge. One such I recollect on a particular, very dark night in the North Sea. It was rough and the visibility was poor. I was on watch as the Principal Control Officer.

'Object ahead,' reported the starboard look-out.

'What is it?' asked the Captain, turning to me.

'Can't see yet, Sir – could be a very dense, low-lying cloud.'

Pause, then peering again through binoculars: 'No, Sir, it is a battleship – no, two battleships – Action Stations, Sir?' With my hand on the Alarm push and sharp prickles down the spine: 'Make the challenge?'

Vian had his own glasses on the ship now: 'No,' he said, 'it's our own battle fleet.' Then, to the Signal Officer: 'Turn the Flotilla 180 degrees to starboard and increase speed to twenty-five knots.' Then he turned back to me and said: 'They bloody well should have told us the battle fleet was at sea but we won't say any more about it or it will start a flow of useless bumph.'

This was a time of non-stop activity for us in the 4th Flotilla, mostly in the northern part of the North Sea. It included two forays over to the Norwegian coast to try to rescue the crews of British submarines which had been attacked and forced to surface. In both cases, I knew the Commanding Officers; in both cases, we failed because we were not told in time. On one of those occasions we were given air cover and, while under attack from German aircraft, one of our Blenheims was shot down. The First Lieutenant, Peter Gretton, dived over the side and swam to the burning aircraft to rescue the pilot; the Captain stopped me from following Gretton – quite wrong I thought, because I was a much better swimmer!

Jan Mayen Island, in the Arctic Circle north of Iceland, was for some reason in part of our area of activity and the Germans were known to have a weather reporting station there, and, as we were passing, I said to the Captain: 'Why not send a party ashore to capture it and break it up, Sir?' Vian agreed 'Yes, you can go. Take a whaler and a few sailors.' But he changed his mind, rightly no doubt. It could have been a failure; and it could have left him with a commitment to get us back on board again.

The most dramatic action of my year in *Cossack* was against the new, fast, large, very heavily armed and armoured, magnificent German battleship, *Bismarck*. In May 1941, the ships *Cossack, Sikh, Maori* and *Zulu* from the 4th Destroyer Flotilla with the Polish destroyer *Piorun* and the anti-aircraft cruiser *Cairo* were escorting a fast southbound convoy of troopships. The convoy had been located by the enemy and attacked by aircraft, one troopship being damaged. In the meantime, it became known that *Bismarck*, accompanied by the cruiser *Prinz Eugen*, had broken out of the Baltic and had been sighted in the Denmark Strait north of Iceland.

On 23 May, our battle cruiser *Hood* – the 'Mighty Hood' as she was known to us – with the battleship *Prince of Wales* in company, engaged the German ships. It left us all horrified – shaken – aghast to learn that *Hood* had been sunk, sunk quickly with nearly all hands. And the Germans had successfully withdrawn. Contributory factors seem to have been that both HM Ships were initially told to concentrate their gunfire on the leading ship; both the German ships had similar silhouettes and the leading ship happened to be the cruiser *Prinz Eugen* – not *Bismarck*. In addition, *Prince of Wales* was not fully worked-up – that is to say, she was not fully trained for battle.

Bismarck then disappeared and was lost. This threatened our convoy with potentially catastrophic consequences. The next event for us in *Cossack* was, however, an order from the Admiralty to Captain(D)4, namely Vian in *Cossack*, for his destroyers to join the Commander-in-Chief, Admiral Sir John Tovey, flying his flag in the battleship *King George V*, as the C-in-C was short of destroyer escort to protect his ships against submarine attack. A few hours after receiving this order, *Cossack* intercepted an aircraft report of *Bismarck* to the southward and the deduction was made that the German ship was making for the safety of a Biscay port. Vian's choice now lay between either obeying the Admiralty's order to provide anti-submarine escort for the battleships and so leave the enemy perhaps to escape, or leaving the battleships short of escorts and going straight for the enemy.

As the A/S Officer, I submitted that it was justified that he risk leaving the battleships short of escorts. The Admiralty had not warned by signal of known U-boats in the area which might threaten the C-in-C and his big ships. In fact, it was the advice of Robin Maurice, the Navigator, that Vian was more likely to take but he must have said the same as I did. Vian went to find *Bismarck*.

A gale was rising as the destroyers set course to intercept the German battleship. Steaming at speed with a nasty sea on the quarter, the ships yawed widely, as much as one hundred and forty degrees off course, Vian says in his book. Some men were certainly hurt and one was lost overboard as the weather continued to deteriorate. There were periodic rainstorms and the visibility was chancy as the destroyers steamed, spread out in line-abreast. Quite suddenly, almost unbelievably, in the failing evening light, the wing ship, the Polish *Piorun*, opened fire. Action was joined.

By this time, we in *Cossack* knew that *Bismarck* had been attacked by torpedo-carrying aircraft, the old, slow Swordfish – 'Stringbags' they were called in the Fleet. I do not think that Vian knew what damage, if any, had been inflicted by the attacks. The standard tactics under the circumstances might have been for destroyers to go for the enemy in line ahead and then turn and fire torpedoes. However, Captain (D) thought that perhaps the more vital role was to maintain contact until the arrival of the big ships in the early morning. It was presumably on this basis that he ordered his ships to surround *Bismarck* in a ring and to carry out independent attacks with torpedoes and gunfire during the night. Such tactics were (unless I had failed to read the right books and papers!) entirely unorthodox; but they worked. When it came to contact with the enemy, Vian was gifted as few before.

Throughout the night, all destroyers made a series of attacks, the Polish ship pressing her attacks home particularly closely. As an observer, I was not impressed with our ship's torpedo fire. All underwater noises were, of course, audible on the asdic and not more than two underwater explosions were recorded in the asdic cabinet log; one of these was, I thought, a torpedo fired by *Maori*. As it happened on this occasion, *Cossack*, one of the first destroyers to be so fitted, had a form of radar known as RDF – radio direction finding. The aerials would not rotate and the equipment would only transmit ahead and on the beam; thus the RDF would give range – that is, distance – but no positive direction or bearing of the target. The Captain ordained that the operation of this mystery box should be mine. There were two rating operators but, because the box was so temperamental, I sat with them in their minute office at the back of the bridge for much of the action that night. The big German ship was on the screen most of the time as a thumping large fluorescent echo while lesser echoes were given off by our

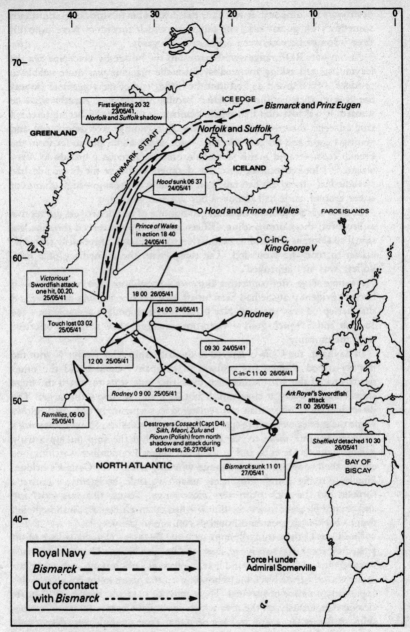

Map 3. The _Bismarck_ Hunt, 1941
The wounded _Bismarck_ was brought to bay in darkness by destroyers on 26/27 May and despatched by the Home Fleet the next day. She died hard.

destroyers in company. It was thus that I was able to work out, admittedly sometimes by guesswork, the ranges at which torpedoes were probably fired – somewhere between 3,500 to 5,000 yards.

At the start RDF ranges were passed to the bridge by voicepipe but the Captain started asking for results which the machine was quite unable to produce. I then found he had shut the bridge end of the voicepipe! He was bored with such equipment, which would not produce exactly what he wanted. It was just after that when, glancing at the green flickering screen, I saw an echo directly approaching the ship, going exceedingly fast and getting bigger and bigger. Aircraft? – no, not at night, not so far from the French coast – rapid maths – it could only be an enemy broadside! Very alarmed, I looked outside into the darkness and saw the broadside had straddled us – the shells had fallen on both sides of the ship – high plumes of water around us. It had removed our wireless aerial!

Cossack was not otherwise damaged but one of our destroyers did receive a direct hit; the Commanding Officer of the ship concerned then made a signal to Captain (D) asking permission to withdraw temporarily from the action to tend the wounded. The reply, with the immediacy of a half-volley, was 'not approved'.

At some stage after contacting *Bismarck* – I could not say exactly when – it became evident that she had been hit aft, that her steering was defective and that her speed was reduced. Her primary and secondary armaments – the 15-inch and 5.9-inch guns – were not impaired; they remained effective until the morning.

In daylight, the C-in-C arrived in the battleship *King George V* with the heavily-armed *Rodney* and cruisers in company. *Cossack* and the other destroyers of the 4th Flotilla then took ring-side seats to watch the huge ships banging away at close range, hitting – and missing – the target. The direct hits more often than not registered as surprisingly dull, fiery glows while the misses were more spectacular plumey splashes. Slowly, *Bismarck*'s gunnery became more feeble and inaccurate but the ship put up a truly gallant fight to the end, and in the latter stages I remember watching one enemy shell toppling with a strange whirring noise over *Cossack*'s bridge. Finally, our big ships' guns being unable to sink the enemy, a cruiser's torpedo did the trick from very close range. To us, this was satisfying and yet not pleasant to watch. *Bismarck* had taken a hideous punishment and fought back with great and hopeless courage to the very last.

The C-in-C then told all ships to leave the area. *Dorsetshire* and *Maori* picked up some 100 survivors; later, the Spanish cruiser *Canarias* may have rescued more. I, for one, found it an unpleasant sight leaving such a number to drown – the little black blobs bobbing up and down in the rough sea with apparently no hope of survival. There may, or may not, have been U-boats closing dangerously on the area which could have been a threat to our big ships. A firmer fact seems to have been that Tovey's ships were desperately short of fuel.

Soon after the *Bismarck* action, I received, greatly incensed, news of a shore appointment to the staff of the C-in-C South Atlantic. Vian did his best to keep me in the ship or to get me a command of my own, as he had done for Peter Gretton. In saying good-bye, the Captain descended from his high horse surprisingly. 'I thought of awarding some seniority,' he said, 'not two years like I gave Gretton because he is outstanding but six months or so. But I won't give you any. It would bring you into the promotion zone when you are in a shore job and could do you more harm than good.'

This was pleasing beyond any expectation; advanced seniority was very unusual. Gretton, after being awarded his two years advancement, was promoted earlier to Commander than any officer for very many years. As a senior officer of escort groups he was a marked success, though it must have imposed a heavy strain as he was always so much younger than the commanding officers under his command. Very highly decorated, he finally retired voluntarily as a very young Vice-Admiral.

As to Vian, as a Captain, he was unbelievably rude, hot tempered and frequently needlessly offensive; one had to stand up to him and be right – or make him think so. In action, he was quiet, calm and very, very quick; and anyone who raised his voice unnecessarily at any time did not do it twice. Otherwise, some distance beneath his ferocious exterior, he could be a man of surprising kindness. In some ways, he was a genius. He had no surfeit of false modesty and yet his written reports were brief to the point of being self-effacing.

Promoted to Rear Admiral, Vian left *Cossack* soon after I did. Within a very short time, *Cossack* was sunk by a U-boat. The new Captain, the new First Lieutenant and my successor Lieutenant Commander Isaacs were among those lost, together with Leading Seaman Lamb, the HSD (Higher Submarine Detector). My thought when I heard this news was that if I had been still in the ship, we would have detected the torpedo and got the U-boat. Conceited, you may say, after all these years? No, not at all, just optimistic; it was surely the way most of us thought.

Thus far in the war, gunnery, the 'trade' of the elite of the Navy, had shown up well. In seamanship and the ability to cope with the unexpected, though, there was too often a lack of imagination, an unreasoning adherence to the book and to the pattern of peace time exercises. Captain Vian, of course, was quite certainly not in this category. However, with respect to so great a man, he was among the many who lacked knowledge of anti-submarine work and definitely under-assessed its importance. It is of passing relevance that a few months after the loss of *Cossack*, *Maori* from our Flotilla was also sunk by a U-boat; and the tall, red-haired, so very popular and up-and-coming Captain 'Beaky' Armstrong was among those lost.

As to the great PLV, he went on to serve with invariable dash, distinction and success in the Mediterranean, the invasion of Europe and the Far East. He ultimately became Admiral of the Fleet Sir Philip Vian, GCB, KBE, DSO and two Bars. Years later, I met him in retirement. He said he had just become a Director of the Midland Bank. When he told me I laughed. So, to his credit, did he.

7. WEST AFRICA

There were not all that many of us anti-submarine specialist officers but each of us closely followed the war against the U-boats, even where we were not, as individuals, concerned.

In the first days of the war, the U-boat offensive against our merchant shipping had been with torpedo and mine in our coastal waters but, even in those days, the U-boats attacked ships which were 'independents' – independently routed – rather than those which were sailing in convoy because it was both easier and safer. Also, in those first days, enemy submarines could not, for lack of fuel, operate too far from their bases in Germany.

With the fall of France in the summer of 1940, Lorient and other bases on the French coast gave the enemy direct access to the Atlantic which, of course, extended the range of the U-boats. It did not take the U-boat Command long to discover that the same tactics as they had used in World War One, namely attacking on the surface at night, paid off best. The surfaced U-boat's low silhouette could not be spotted in the dark and the small target offered by the U-boat on the surface could seldom be detected by asdic, especially with ships so poorly trained as our escorts then were (escorts were not then radar-fitted); nor did it take the U-boat Command, under Grand Admiral Dönitz, himself a World War One U-boat CO, long to establish the weak points where attack was most profitable.

For Britain, which would starve without imported food, her merchant shipping losses in 1941 and 1942 were truly alarming. As mentioned in the Author's Note, Winston Churchill wrote that the only thing that ever frightened him during the war was the U-boat peril.

An immediate problem had been the shortage of suitable convoy escort vessels. The Admiralty met this by expediting the building of a number of corvettes, small asdic-fitted vessels, slow at 16 knots but equipped with one 3-inch gun and a number of depth-charges. These little ships, excellent sea-boats for their size, were to form the backbone of our escort forces. We also had the fifty Lease-Lend American 'Four-Stackers' – old four-funnelled destroyers, and in many cases useless destroyers, or so I thought. Most important, at that time, the potential of RAF Coastal Command was greatly improved. One German answer was to attack even further afield and thus to force us to disperse the protection we could give our shipping. Another was to adopt the 'wolf-pack' attack whereby one U-boat, or a

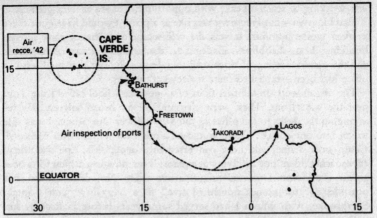

Map 4. South Atlantic Anti-Submarine Duties, 1941-2
As the Fleet Anti-Submarine Officer, Freetown, the author made air inspection
flights to West African ports and, on orders, a compromising aerial reconnaissance
of the Cape Verde Islands in search of U-boat bases.

German aircraft, would home all other German submarines in the area on to
a convoy; and then they would attack in strength. This meant breaking
wireless silence which at least enabled the Admiralty to track U-boats and
warn convoys in danger.

With too few warships in the convoy escort and, especially to start with,
too little training for the officers and men of those ships whose convoys
were under attack, the senior officers of escort groups and the commanding
officers of escort ships had to face great difficulties. Often with impotence
and confusion, they saw the ships they were trying to protect being sunk
while they were unable effectively to hit back.

Freetown, Sierra Leone was of course a focal point for shipping bound for
the West African ports, for the Cape or for the Mediterranean via the Cape.
Before I arrived, a number of commerce raiders including *Graf Spee* and
some U-boat supply ships had been dealt with by our cruisers in the South
Atlantic. More immediately before I arrived, a number of sinkings, mainly
of 'independents', had occurred in the approaches to Freetown. The U-
boats concerned had refuelled from smallish German ships, from the
Spanish Canary Islands, possibly from the Portuguese Cape Verde Islands
and from Vichy French-controlled Dakar, just up the coast. Much of the U-
boat effort, however, in the out-field, was then diverted to the Greenland
area, though patrols were continued on the West African coast and later
spread well into the South Atlantic. The threat from German submarines
had very greatly spread.

While we all watched the pattern of development, no officer who had
been trained as an anti-submarine specialist could possibly feel anything but
fury at being taken from a ship to go to a shore job when the U-boat war

71

was working to reach a peak, with opportunities at sea at their greatest.

Had I known what Freetown was like as a place, I would have gone there in even worse humour. It was the wet season with heavy rain, intense humidity, heat, shabbiness, inadequacy, the lack of any sort of smartness and the general feeling of sloth – all this despite the fact that the C-in-C's office had been established there for several months.

The offices were on the first floor of a one-time school called King Tom near the waterfront. They were surrounded by a broad balcony. By re-arranging the desks in the office of the Staff Officer Operations, I was able to get into one corner. There would be a cabin for me in HMS *Edinburgh Castle*, once a liner and now converted to a depot ship. She was dirty, cockroach-ridden, hot and lying at anchor; it would mean asking for a boat ashore every time I wanted to go to my office. No, definitely no, not possible; so, for some months, I lived in a bungalow with Captain Sherbrooke, with whom I had served some years before in *Rodney*, and with two over-zone lieutenant commanders.

The C-in-C was, for the first few weeks, Vice Admiral Raikes (Admiral Sir Robert), a distinguished World War One submariner who, I thought, had an understanding of the U-boat war. He was relieved by Vice-Admiral Algernon Willis (Admiral of the Fleet Sir Algernon) who had a reputation for being most aggressively puritanical and was known in the Navy as the 'Desiccated Admiral'. He had held some distinguished appointments, was politically well-connected and he and Mr Attlee, the Socialist, then Deputy Prime Minister to Winston, had married sisters.

It was then – and still is – part of my contention that very few senior officers of that day, with the exception of submariners, had an understanding of, or even enthusiasm for the anti-U-boat war or for A/S tactics; nor, so far as that is concerned, do I think they appreciated the dangers of the U-boat. Once again in such category, with due reverence and much respect, I include the great P. L. Vian. In *Cossack*, after much nagging, I once got him to the Asdic Attack Teacher in Scapa Flow. Attendance at this synthetic teacher (simulator) was essential for every Commanding Officer whose ship might contact a submarine. Vian stayed for half an hour, turned and said: 'If we get a contact with a U-boat, you can handle the ship and get on with it.' He then left. 'Like hell,' I thought.

There is little doubt that this attitude, this apathy of almost all officers, emanated from the pre-war A/S training and understanding – or rather the lack of it – except, once more with the submariners. Such criticism applied, I thought, to the new C-in-C, a clever man who knew the book, the pre-war book. He was severe, unbending and very thin, ashen, unhappy-looking, possibly operationally tired, possibly not fit. What a choice where the crying need was for driving, but essentially benign, encouraging leadership!

The Chief of Staff to the C-in-C South Atlantic was not much involved operationally and he was relieved by an officer from the Retired List, who similarly kept rather away from operational affairs. Then there was the Staff Officer Operations, a commander, a very hard-working, well-balanced officer and three lieutenant commanders, all superannuated, all retired and all bloody-minded. My job was to advise on A/S matters, in particular to help train the Local Escort Force, to help compile local anti-U-boat intelligence and periodically to interrogate survivors from sunken merchant ships.

With few exceptions, the officers at Freetown were then the unhappiest collection I had ever met or was to meet in my whole Service career. There were several reasons for this. Certainly the climate was one of them. It was very debilitating due to the heat, the humidity and the prevalence of malaria. The living conditions were appalling; recreation was almost nil and social life did not exist. To cap this, it appeared that it was to Freetown, where the drink was duty-free – gin two pence a glass – that a number of officers who had been in recent trouble, including over drink – were sent. In many cases, too, these poor chaps had not enough to do. Let it hastily be added that I was not in such a category! Finally, Freetown was not an area of hot war and so got little priority from the Admiralty; and to cap the lot again, there was no inspiring lead from the top.

Against the foregoing, I was lucky in that Captain R. St V. Sherbrooke, once my Divisional Officer in *Rodney*, was Captain(D) of the Local Escort Force and I had to work with him in the training of local escorts. Then there was Lieutenant John Kennard, the Signals Officer, a most likeable and very promising officer who was so sadly to die early and who had been a midshipman with me in the *Rodney* Gun Room. Sherbrooke was as easy to work for as he had been in *Rodney*. Since those days, he had had an interesting career. At the time of the Abyssinian Crisis in 1935-36, he was sent as a commander to be Boom Defence Officer, Mediterranean, and anything to do with Boom Defence was then equated to the end – superannuation. It was one of the 'Second Sea Lord's Office non-promotion appointments', so it looked like curtains!

His first job, so the story goes, was to lay the anti-submarine and anti-torpedo boom across the entrance to Alexandria harbour. The boom, a vast complicated jangle of heavy wire mesh, had been loaded into the transporting ship with all those components needed first at the bottom and all those needed last at the top. The C-in-C Mediterranean, when told this, was not in the least sympathetic and gave an almost impossible time in which to sort it all out and get the boom in place. Sherbrooke was successful in this and was later promoted to captain. When, in 1942, he left Freetown, he got command of a destroyer flotilla and won a very fine Victoria Cross in defence of a Russian convoy against superior German forces – an action in which he lost an eye.

Operationally, the Admiral at Freetown, the C-in-C South Atlantic, was concerned with the German raiders, warships and armed merchant ships, often disguised, which preyed on our merchant shipping. That, for the most part, was well-controlled when I arrived – but not so the problem of the U-boat threat. Freetown was an important port of call for shipping to and from the West African ports as well as to and from the Cape for the British forces in Egypt. One outstanding difficulty for the C-in-C was, without question, a lack of anti-submarine escort vessels. Frequent letters and signals went off to the Admiralty emphasising the U-boat threat to merchant shipping in the area. Little notice was taken but, in the event, the threat never very seriously developed. There were some losses off the West African coast admittedly, mostly 'independents', just before I arrived in Freetown. It was fortunate the Germans never realised how very weak we were and returned in force.

To compensate for the shortage of larger and more effective escort vessels, I suggested – and the Admiral agreed – making use of the 112-foot Fairmile motor launches in the approaches to the port. Gradually, he was persuaded to accept the use of these boats further afield but the difficulties were that they were petrol-driven and, thus, a definite fire risk while only having a limited range. My offer to be entirely responsible for fires, explosions and other disasters was accepted and extra upper deck fuel tanks (oil drums) were fitted. Nothing went wrong – to my satisfaction and relief. However, after presentation of countless papers (drafted by me), the Admiralty sent out a number of the smaller diesel driven Harbour Defence MLs. They were found to have remarkable sea-keeping qualities. With such tiny vessels, the asdics were not sophisticated: their sets could only transmit ahead and on the beam and could not sweep through an arc like larger vessels. Even supposing they did get a real submarine contact, the depth charges they carried were small as compared to the standard 300 lb charge used by all larger escorts – and these only had a lethal range of thirteen yards.

The real merit of these little MLs as convoy escorts was their presence. They could dart about, admittedly not very fast, around a convoy, forming a potential physical obstruction to an attacking U-boat; then, too, the sound of their asdic 'ping', audible on the U-boat's listening apparatus, was in itself off-putting. One technical snag did arise with underwater asdic works of these boats: a component which had to be watertight was found to be leaking. The problem was overcome by encasing the part in question in a Naval medical store, namely a 'french letter'. This had to be formally promulgated by the C-in-C. Algy did not like such an unseemly idea but accepted it, *faute de mieux*. These little boats did trips of a thousand miles down the coast; they were a much decreased fire risk compared to the petrol bigger boats. At least on that score everyone was happy.

Willis was the only Admiral I ever met who did not like his staff to stand up to him. After an exhausting service in the Mediterranean before he came to Freetown, he may have been on edge; possibly he was ill – none of us were too fit in that climate; it is certain that he was ill-humoured. Take this case. Something really rather trivial had gone wrong during the previous night. We always started work early and when the C-in-C arrived at 8 am, he said he wished to see the Duty Commander who had been on night duty and had just gone off. Three quarters of an hour later, Lieutenant Commander Mackenzie, the officer concerned, reported and the conversation went thus:

'Where have you been? I sent for you some time ago.'

'Having a bath, shaving and breakfasting, Sir.'

74

'When I was your age, my boy, I'd do all that and be back on duty in a quarter of an hour.'

Mackenzie was a smallish chap, mild and affable, who looked rather younger than his years. He had retired voluntarily before the war in order to run a family wool business and was, in civilian life, a man of consequence. Recalled to the Navy for the war, he was a man with a good brain and shrewd judgement.

There was a pause before he answered, slowly and firmly: 'Sir,' he said, 'firstly, I am not your boy. I am nearly as old as you are. Secondly, I cannot have a bath, shave and have breakfast in a quarter of an hour and I'm not going to try.'

He then walked away.

In falling out with the Admiral, I made more of a job of it than had Mackenzie – and did it at least three times. On the first occasion, I came on as Duty Commander one evening to find that the Admiral had despatched two of our hard-pressed destroyers from Local Escort Force some three hundred miles to a merchant ship which had made a signalled report to the effect that a possible submarine periscope had been sighted. Such reports were both frequent and false from unescorted ships which inevitably felt vulnerable. This report was indeed false. The Admiralty disposition of U-boats, passed out daily by signal, had put no U-boat anywhere near the relevant position; secondly, there had been no follow-up to the merchant ship's vague and uninspiring signal – and several hours had passed since that signal had been received. I therefore recalled the two destroyers, telling the Admiral next morning my reasons for what I had done and adding, perhaps unwisely, that even if there had been a U-boat there, the chances of the destroyers contacting it so many hours later would be virtually nil. He did not agree but was abundantly clearly wrong, which made it worse!

The next time I was to be in the dog-house was when rumour had it that the U-boats might be using the Cape Verde Islands as some sort of base, probably for refuelling. I was sent off to the Gambia where the RAF's Sunderland flying boats were based. The Admiral said I was to investigate, to be in complete charge and give whatever instructions I thought appropriate to the aircraft's pilot. I thought we should make three sorties, two in bright moonlight and one by day. That is what we did – twice making forced landings because of water in the petrol! The night sorties revealed no activity and we had a good close-in look. On the day sortie, I saw a large seaplane hangar which could conceivably have been an improvised submarine pen. However, it had sliding doors, one of which was shut. I asked the pilot to fly low and at an angle in order to see behind the closed door. There was nothing there! Unfortunately, at that very close range the Portuguese had no trouble in getting the flying boat's number and, through the usual channels, came a diplomatic raspberry for the C-in-C who passed it on with added acid to me. To imagine that a recce of any value could be made without going into neutral waters was not sense. The sin, of course, lay in being bowled out.

Then came the third fall from grace. Each morning, the Admiral held a

Staff meeting, which was never entertaining or encouraging. When they ended, we were thankful to be dismissed. One morning, not without the customary air of aggrieved ill-humour, the Admiral announced that a plague of ants had invaded Admiralty House. No one liked to comment. The Admiral then told us that they had advanced on one of his daughters. The melancholy of the ludicrous scene was so provoking that, driven by a forceful if tactless attempt to break it, I said: 'Not ants in the pants, Sir, I hope?'

Truly expensive this ill-controlled quip later proved to be.

Most of the Admiral's Staff worked really hard and some, like myself, very hard indeed! Morale was however low; it was so low that when the Admiral left the South Atlantic Station, the Secretarial Staff allowed some of us to see our Confidential Reports. This was, of course, strictly against the rules and the sort of thing I had never heard of happening in any other ship or establishment. My confidential report was slightly above the average but, at the foot of the document, where there was a space for remarks by the Admiral, he had written in his own hand: 'This officer wants command of a destroyer. He is not recommended.'

Briefly, Vice-Admiral Sir Campbell Tait, known in the Navy as 'Tufty Tait' because of the abundant fur in his ears, then arrived but almost at once transferred his office to Simonstown in South Africa and Rear Admiral Pegram took over at Freetown as Flag Officer, West Africa. This largish, bright-eyed, rotund and cheerful, humane but hard-driving boss, who joked with officers and men, and who drank and had a rich flow of invective, brought instant change to Freetown. Those of us who worked at all close to him would readily and happily bust our guts to get the right answer; yet one of the first jobs he gave me was only a qualified success.

'You fly up and down the coast,' he said. 'I'd like you to go to Liberia and call on the American General in Monrovia on my behalf.'

'Anything special, sir?'

'No, no.' He was in a hurry. 'I'm not going to scratch your arse for you, old boy. You know what to do. Go and be polite and come back and let me know what's going on there.'

On arrival by RAF Anson at the desolate airfield, cut out of the bush, I asked for the General's Aide. 'The British Admiral regrets he cannot leave Freetown and has sent me to call on your General,' I told him.

There was a pause, then, anxiously: 'Call? Say what does your Admiral want to call our General?'

'No, my Admiral wishes me to bring his respects to your General.'

Another pause and then, more happily: 'Sure our General knows your Admiral respects him.'

Trying again: 'My Admiral told me to pay his official call on your General.'

This was a linguistic error. 'Pay? Pay? Our General is paid by the United States!'

I was getting nowhere. 'Can I see your General please?'

'No.'

'Why not?'

'See the General? No you can't see the General. He ain't here.'

But I did manage to stay the night and meet some of the American staff.

For us, the British, the overall picture in the latter part of 1941 had not been too bright. On land, Hitler virtually controlled the whole of Europe except for the United Kingdom, and Portugal and Spain, although Spain favoured his cause anyway. His armies were marching with confidence against Moscow while ours in North Africa were not doing well. At sea, our merchant shipping losses remained perilously high, mainly through the U-boat offensive. The threat posed by the battle-cruisers, the battleships and the cruisers of the German Navy existed all right although it was nevertheless mitigated by temerity to risk damage far from home by engagement even with our less powerful warships.

The U-boat diversionary effort had gone partly to the Mediterranean resulting in the sinking of our battleship *Barham* and aircraft carrier *Ark Royal*, although the latter had already been sunk several times in German propaganda by the voice of the first 'Lord Haw-Haw' (who for a time, at least, seems to have been Baillie-Stuart, my Dartmouth Term-mate).

The sinking of HMS *Barham*, with the loss of her Captain, G.C. Cooke, and 861 officers and ratings is a sorry tale which may be thought to bear out much of what is in this book elsewhere. The battleships *Queen Elizabeth* – the Fleet Flagship – *Barham* and *Valiant* were at sea with a protective anti-submarine screen of destroyers spread out, fan-shaped, ahead of them. All the destroyers were, of course, sweeping the water with their asdics. Barring unusual circumstances – and it does not seem there were any – no enemy submarine should have been able to get through the screen undetected and it would thus automatically have been attacked with depth charges. History records, however, that *U-331* did pass successfully through the destroyer screen. Worse still, one destroyer did, in fact, contact the U-boat but classified it as a non-sub echo and so did nothing about it! Several days after this event, John Mosse, my friend from earlier days, was sent out to the Mediterranean Fleet for anti-submarine duties, and was thus in a position to make first-hand observations. He was a reliable and qualified judge. He told me sometime later that the anti-submarine warfare standard in the Mediterranean had then been low and that the ships were always looking upwards, obsessed by the constant threat of air attack, to the detriment of their attention to the threat from underwater.

In addition to the Mediterranean, the North West Atlantic was again bearing the brunt of the U-boat diversions. The heat was not seriously on us in the South Atlantic but we were desperately short of proper escorts: destroyers, frigates, corvettes – a weak spot which the U-boat Command could have exploited to our great cost.

In December of that same year, the one-time Corporal in World War One found, as '*le petit Caporal*', Napoleon, had found some years before him, that he had made a mistake in sending his armies to conquer Russia; they were being driven back in defeat. More or less concurrently, Hitler persuaded the Japanese that a successful assault on the American Fleet would end the influence of the United States in the Pacific. The air attack on the American Fleet in Pearl Harbor resulted. It was followed by the sinking off the Malayan coast of our battle-cruiser *Renown* and the battleship *Prince of Wales*. Four days after Pearl Harbor, Germany declared war on the United States. 'At long bloody last, the Yanks have been forced to come in' was what we said with relief, feeling at the same time it would have been in their own interest to have done so much sooner.

No particularly critical U-boat threat had as yet been posed to the South Atlantic. However, with the American entry into the war, the heat was switching to American spheres in the West Atlantic, to the Caribbean and the Gulf of Mexico with truly shocking losses to merchant ships, especially tankers, and, with less effect, to the area of Ascension Island.

Then, as a new development, from the spring of 1942, the U-boats were being refuelled by 'Milch Cows'. These are not to be confused with U-boat supply ships. They were largish submarine oil tankers-cum-supply vessels. This arrangement allowed for each U-boat to remain marauding for far longer and, of course, for an increased number of U-boats to be at sea on the job. The heavy West Atlantic losses continued until the Americans learned to institute an effective convoy system in their own waters.

We had to contend with 'Milch Cows' fuelling U-boats in the South Atlantic and off the coast of West Africa but our brave baby escorts, the MLs, now ocean-going, helped our few larger escort vessels protect the ships in convoy down the coast from attack. In September 1942, there was, however, a hideous, harrowingly unpleasant event south-east of Ascension Island, just outside the operational control of Admiral Pegram.

My description of this is a personal one rather than one which might be fully confirmed by formal account. It is based on local knowledge at the time, on seeing the signals immediately they came in and on interrogating survivors after the event – and other limited information. It was known to us at Freetown, in the Operations Room, that SS *Laconia*, a large troopship of 19,695 tons, was, like other ships of her size and speed, sailing independently northward bound from Cape Town. She was unescorted – not in convoy – though it was known there might be U-boats in the area through which she would have to pass.

About 9 pm on 12 September, some 300 miles north-east of Ascension Island and well south of the Equator, *Laconia* was hit by two torpedoes fired by *U-156*. On balance, it seems that the ship did manage to make a signal on reduced power but the signal she made was one just meaning that she had *sighted* a submarine. This signal was never received directly at Freetown. Again, rather as surmise based on reports, it seems probable that the ship never made a *distress* signal at all. In any event after the sinking, the Commanding Officer of the U-boat certainly made a report of it to the Flag Officer U-boats but this was, of course, in code.

It was when cruising in the dark among the life boats, the life-saving rafts and the swimmers that the German Commanding Officer discovered that *Laconia* had been carrying the 1,800 Italian prisoners of war as well as an

HMS *Wanderer*: Long-Range Escort Conversion

The 'V' and 'W' classes were built during World War One in quantity as fleet destroyers. Modifications were introduced in successive orders, and dimensions differed, but the design pattern remained basically the same. HMS *Wanderer* belonged to the Admiralty Design 'Modified W' Class, the thirteenth 'V' and 'W' order, placed in January 1918 and termed Group VIII. They introduced 4.7-in guns, replacing the 4-in weapons of earlier 'V' and 'W's. She was built by Fairfield and launched on 1 May 1918. The average cost of the class was £262,478 (hull cost £104,726, weighing 548 tons; machinery cost £109,308, weighing 417 tons).

By the time that the U-boat menace in World War Two had become very serious, the Royal Navy was short of escort vessels. The 'V' and 'W' classes were out of date but still had some good life in their hulls and several were converted to make them useful as fast escort vessels with a greater operational range and appropriate weapons. Six Admiralty 'Modified W' Class fleet destroyers were converted into Long-Range Escorts: *Vansittart*, *Venomous*, *Verity*, *Volunteer*, *Wanderer* and *Whitehall*.

Wanderer's appearance in the 1920s is here contrasted with her appearance after the LRE conversion, with alterations annotated on the 'IN' and 'OUT' basis.

Wanderer was converted in January–May 1943. All changes stemmed from the removal of No. 1 boiler 'A' and 'X' guns and the torpedo tubes, and fitting new A/S armament. The latest asdic, radar, W/T, R/T and H/F D/F equipments were installed. The removal of No. 1 boiler (below the forward funnel) reduced the speed to 27½ knots but allowed an extra fuel tank to be installed in the lower half of the stokehold which appreciably increased the range. 'A' and 'Y' guns and mounting and the torpedo tubes were landed. Additional AA guns were installed. The depth charge battery was greatly augmented and stowage considerably increased. Designed to carry a war complement of 134 without alteration – although the H/F D/F office lost two officers bunks! – *Wanderer* now had a complement of 193. *Wanderer* was ballasted to compensate for the alterations.

	Armament	
1919		*1943*
4	4.7–in BL Mk I gun	2
A, B, X, Y	on CP VI* mounting	B, X
2	2–pounder	–
1	.303–in Maxim machine gun	–
4	.303–in Lewis machine gun	1
6	21–in torpedo tubes in 2 × triple mountings	–
–	twin 20 mm Oerlikon	4
–	single 20 mm Oerlikon	1
–	'Hedgehog' A/S mortar, firing 24 x 32–lb–warhead spigot-mounted bombs	1
–	double depth charge throwers	2
–	double depth charge chutes	2
1	single depth charge chutes	–

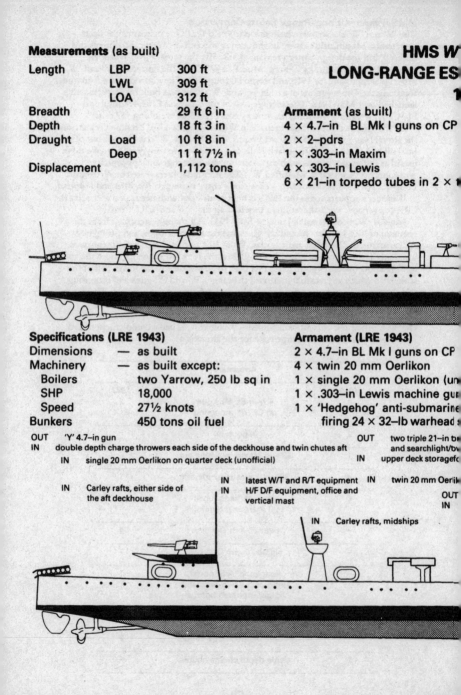

Measurements (as built)

Length	LBP	300 ft
	LWL	309 ft
	LOA	312 ft
Breadth		29 ft 6 in
Depth		18 ft 3 in
Draught	Load	10 ft 8 in
	Deep	11 ft 7½ in
Displacement		1,112 tons

HMS W

LONG-RANGE ES

Armament (as built)

4 × 4.7–in BL Mk I guns on CP

2 × 2–pdrs

1 × .303–in Maxim

4 × .303–in Lewis

6 × 21–in torpedo tubes in 2 ×

Specifications (LRE 1943)

Dimensions	— as built
Machinery	— as built except:
Boilers	two Yarrow, 250 lb sq in
SHP	18,000
Speed	27½ knots
Bunkers	450 tons oil fuel

Armament (LRE 1943)

2 × 4.7–in BL Mk I guns on CP

4 × twin 20 mm Oerlikon

1 × single 20 mm Oerlikon (un

1 × .303–in Lewis machine gu

1 × 'Hedgehog' anti-submarine
firing 24 × 32–lb warhead

OUT	'Y' 4.7–in gun	OUT	two triple 21–in b
IN	double depth charge throwers each side of the deckhouse and twin chutes aft		and searchlight/b
		IN	upper deck storagefo
IN	single 20 mm Oerlikon on quarter deck (unofficial)		

IN	Carley rafts, either side of the aft deckhouse	IN	latest W/T and R/T equipment	IN	twin 20 mm Oerli
		IN	H/F D/F equipment, office and vertical mast	OUT	
				IN	
		IN	Carley rafts, midships		

NDERER
ORT CONVERSION
43

I* mounting

ole mountings

Machinery (as built)

Engines	Brown-Curtiss geared independent reduction oil-fuelled turbines
Boilers	three Yarrow, 250 lb sq in
Shafts/screws	two
SHP	27,120
RPM	260
Speed max.	34 knots trials 32.84 knots
Bunkers	374–353/324–318 tons fuel oil

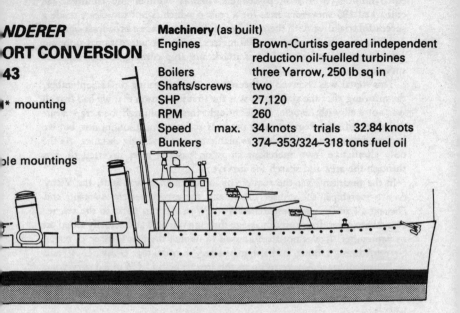

* mountings

fficial)

mortar,
igot-mounted bombs

d o-tube mountings

0\5 depth charges

either side abaft funnel

forward funnel and No. 1 boiler
xtra fuel tanks

2 × double depth charge throwers
2 × double depth charge chutes

IN   latest Type 144 asdics with control cabinet at the back of the bridge

IN   Type 271 surface warning radar on the bridge

IN   Type 293 air/surface radar above bridge

IN   Carley rafts, either side below the bridge

OUT   Gunnery Director tower from the bridge

OUT   torpedo control on the bridge

IN   single 20 mm Oerlikon guns either side of the bridge wings

OUT   'A' 4.7–in gun

IN   'Hedgehog' A/S mortar and ammunition lockers

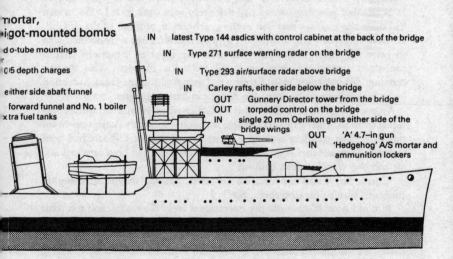

equal number of British passengers, mainly women and children. He embarked 193 survivors and, for a reason which is not too clear, made a successful trial dive with them on board. He then made a broadcast signal in English, in plain language on 600 metres, using the international shipping wave, to say that he would not attack any ship coming to the rescue of survivors.

This signal was received in Freetown in mid-morning on 13 September, the morning after the sinking. It was the first intimation that we had that all was not well with *Laconia*. Some thought this signal might be a trap, a *ruse de guerre*. Admiral Pegram, now the boss at Freetown, thought not, but we had no destroyers or fast ships available to send that long distance. As the only alternative, two merchant ships on passage were diverted to pass through the area and search for survivors.

In the meantime, at the request of the German Naval Staff, the Vichy French warships, the cruiser *Gloire* and the escort vessels *Annamite* and *Dumont d'Urville* were despatched from West African ports to the rescue. They were given freedom of passage through our area and actually sailed on 14 September. It was not then known to us that the Flat Officer U-boats, Grand Admiral Dönitz, had also instructed, in code, that *U-506*, *U-507* and an Italian submarine were to go to the area to help *U-156* to aid survivors. Another source reported that a further four U-boats were originally told to join the rescue but later ordered to proceed further south to their war patrols.

It was thought that a distress signal from *Laconia* was received in Freetown two days after the sinking. Maybe this was the submarine *sighting* (not distress) signal made on low power, picked up and relayed corrupt (distorted) after a delay. All that anyway I knew on the morning of 16 September was that *Laconia* had definitely been sunk; that *U-156*, which had done the sinking, was still in the approximate position of the sinking, assisting survivors, and that three Vichy French warships were on their way to help. An intercepted signal that morning from an American aircraft confirmed that the U-boat was still with the lifeboats. This aircraft certainly did not come from Freetown. I assumed it came from Ascension but it might have come from the American base in Liberia.

An hour later, I was in the Admiral's Office when yet another intercepted signal from an American aircraft came through – definitely Ascension-based this time. The wording was very excited – a group of U-boats had been sighted. Then another signal: the group of U-boats had been attacked and hit and one was 'last seen belly-up'.

'Christ, Sir,' I said in nauseated, horrified anguish, 'they're attacking the lifeboats. Can't you stop them, Sir?'

'No, old boy. It's outside my operational area. We really can't tell what may be happening at their end. I cannot interfere.'

I could see that, on the information available, the Admiral was right. Later, we confirmed that the aircraft had bombed the lifeboats, killing survivors, while *U-156*, which was displaying a large Red Cross flag and had some lifeboats in tow, had had to cut the tow and dive to escape damage.

This attack was followed by a later air attack on *U-506* which was also in the vicinity helping survivors and which also had to dive this time with a number of survivors on board.

Of the total of 3,500 men, women and children from the *Laconia*, the Vichy ships rescued over 1,000 (some 600 of them being British), including those transferred from U-boats. Then sixteen British in one lifeboat made the West African coast after a truly gruelling arduous twenty-eight days and some deaths at sea, while another lifeboat made it with only four survivors after thirty days.

How can it ever have gone so wrong for the American aircraft from Ascension Island? It can only have been through communication failures. The attacking aircraft, and presumably the operational control, cannot have known the gist of *U-156*'s broadcast English plain language signal, nor can they have known of the first American aircraft's report. Thus the true situation must have been unknown to those in control on Ascension Island. But then, what about the American pilots who attacked the lifeboats in error? Was it misleading briefing? Was it inexperience? Aerial recognition over the sea was not a simple technique easily acquired.

Some half of those shipwrecked were Italians. But it has to be fully admitted that the Germans, both at their headquarters and in their U-boats, behaved most compassionately, not differentiating between British and Italian prisoners of war, while at the same time putting their submarines at risk. A consequence of the event was that the Laconia Order was issued by Grand Admiral Dönitz, to the effect that survivors were not to be rescued after such sinkings. At the Nuremberg Trials after the War, it was held against Dönitz that this order was indictable. The Court disagreed, though Dönitz was sentenced to ten years imprisonment on other counts.

Though it had become so very much more congenial during the Pegram regime, I felt badly being out of the war at sea. The Battle of the Atlantic was still going hard and in the Mediterranean there was fierce non-stop naval activity in actions large and small. Among the melodramatic, small, but also effective actions, was an attack by Italian charioteers, that is to say human torpedoes – torpedoes straddled by the driver and his mate. Two of these craft successfully and courageously fixed limpet mines to the bottoms of our much needed battleships *Queen Elizabeth* and *Valiant* in Alexandria harbour. The chariots had come through the gate in the anti-submarine boom immediately after it had been opened for some of our ships to enter harbour. The limpet mines duly detonated, holing our ships and leaving them unfit for sea. The crews of both chariots were captured and when searched were found to be equipped with iron rations, English and Egyptian money and, with national, characteristic optimism, a supply of contraceptives.

At the end of 1942, the Admiral agreed to apply for my relief after only fifteen months on the Station. Few officers lasted the course of a two-year appointment in that climate and I had been sick several times with malignant malaria. Admiral Pegram had been a remarkable example of what leadership could do. As an instance, I remember one afternoon he sent for me: 'Haven't we made a slight balls here, old boy?' he said, pointing to a signal.

With guilt, I apologised profusely at once. No, no, it was nothing to worry about but perhaps I would put it right, he said.

He was again a boss for whom one would bust one's guts and be personally upset at failing in any way – and how different from his predecessor! Little doubt of the difficulties in West Africa with no Admiralty priority, very very limited local resources and – in repetition – the heat and high, hideously debilitating humidity. Yet Admiral Pegram got things done and I never heard him swear at any officer or rating – and that was no reflection on his vocabulary of invective. Ultimately, Pegram became the Controller of the Navy, approximately the boss of all ship building and material – a particularly exacting job. I believe he died from overwork.

My successor was another non-friend of the powerful lieutenant commander who nominated all A/S officers for appointment. He did his best, my successor, to duck the job – and who could blame him? He arrived a month late. I left with an incurable taste for avocado pears – the sole mitigation of the misery of Freetown – a vast bunch of bananas, recurrent malaria and a recommendation for command of a destroyer.

It was elating to get away from West Africa but it meant a homecoming to a situation different to the one with which I was familiar. My mother's flat in London had been destroyed in an air raid, fortunately when she was out playing bridge. Refusing to leave London, she had moved to another near Harrods. Joan, who had written in the usual way when I had been away, was still driving a Red Cross ambulance in the London blitz and was still living at the top of a block of Kensington flats and in constant danger. Jimmy, with her parents in Dorset, had written of her wartime problems. Civilians were certainly having a hard time.

Food and clothes were, by then, rationed and in short supply. For food, there were different coloured ration books in different categories – pregnant women, young children and the ordinary citizen, with special allowances of, say, cheese for manual workers. Those in the Armed Forces were on two levels. We, on active service, did quite well though I remember sometimes being hungry at sea. Part of everyone's ration would be made up from substitute food. Those old enough will remember the dried egg – grey slime when scrambled. So far as it is possible to generalise, the weekly ration of most types of food for the civilian was about the same as what is now eaten in a day. Some things which came from abroad though were almost unobtainable, hence the large bunch of bananas. Undernourishment was reported among the poorer people living in the towns, as opposed to those living in the country. Considering that about half of our food in the United Kingdom had to be imported, Lord Woolton, the Minister of Food, and those who helped his organisation to make the food go round, did a most successful job.

Soon after my arrival in England, I was sent first to the Hospital for Tropical Diseases in Liverpool and then to a hospital in Dorset for treatment. The malarial victim started with pills which turned him yellow; then he was released from hospital and thereafter continued for some months to take pills which turned him blue. On leave in Dorset later, I spent much time shooting rabbits, pigeons and anything else which could reasonably go into the pot. This was very popular. Game and edible vermin were 'windfalls'.

On the subject of windfalls, there was the story of the officer who sent his mother a smoked salmon from Iceland, on the strength of which the old lady decided to give a lunch party. Six generous helpings of smoked salmon had been laid out when the elderly domestic found that Tomkins, the cat, had leapt up and finished one of them off.

'Divide the five into six,' said the lady of the house, accustomed to handling emergencies and they all sat down, quickly to polish off this very unusual luxury.

'Perhaps you should know, Madam,' whispered the elderly domestic, bringing in the rabbit stew, 'that Tomkins has dropped down dead.'

With ashen face and thoughts of ptomaine and salmonella, the hostess broke the news and the whole party at once repaired in psycho-somatic pain and panic to the local hospital.

'Perhaps you should know, Madam,' said the elderly domestic the next day, 'the Veterinary Surgery which did the post-mortem has just rung up to say poor Tomkins died of a heart attack.'

Even after a few days of leave, time started to hang heavily and when Lieutenant Colonel Bullen-Smith, then commanding The Kings Own Scottish Borderers, stationed nearby in Dorset, invited me to come out with him on a big Army exercise I readily accepted. The aim of the side to which the KOSBs were attached was to advance on and cross the Thames. It was known that the river was then in spate. We might be living rough, Bullen-Smith had said, and there were reasons for thinking he might be right. I had found, on previous occasions when dealing with the Army, that they had an almost masochistic approach to discomfort. Admittedly, the open bridge of any of HM destroyers – and they were all open then – was not the same as a club armchair but there was nothing to be done about that. A second reason for expecting it to be rough was that the Commanding General was 'Monty', later Field Marshal Viscount Montgomery of Alamein.

The so-called evening meal we were given 'in the field' proved my first point. It was watery, lukewarm, greasy stew, reasonably enough, the same for officers and men. No untrained Ordinary Seaman acting as a temporary cook in a small ship would have been allowed by his messmates to get away with so nauseous a production in the Navy, whatever the circumstances. The next morning Monty convened a conference in a local school to discuss the river crossing with his Commanding Officers.

'I have a Lieutenant Commander RN with me,' said Bullen-Smith from the door of the school, 'shall I bring him in, to advise on the crossing, Sir?'

'No,' said a loud squawky voice, 'certainly not. We don't want any bloody sailors here.'

8. COMMAND

There can be no inspiring, entirely absorbing thrill comparable to that of being appointed to command one of HM Ships, especially in war. The ship, the crew, the fighting equipment and the general safety are yours for success – or failure. Not many can, surely, think about failure though.

Join *Wanderer*, they said. She is in Devonport Dockyard; she is refitting, converting to a 'longlegger' and is Job No. 345678; go and find her and get on with it.

In the Dockyard, on a wet, dismal afternoon day in March 1943, it took some time to locate the ship. She was in dry dock, barely recognisable as a ship at all. Right forward and right aft there was some steel plating on the ship's side. Amidships there was no plating; nothing to see but a mass of confused pipes – large and small. The deck, where there were no large holes in it, was wet. It was also greasy, covered with dirty torn paper, cigarette ends and cluttered with compressed air hoses. There were more pipes – either removed or ready to replace old ones – steel plates, component parts, packing cases, cardboard boxes under tarpaulins – and all the accompaniment of strident noises of hammering, electric drilling, riveting and welding arclights burning with showers of sparks and their own special intrinsic smell. The Dockyard mateys were at work in their old brown, or more often oil-stained, canvas overalls and a small group of Dockyard officials were in a cluster making notes.

On the gangway was an Able Seaman in a duffle coat and seaboots. Yes Sir, he thought the First Lieutenant might be onboard, that was if he was not in the Dockyard. Then the Engineer Officer; he'd been with the ship some time and he was probably down in the engine room. Otherwise there was only the skeleton crew present. Oh, there was the new Doctor and he'd arrived and gone to the Naval Barracks. That's where the First Lieutenant was living, Sir. No one could live on board at present, Sir, could they? There was no water, heat, or lights after the Dockyard workmen had gone in the evening. No, he had not heard when the ship might commission and it looked as though there was a lot of work to be done before anyone could live on board, didn't it, Sir?

This took away any surplus puff. Antrobus, the First Lieutenant, and I soon met and he told me of his problems in trying to get the major dockyard work done; to get one boiler removed and extra oil fuel tanks installed; to get two of the four 4.7-inch guns removed as well as the fire control equipment; to dispense with the torpedo tubes and replace them with long racks of depth charges on the upper deck. Then, thrilling stuff this, there were two radar sets to come in: the Type 293 was an air/surface detection set with which I was reasonably familiar. The Type 271, a surface, high definition set, was brand new and had shown a very promising performance on trials. The newest W/T and radio-telephone equipment was coming to us as well. The asdic set Type 144 was the latest thing and I knew it worked admirably.

'Where are you going to put it?' I asked the Dockyard.

'Oh, we'll build a small steel-plated compartment by the foot of the foremast on the upper deck.'

'No, put it on the back of the bridge.'

'That would be too much top weight.'

'Well, make the compartment of wood, so long as it is warm and dry.'

How thankful we were later to be able to be in direct personal touch with the asdic team from the bridge.

At more or less the last minute, the bits and pieces for an ahead-throwing anti-submarine mortar code-named 'Hedgehog' arrived. It was put together and then a four-stripe Captain arrived to look at it.

'How does this thing work, Sir,' I asked, 'and when are we supposed to use it?'

'You'll get full instructions,' he said and disappeared. I was mildly suspicious.

As a solace, when looking at this foully untidy, complex mess which was *Wanderer*, one could only say that this was a *big* refit to achieve a complete change of function of this class of ship. They, the old 'V' & 'W' destroyers, had been built twenty-five years ago as fleet destroyers. Their purpose then had been to work in flotillas of eight under a slightly larger leader ship, to make co-ordinated torpedo attacks on the big ships of the enemy during major fleet actions. Now, these same ships, old but well built, were to fulfil a quite different role. They were to be fast escorts to convoys of merchant ships; they were to be given the latest anti-submarine detection and attack weaponry and radar. Further, they were to have extra oil fuel stowage to allow them to cross the Atlantic.

The conversion was a large undertaking for the First Lieutenant, aged about twenty-five, and the Engineer Officer. It all conjured optimism for the days to come with our new bunch of sophisticated tricks; it seemed impossible that we could ever fail.

Comparatively quickly, the ship's side plating was replaced. The constructional work neared an end and the Royal Naval Barracks – after persuasive pressure – sent working parties of sailors to help clear up the revolting mess and living quarters on board to become habitable. We commissioned with a crew of about a hundred and eighty – well in excess of the numbers for which the accommodation was designed. We stored ship and were nearly a going concern.

The average age of the Ship's Company, including their elderly Commanding Officer (myself at thirty-four) was twenty-two. The other officers were all in their twenties except for the Engineer Officer who was even more ancient than myself. Two thirds of the ratings had never been on the sea before in their lives.

In the finishing stages of dockyard work on board they invited me to sign for the air pressure testing of watertight compartments as having been done. But, with *Duncan* so nearly sinking in mind, I said no, this test had to be properly done and under our supervision.

Then came the need for officers to be given their action duties. The First Lieutenant had, by custom, to be positioned aft well away from the Captain in case the latter were slain on the bridge. Bower, a professional Merchant Service Officer in the Royal Naval Reserve, was a natural for the job of Navigator and charge of the Action Plot. Frost, Royal Naval Volunteer Reserve, fell into the slot as Action Officer of the Watch because he had served at sea in the Western Approaches before. The A/S Control Officer was perhaps the key job and, being an A/S specialist myself, I wanted someone who would be quick and who would do it my way. Sub Lieutenant Kidd, RNVR, who had an interesting personal background, was to prove a most fortunate selection.

In passing, it should be noted here that during the war we had officers from the Royal Naval Reserve (RNR), who were all from the Merchant Navy, and officers from the Royal Naval Volunteer Reserve (RNVR), who came from other professions, as well as the regular RN officers serving in HM ships. Many of the RNR officers had belonged to the Reserves before war broke out and, as to the RNVR, a few belonged to it pre-war, like the Territorials. Many were chaps who gained RNVR commissions on joining up or were promoted through the Lower Deck later. It was said that the RNR officers were seamen but not gentlemen; the RNVR officers were gentlemen but not seamen and that the RN officers were both – or neither – depending on how the observer saw it. Today, for good or ill, all Reserve officers are RNR. The interlaced stripes of the wartime RNR and the wavy stripes of the RNVR are gone. It is now straight stripes for all with an 'R' in the curl for RNR officers.

The A/S team, Kidd, Leading Seaman Cocks, RNVR, the Higher Submarine Detector, the six junior operators with myself, were then ordered off to the A/S School in Scotland to practise on the excellent synthetic trainer, with our new Type 144 asdic set. It was then that we also learned the use of the Hedgehog, the multiple mortar mounted on the forecastle, so named because when loaded with its twenty-four mortar bombs, all standing up and angled forward, it did perhaps look like a giant hedgehog going astern (that is if you ever happen to have seen a hedgehog in reverse). Anyway, the Hedgehog involved a new concept of attack on a submarine.

In the previous, established form of attack with depth charges, the ship held contact with the submarine and approached with the asdic control equipment computing to allow for the movement of the submarine in the final stages of an attack and also to give the time to fire. To defeat this, the U-boats had taken to diving deep when under attack so that, when the ship got close, the cigar-shaped asdic beam would go over the top of the U-boat and the attack would thus be blind – or rather deaf – for several hundred yards and would thus be inaccurate.

With the Hedgehog, the surface ship would come in slowly, at eight knots and, when the range was about 250 yards, the mortar would be fired and the bombs would go rippling off through the air landing on the perimeter of a fair-sized ellipse ahead of the ship; quite spectacular this looked. The idea was that one or more of the bombs would hit the U-boat and the explosion would cause all the other bombs to countermine. The nice healthy explosion of the twenty-five bombs would finish the U-boat off. Later, we tried this for real!

While the Dockyard completed the final touches – more often bashes – I was sent off to the Tactical School at Liverpool. Like the school at Londonderry, it was run by Captain Gilbert Roberts with a small staff and some very bright Wren ratings. Lectures apart, we, all Commanding Officers, would be placed in small cubicles able to see only a small portion of the ocean 'battlefield' laid out on the floor; and each would have to tell an attendant Wren what we would do under a series of different circumstances as the battle progressed. I remember once handing my written answer to a particularly clued-up girl.

'No, Sir, I do not think you should do that,' she said, firmly and politely.

'Good God,' I thought, 'what on earth does this girl know about it?'

Such was her confident, tactful tone, however, that, meekly, I said: 'Oh, why not?' She explained convincingly. This young lady later married Peter Gretton who covered himself in glory in the Western Approaches.

It was an astonishingly effective set-up: more of it later but Roberts must have contributed very greatly towards the operational success of HM Ships in the Western Approaches.

Back to the ship in Devonport, the last event alongside the Dockyard wall to prepare us for war ammunitioning. This was a slow, painstaking business with ammunition lighters alongside the ship, red flags everywhere, no smoking strictly enforced. It involved checking and allocating precise stowage of 4.7-inch shells which were semi-armour-piercing, high explosive, delayed action and shrapnel; Oerlikon 20 mm and Lewis gun belts; Verey lights and minor fireworks; Hedgehog bombs; and over one hundred depth charges, mostly stowed on the upper deck. How much of this would we chuck at the enemy and how soon?

'You were in the business of killing,' a lady said to me not long ago, referring to World War Two. It is rather a catchy phrase today – sounds nasty – of 'pacifist' origin perhaps. 'Destruction of the Enemy' was the aim of HM Ships in war, and always has been, though in the Western Approaches, and elsewhere, there was also the duty of escort vessels to ensure 'the safe and timely arrival of the (merchant ship) convoy'. That was why we were embarking ammunition. It was not with the implied blood-lust of the current quip.

Sea trials of the guns, depth charge equipment, the much-vaunted Hedgehog, the asdics and the two radars – the lot – came next. If there was one regret it was that we were not getting going earlier. By that time, the spring of 1943, the tide of the Battle of the Atlantic was turning in Britain's favour. After the very heavy losses in our convoys – over 800,000 tons of merchant shipping in one month – from U-boat attacks, the heat had effectively been turned on and the trend was being reversed.

Escorts were at last getting radar, enabling them to 'see' in the dark. Commodore 'Monkey' Stephenson had his working-up base at Tobermory going full blast and was violently shaking any lethargy out of ships sent to him before they were employed operationally. The shore synthetic training facilities, especially at the Londonderry escort base, were excellent. There was no doubt that the appointment of Admiral Sir Max Horton, a one-time submarine officer and thus a real professional, had an enlivening effect on general efficiency. He was to send for me once: a stocky, dark man, seated at his desk, he proffered a cold, limp hand (to be shaken) – and a piercing glare. Like a menacing spider he seemed but on that occasion he was not dangerous – on the contrary, very friendly.

Once the ship was operational, we were sent off to join the escort force at Greenock, on the Clyde. Of the Captain(D), the boss ashore, I thought nothing – a nervous and rather ignorant fellow, out-of-date and lacking in confidence but, be it noted, this was not Captain Gronow Davies who came later and who certainly *did* know his stuff. With him it would have been very different. Almost immediately after arrival in the Clyde, *Wanderer*, a very newly commissioned ship, was detailed to do the trials at sea of transferring ammunition under way from a merchant ship. Later this operation became standard practice. Today (forty years later) all of HM Ships do it as a matter of routine but then, for a raw ship with a gallery of brass hats watching from the merchant ship, it was a mild ordeal.

There was a moderate sea running and the merchant ship, a Norwegian, chose, for this operation, to have the sea astern, making the steering the more difficult for us. Approaching and overtaking the Norwegian I swapped these signals with her:

'Are you steering by gyro or magnetic compass?'

Reply: 'Magnetic.'

'I am afraid your compass will be thrown out as I come alongside.'

'Do not be afraid,' replied the merchant ship.

Nettled, I never again used this colloquialism. The operation went well, though in the course of it, Captain(D), who was among the spectators onboard the merchant ship started shouting orders across. Seizing a megaphone, I said:

'Leave us alone to do the job, Sir.'

He did not like this – the Chief of Staff, Western Approaches, a Rear Admiral, was among those watching.

The ship's first operational job was to escort the monsters, the really big liners, carrying troops out for the invasion of Sicily. There was much secrecy about this in advance and the ships of the escort were even issued, very ostentatiously, with khaki tropical kit – just the stuff for fighting up-country in the Malayan jungle it looked. *Wanderer* was to be Senior Officer of the escort but, to my annoyance, at the last moment Captain(D) put in a retired lieutenant commander over my head. It was not a happy arrangement. He was a nice enough chap but not up to the job. One satisfactory element was that one escort, *Inconstant*, sank an Italian submarine on the return journey.

One small but memorable event of that trip occurred one night when the Surgeon Lieutenant woke me up in my sea cabin.

'What is it Doc? Someone hurt? Someone ill?'

'It's a cypher, Sir – had to be unbuttoned by an officer.'

In addition to his not too onerous medical duties and looking after the Ward Room wine books, the 'Young Doc' was also the ship's Cypher Officer. An infringement of the Geneva Convention? Well, maybe, but if so, not a serious one nor an uncommon one in those small ships at that time.

'O.K., what's it about?'

'It's very corrupt. Parts of it won't come out. It seems to refer to a threat from a Japanese submarine.'

'No, I don't think I can believe that. Wake up the Watchkeeper' – an officer – 'longest off watch and get him to check with you that you're using the right book and the right decyphering tables.'

He did. The true contents of the signal did not really concern us. It happened occasionally that we got signals which could only be dealt with by an officer, as opposed to the ship's normal coding staff who were ratings and from practice, usually quicker and better at the job.

After arrival home from the Mediterranean we were, with great thanksgiving and relief, transferred from Greenock to Londonderry to come under the authority of the Commodore(D), Western Approaches, another one-time submarine officer like Max Horton. It was clear from the outset that Commodore 'Shrimp' Simpson was a leader, firm, sensible, reliable and very likeable too.

It was also soon clear that he had an efficient and conscientious hard working and driving shore staff who were easy to work with. The Base Anti-Submarine Officer, Lieutenant Commander Michael Lee, RNVR, a barrister pre-war and a judge post-war, made sure that all ships fully used the shore training facilities. Depth charge crews had to persist until they could do a complete reload within a specific time on the shore training equipment. The ship's asdic team had to attend the Attack Teacher house, a trainer which precisely simulated attack on a submarine using the asdic, with the movement of the ship and the submarine exactly represented.

Excellent this was for the Commanding Officer, the A/S Control Officer and the asdic operators. For success, the whole team needed to be, and had to remain, fully familiar with the established procedures and any changes imposed to meet altered U-boat tactics. To this end, there was the Night Attack Teacher, housed in a largish building. Very sophisticated for its day, it consisted of a mock-up of an unlit escort's bridge at night and attached to it were separated mock-up asdic cabinets and radar sets. The movements of one's own ship according to what was ordered from the bridge and the movements of an enemy were automatically incorporated, as were the various effects such as imposed asdic echoes and echoes from the radar, reports of such contacts coming to the bridge and to the plot mock-up below. Star shell could be shown and heard and the bridge even rolled! The officers on the darkened bridge, the officer on the plot and the various rating operators behaved exactly as in a night action.

Today, the Commanding Officer may fight his ship from an operations room where he has every form of information coming in straight to him. In those days, he was on the open bridge, reliant on voice pipe reports. Night action was almost invariably confusing: almost invariably, too, it called for quick decisions. The Night Attack Teacher was thus invaluable. It turned the real thing into *déja vue*.

Wanderer joined B1 Escort Group, with Commander E. C. Bayldon as the Senior Officer of the Group. That was good news. Bayldon himself was an A/S Officer, he knew his stuff and was, like Commodore Simpson, easy to work under.

We soon settled down to the standard routine of convoy work in the North Atlantic. The day started just before first light. The Captain appeared on the bridge and, if there were any potential dangers to the convoy, the ship would go to Action Stations. Some ships always went to Action Stations just before dawn – really a relic of World War One – but, with the advent of radar, this seemed a needless nonsense for the whole ship's company though not for the Captain. To me, that first cup of over-stewed, over-sweetened tea made with condensed milk and drunk with a cigarette while one waited, usually in silence, peace and quiet, to see what the daylight might bring, was always pleasant and relaxing.

When the convoy was in good working order and there was no merchant ship straggling behind which needed to be rounded up, a series of administrative signals would be flashed by signal-projector from the Senior Officer's ship – which escorts might need to refuel? Which might have defects? Then there might be operational matters of a non-urgent nature. False alarms were invariable: asdic echoes which proved to be fish shoals; radar echoes which were caused by atmospherics or small, harmless objects; doubtful sighting reports. Many of such reports, incidentally, came from junior ratings but every one of them had to be considered analytically. Also during the forenoons, ships would carry out depth charge drills and would test armaments as well as, where necessary, refuelling.

The method of refuelling then used was for the escort ship to come up from astern of the oiler (tanker) to pick up a heavy hemp rope. The oil hose was then separately hauled across from the oiler and connected up. Pumping oil then started while the ship being oiled steamed astern of the oiler at such a speed as to keep the hemp just slack. That was the idea but it was not always all that easy; if too much strain came on the hemp and the strain then came on the oil hose, the latter would break. This was said to be very unpopular and messy. Luckily, we never experienced it, though we oiled at sea often enough.

None of the officers or ratings ever normally had an unbroken night's sleep because a part of the Ship's Company were always at cruising stations and because everyone turned out for Action Stations for false alarms. Therefore, afternoon organised activity was avoided as much as possible. For the rating not on the Watch there was their tot of rum, dinner at midday and, if possible, 'head down' till four pm. For the officers who worked in three watches there was, of course, no tot – no liquor at sea at all. (Very recently, the young Doc told me that the Wardroom bar closed as soon as the ship went to sea and did not re-open till return to harbour.)

Except during a severe gale, that was the way the day might go. Most of it I spent on the bridge – sandwiches for meals if there was anything going on, otherwise, a meal in my sea cabin just below the bridge. About eight by five feet with bunk, wash-stand and folding table, this adjoined the wheelhouse. Remembering poor Robin White, shut inside his sea cabin with the sliding door jammed shut when his destroyer *Duchess* was rammed and sunk, I had the door of my sea cabin removed altogether. Through the open doorway came the stink of cigarettes from the wheelhouse and the wailing note of the asdic beam, the 'ping' as it went out every three seconds. If the note changed or there were an asdic echo, I would be aware of it at once. The same would apply if there were an increase in the ship's speed as indicated by the ringing of the revolution counter – or even if an unusual helm order were given by the Officer of the Watch as the ship followed the convoy's zigzag course. All Commanding Officers must have adapted to reactions something like that.

The ordinary day ended with bed about eleven pm, taking off nothing but a cap. Retrospectively, it is surprising how each of us, officers and ratings with different backgrounds in our different jobs and in our different ships, came to accept a life in which, for ten days or so on end, we were always fully dressed, often wet and cold and being chucked about by the sea, and were yet able so quickly to be alerted. Ultimately, in *Wanderer*, within two minutes of the alarm rattlers suddenly going for Action Stations, everyone would be 'closed up' and ready for whatever was coming.

9. CONTACT

Wanderer had done a couple of UK to Halifax convoys with B1 Escort Group and we had our share of alarms but no real excitement. Now the convoy had just arrived off Halifax, the ship was in a position ahead of the merchant ships and we got a firm asdic contact. The echo came back with a resounding wallop. The Admiralty daily U-boat disposition signal had put nothing in the area. However, rather than wait, I went to Action Stations.

'What do you think of it?' I said to Kidd.

'Seems much too big, too wide a target for a submarine.'

'It's fish,' said the Officer of the Watch. 'I can see them.'

'Ask the Senior Officer for permission to test smoke-making apparatus,' I said to the Yeoman of Signals.

After approval of this request and after laying a smoke screen to hide our activities, we attacked the fish shoal with a depth charge. The result was an area of the sea around the ship covered in dead and stunned cod! A boat was lowered. The scrambling nets – contraptions intended to allow survivors in the water to clamber up the ship's side – were lowered. Then men came with improvised nets, buckets and baskets, they slid down ropes to the water – anything went – to recover the fish. The consequence of some ten minutes of uncontrolled hilarious activity was a pile of fish six feet high on the upper deck. The result was enough fish for our own ship, all the other ships in the Escort Group and even for the local hospital.

For the next trip, the Escort Group was transferred to do a UK to Gibraltar convoy. Better weather, not so cold, the prospect of getting ashore somewhere where there was some chance of shopping, this had some appeal. Bananas, thought some; sherry, thought others; beer and girls for the asking – well, no, but very nearly – thought some of the young men.

The convoy totalled about forty merchant ships. One calm, starlit August evening with the convoy southbound some miles off the coast of Spain was particularly pleasant and balmy. At about 11 pm, I said to Frost, the Officer of the Watch: 'I'm turning in now. Stay ahead of station during the night and call me earlier than usual, an hour before first light.'

'Any particular reason, Sir?' he queried. 'Do you expect anything to happen?'

No, I did not. The ship was ahead of the convoy to port, playing left wing, so to speak. There were no U-boats, nor any other ships of possible threat according to the Admiralty's daily disposition signal. The instruction I had given in no way related to reason!

I was asleep in my sea cabin when, about 4.30 am, Foster, the Sub Lieutenant, now the Officer of the Watch, called down the voicepipe conversationally:

'Captain, sir, I was going to call you soon anyhow but we have just got a very small echo ahead at 14,000 yards.'

'That's a hell of a distance for a small echo. Sure it's not a ghost echo or something phoney?'

'Able Seaman Herbert picked it up. The leading hand is in there now with him. Both of them say it's a true echo.'

Fourteen thousand yards – seven miles – a small echo when there should be nothing there? Eight to ten thousand yards was the officially stated maximum range at which we could detect a surfaced U-boat with the type 271 radar. Very puzzling: it could not be anything that the Admiralty knew about or we should have been told. Just possibly it could be some sort of enemy Q-boat; but, if it were enemy, I wanted to capture it and especially its signal books. The idea of a short action, sending a boarding party and then taking a vessel in prize had a strong appeal.

From the Officer of the Watch: '271 reports echo firm – increasing in size – bearing moving steadily right to left, Sir.'

'Officer of the Watch, increase to twenty-two knots and pass by R/T to the Senior Officer, am investigating radar echo – give the range and bearing.'

'What d'you think it is, Sir? Press the alarm rattlers?'

'No. We'll not be near it for a few minutes. Might still be something innocent. Send the Bosun's Mate round the mess decks and the bridge messenger to tell the officers we may be going to action shortly. Warn the engine room. And you may as well tell the galley to stew up lots of tea – just in case.'

All was quite still: the shsh–shsh–shsh as the ship cut through the slight swell, the hum of the boiler room fans and the muted talk of the men at B gun directly in front of the bridge. Then, as the men, surprised at the long warning, drifted quietly to their Action Stations, came the *sotto voce* muttering audible on the still night: 'What's the Old Man doing? There's no alarm yet is there?'

Bower, the Navigator, was on the plot now. He would not get it wrong. 'Target's moving right to left. Course easterly. Speed twelve knots,' he reported.

It looked like a gun action to come.

'Press the alarm rattlers,' I said.

There followed the immediate shuffling of feet and rattling of iron ladders as the remaining officers and men dashed in the dark to their Action Stations – no shouting, no needless noise. Then came the steady flow of reports to the Action Officer of the Watch from the guns, the radars, the asdics, the plot, the depth charge crews to say they were 'closed up and cleared away'. All necessary voicepipe and telephone communications were tested. It was quick, calm routine procedure. Within seconds all was quiet again: back to the same sea and machinery noises and the very quiet mumbling background talk from B gun's crew.

From me: 'B gun star shell load star.'

The First Lieutenant arrived on the bridge.

'Fire star shell, sir? and find out what it's all about?'

'No. I want to get right up to it undetected,' and, to the Officer of the Watch: 'All guns load.'

For the first time in the procedure – anticlimax – the order rang out loud around the ship: 'All guns. Load – load – load.'

Bower, from the plot: 'Target's course 065 degrees. Speed twelve knots. Good plot. We're in to six thousand yards now, sir.'

The temptation to open fire was there all right. But with fire control equipment no longer fitted in the ship, we were very unlikely to hit any target except at point blank range. Then, supposing it *were* a U-boat, it would be alerted by gun flashes and would dive at once well out of asdic range; it might use the advance warning to fire a torpedo at us; and it would, anyway, get a start on us in making an escape before we could pick up asdic contact.

Radar: 'Range 3,000 yards. Target very firm. Increasing in size.'

Despite the Admiralty Intelligence this could still be a U-boat: the ship should slow to maximum asdic operating speed. 'Eighteen knots,' I ordered.

'Cuppa, sir?' from Cartwright.

'Thanks. ... Frost, you and the look-outs keep your eyes skinned ahead.'

Radar: 'Range 2,800 yards – target's getting smaller – it's fading – it's gone – last bearing 215 degrees.'

'Plot, give me a course to steer till the asdics pick it up.'

Asdics: 'Echo bearing 205 degrees. Range 2,400 yards.'

Two thousand four hundred yards, at eighteen knots – ten yards a second – that would be four minutes or thereabouts before firing a depth charge pattern.

To Frost, the Officer of the Watch: 'I'll take her now.'

To the Cox'n: 'Steer 205.'

'Steer 205, sir,' he repeated back.

Then: 'Stand by depth charges set at 100 feet.'

The ping-echo ever faster as the range decreased. Building tension. Must be nearly there.

Asdic: 'Range 200 yards.' Then: 'Simultaneous echoes.'

Kidd: 'Stand by – fire.' And he pressed the firing buzzer. Seconds — then C R A S H E S!

The stern of the ship rose and shuddered with the explosions. Plumes of water rose astern.

'Bugger. I did not lay off enough. Not a kill,' I said.

Plot: 'Looked like a good attack from down here but slightly behind him. He put on a last-second burst of speed.'

The explosions of the charges disturbed the water. This blanked, temporarily, the U-boat from detection; but the asdics got him again. Great relief: we were to have another chance.

This time we would make a sedate, deliberate attack. We would go by the book, use the Hedgehog mortar and, as instructed, approach slowly.

Asdic: 'Echo regained, bearing 040, range 1,200 yards.'

Myself: 'Attacking with Hedgehog. Speed eight knots.' Then, turning to Cartwright: 'Get me another cup of tea and my cigarettes', and, to Frost, 'See everyone knows what's happening, including the engine room.'

Slowly, and with great concentration, we approached the U-boat. The asdic operating conditions continued to be excellent, and the operators themselves provided their steady flow of precise and accurate information.

The plot, based on the asdic information, had the U-boat's movements exactly taped.

Asdic: 'Range 500 yards.' We were coming up to it. The firing range for the mortar was 250 yards plus or minus a few yards to allow for the movement of the target. The Hedgehog's crew on the forecastle were all prepared. We should just about get the attack completed before the convoy caught up. 'Go on Kidd, fire when you're ready.'

From Kidd: 'Stand by – Fire.' He pressed the fire buzzer and the twenty-four mortar bombs, ripple-fired, sailed into the air. Even in the dark, the pattern they formed on hitting the water was visible. If one bomb hit the target, the lot would countermine. We waited. Nothing happened. Then, one small, not convincing pop. The whole pattern of bombs had certainly not gone off.

'But that was a good attack, Sir,' said Kidd, somewhat indignantly.

'It was first class. Tell the asdic team. It's that goddam bloody useless ammunition. The whole f'ing lot we've just used is to be sent back to the Armament Supply Officer for test and report,' I said, temporarily livid with fury.

Asdic: 'Target's turned towards the convoy.' The asdic operators in contact with the U-boat could hear the 'hydrophone effect', the heavy throbbing of the approaching merchant ships' propellers the far side of their target.

Plot: 'We confirm the U-boat's heading to get under the convoy.' Damn and blast. Anger gone now. This was going to be nasty in the dark. U-boats had done this before. It was a means of usually successful escape. The problem was how to keep asdic contact. For the operators, the distracting hydrophone effect, the distracting thump-thump-thump of merchant ships' propellers and the aerated water the ship's wake would cause, would mask and deaden, if not completely stop – cut off – the asdic beam.

'Asdics, we're going in among ships of the convoy now. Do your best to hold contact. If we have to cross the columns, I'll tell you before we come to a wake.'

There it was, the convoy of some four dozen black-looking unlit ships on a zig-zag course. Into it we went after the U-boat.

Plot: 'Target's altering course westward, Sir, trying to get the other side of some wakes.'

'Asdics, we're crossing a wake now,' I said.

Asdic: 'Lost contact.' Then: 'Contact regained.'

And I altered course again to pursue.

'Asdics, we're going to cross another wake.'

Once more, the ship had to cross at right angles – more or less – through the advancing columns of the convoy.

'Asdic: 'Lost contact – no, contact regained.'

It was going to happen a third time when, from Frost, the Officer of the Watch: 'Merchant ship to starboard altering course towards us in her zig-zag. She's going to be pretty close.'

We were going to be hit. Full speed, an emergency order, which meant that the engine room was to produce maximum power, might damage the asdic dome in its lowered position.

'Port twenty. Ring on twenty-five knots.' In fact, we always gave orders for ship's speed in terms of revolutions, knowing exactly what revs to order for the required knots. The Wheelhouse below then 'rang on' (ting-ting-ting) the revs to the engine room by speedily winding the rev counter.

Then, when we were clear and able to get round the stern into the next column of merchant ships: 'Starboard twenty. Fifteen knots.'

It was no good. The proximity of that merchant ship and our burst of speed made it impossible for the operators. Asdic contact was lost. We had been out-manoeuvred by the U-boat.

The exacting caper, dodging about, chasing in the blackness through the columns of the darkened merchant ships had taken only some fifteen minutes. I was, though, as never before nor since, in a cold, damp sweat, shaking a little at the legs.

'Plot, work out a search scheme, assuming the target will have gone back to his original course and under-water speed and will be making for Lorient. Give the Officer of the Watch the courses for our own speed of fifteen knots.'

The First Lieutenant arrived on the bridge. 'Would you like a rest, Sir? Shall I take over for a bit?'

'No, let's have more tea and a cigarette. Tell the gun crews they can relax. Stay at Action Stations. No watertight doors to be opened but everyone can smoke. Make the first teams of radar and asdic operators come out for a few minutes of fresh air, whether they want to or not. The second teams can take over temporarily.'

The ship was completing one of the standard square searches of the area recommended for such occasions; no good after half an hour, and the search was nearly over. What next? I went down to the plot to talk it over briefly with Bower, when Asdic reported again: 'Contact right ahead. Echo bearing 160 degrees. Range 2,300 yards. Good echo.' Yes, it was. The echo came back with a firm, convincing click. It could only be the U-boat.

During the early minutes of the square search scheme, we, Kidd, the Gunner, Mr Ellis (a very experienced Warrant Officer) and I held a brief post-mortem upon the failure of the Hedgehog ammunition.

Was the Gunner actually present at the mortar before and when it was fired? Yes, Sir, with mild indignation, certainly he was. Was he absolutely satisfied that all the bombs were fully armed and set to explode? Yes, he had personally supervised that this was done. I, in turn, was satisfied that the last attack was entirely accurate and that the bombs fell just as they should in a good pattern. So what? Well, plainly all the bombs had come from a dud 'lot' – ammunition was always mysteriously divided into 'lots'. There was another fresh lot immediately available, said Mr Ellis. Right, we would do another attack using this mortar weapon of such high repute.

Here was a second chance.

'Attacking with Hedgehog. Speed eight knots,' I said.

The ship's approach was slow: 2,000 yards – 1,500 yards – 1,000 yards – as the steady, clear reports of the target's bearing and range came from the asdic cabinet.

'Plot. What's the target doing?'

Plot: 'Going slowly away, about two knots on a mean course of 065 degrees.'

Asdic: 'Range 600 yards. Poor echo. Echo fading. Lost contact.'

Oh, bloody hell. Whatever now? Almost at once, the Asdic cabinet reported, 'Contact regained.' Then there was some brief muttering audible over the intercom, Kidd talking to the operators, Kidd talking to the plot, and, thirty seconds later: 'It's a non-sub. It's an SBT and the U-boat's gone deep.'

This was a clever piece of tactics. Knowing that by going deep, the asdic beam would pass over his hull, the U-boat Captain had gone down to perhaps 500 feet. At the same time, he had released a submarine bubble target (SBT) decoy – a canister which would cause effervescence in the water and give a false echo and thus, he hoped, throw us off the metaphorical scent. It was not for long; his cunning was met by the quick, shrewd, analytical team-work of Kidd and Cocks backed by Bower from the plot.

'Contact regained bearing 240 degrees, range 700 yards,' reported the asdics. An immediate attack with the U-boat so close would not be accurate. It was, quite suddenly, daylight and a corvette sent back from the convoy escort arrived to see if help was needed. She at once reported asdic contact. 'Attack,' I said. *Wanderer* would do the next one; but it was unfortunately the SBT which the corvette attacked.

'Plot,' I said meanwhile, 'work on the last definitely known position of the target and give me the dope to get the ship 2,000 yards astern of target, on its mean course. Then we'll come in at eighteen knots and hope to attack from astern – up the arse. The depth charge crews are to fire a pattern of ten charges, then reload at top speed and fire another pattern of ten with both patterns at the deepest settings.'

This was unorthodox. I had heard that Commander 'Johnny' Walker, the great anti-U-boat ace, had done something like this but at slow speed and with several of the ships in his group taking part at a time.

From Kidd: 'Do you think it will work, Sir?'

'If it doesn't, we'll do it again. The U-boat is deep and you'll be out of contact for the last fifty or sixty seconds, so you'll have to work with Bower to estimate the time to start firing. You can fire your Hedgehog, too.'

'That's not allowed at that speed, Sir.'

'The thing is no bloody good when we do obey the rules! It might work if we don't.'

The unsuccessful attempts to attack so far were not heartening but the asdic conditions were so good and the U-boat so plainly on the defensive that we seemed bound to win.

From the plot: 'Ship's in position now. Range 2,000 yards and target bearing 065 degrees. That's the approximate course the U-boat's been trying to make good since we first picked him up.'

'Attacking at 18 knots,' I said. Then the ranges started to come down rapidly: eighteen knots was ten yards a second – 1,500 yards – 1,000 yards – 600 yards – and then, from the asdic: 'Target fading – lost contact.'

There would be some sixty impotent seconds while we were running in blind, or more literally, deaf.

'Time to fire yet?' I asked impatiently. Quickly, rather irritably: 'No, Sir, wait.'

Then, Kidd: 'Stand by. Fire.'

I went to the back of the bridge to watch the depth charge crews doing some beefy manual work to get the double pattern off. There were pauses of seconds before the charges sank to the depths set to explode. Then again came the deep rumbling, thunderous crumps. The mounds of water were forced up from below – not the vast columns of water from charges set to explode shallow but powerful aerated tumuli bursting through the surface.

'Contact regained, 1,000 yards,' from the Asdics. Bugger, we've not sunk it. We'll have to do it again. I reduced speed.

From Kidd, suddenly, confidently, almost calm: 'U-boat's surfacing. We can hear her blowing tanks, quite clear.'

'Keep all guns on the asdic bearing. Get the boarding party in to the whaler. We want some of the German signal books even if we can't capture the U-boat.'

A chorus of reports and cheers from the look-outs and guns' crews: 'Surfacing green four five.'

The black-looking bow appeared at a steep angle and the U-boat levelled off doing some two knots.

'Open fire,' I said. 'Hoist Flag Five' – the signal meaning 'Open fire at once' – half ahead both engines, starboard twenty. I am going to get close.'

From the Coxwain: 'You're crossing her torpedo tubes, Sir.'

'Thank you Cox'n, it'll be all right.' Then: 'B gun, why don't you open fire?'

'Loaded star shell, Sir.'

'Pull the bloody trigger at once.' A hit on the conning tower and a shower of spectacular sparks! Very close now. Then: 'Cease fire.' We did not want to sink the U-boat. To the First Lieutenant: 'Get the boarding party boat away.'

Frost: 'They're manning their guns.' It was a brave act with a destroyer so close.

'Kidd, take the old bridge Lewis gun and keep them away from their guns.'

'It's point blank range, Sir.'

'Do it at once! Spray the U-boat's casing!'

The red tracer bullets from the Lewis gun were too much for them – the German crew jumped overboard.

Frost: 'U-boat's sinking. They've opened sea-cocks – sinking fast.'

Bloody hell! Couldn't we have been quicker? No, we could not. The Germans had beaten us to it. Our whaler, now in the water, could only help the corvette's boat to pick up the German survivors while we lowered scrambling nets down both sides of the ship to help survivors swimming to the ship to get on board.

It was over. It was a pity to be seen off at the last moment and get no capture of the U-boat – not even any German signal books. As a mild consolation, *Wanderer* had been able to hoist the famous Flag Five meaning 'open fire at once'.

I, for one, was mildly relaxed watching the survivors being recovered when suddenly: 'Torpedo approaching bearing 185 degrees' came the report from the asdic operator. There must be a second U-boat! Could we get two in a day?

'Full ahead port engine. Hard-a-starboard,' I ordered.

The Cox'n repeated the order back, then: 'Port engine going full ahead, wheel's hard – starboard, sir.'

From me: 'Midships. Half ahead together. Steer 185 degrees.'

We were now aimed at the source of the supposed torpedo but the report had not come from the action team who were taking a breather. In a flash, Kidd and Cocks were back on the job and they at once pronounced disappointingly that it was a false alarm. Here was an example of how we had so often to rely on the judgement of a young and junior rating in a remarkably responsible position. Recriminations for causing a false alarm were plainly not on – if such a young rating was not up to the job he had to be replaced.

Due to the diversion we only picked up thirteen Germans and regrettably I almost certainly drowned one or two of them who were swimming round *Wanderer*'s screws when the ship had to be turned so suddenly towards the supposed torpedo. However, the corvette picked up twenty or so, including the U-boat's CO.

With survivors on board and boats hoisted we proceeded at twenty-two knots, the maximum asdic operating speed in such fine weather, telling the corvette to follow at her best speed to rejoin the convoy. To cheer up the merchant ships which had only heard a series of unexplained explosions and perhaps seen a destroyer dodging about in the dark in the columns of ships the night before, I had White Ensigns hoisted at the foremast, both yard arms, the gaff and the ensign staff aft.

As a device, maybe not altogether in accordance with the Geneva

Convention, I told the Gunner to fall-in a firing party with Sten guns on the upper deck and to bring the prisoners out, one by one, for questioning; then, to fire a volley over the heads of those who were the least forthcoming. It worked, within limits, but the Germans had been told to expect rough treatment from us – even to having their hands cut off if taken prisoner.

As soon as all was calm again, the inevitable Able Seaman Cartwright appeared on the bridge.

'Cor, Sir,' he said, 'you do look 'orrible. You'd better have some nice bacon and eggs.'

'No. Shaving water. Toast and coffee will do this morning,' I said.

Thinking over the four-and-a-half hour action, I felt it had gone well. We were lucky to succeed against a U-boat so skilfully handled, especially with our dud Hedgehog mortar ammunition. We had had good weather, good asdic conditions and the advantage of the splendid training on the synthetic shore devices – the simulators – at the Londonderry Base. It was gratifying though to see the asdics, the radar and the plot work so well – and so well together – when it came to 'doing it live'.

Later, talking to Antrobus, the First Lieutenant, I said: 'That was all very satisfactory, except that I forgot that B gun was loaded with star shell and we should have cleared the gun at daylight.' (It was impractically dangerous to unload star shell.)

Then I spoke to the Gunner who was responsible for the rum: 'Mr Ellis, Splice the Main Brace.'

With a look of horror: 'You can't do that, Sir, without an order from the Admiralty or the C-in-C, and I have to keep my rum accounts very precisely.'

'Yes, yes, of course, but I will sign to say that a rum jar was broken in heavy weather. You keep some pieces to show the 'pussers' and the First Lieutenant here will testify that I am guilty if we get rumbled.'

Some months afterwards, the Admiralty did actually approve that Commanding Officers could Splice the Main Brace – issue an extra tot of rum all round – when it was confirmed that their ship had sunk a U-boat. But we were never bowled out 'warming the bell' – pre-empting the order.

Now, at last, there was some real medical work for the young Doc to do, with the prisoners wounded – probably caused by our 20 mm Oerlikons when the U-boat first surfaced, as opposed to Kidd's spraying the submarine's upper deck with the Lewis gun. Two of the wounded died and, just as any of us would have been, they were sewn up in seamen's hammocks weighted with iron fire bars. By custom, this was the coxwain's job: he was the ship's undertaker – the funeral director, if you prefer it. His final act, again by custom, was when sewing up the hammocks, to put the last stitch through the nose of the deceased, just to ensure against mistakes.

The funeral, later, was attended by all of the prisoners of war and, voluntarily, by most of the Ship's Company off watch. The Service was taken by the First Lieutenant as I seldom left the bridge area at sea. The dead

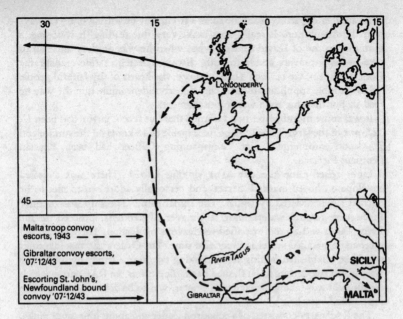

Map 5. HMS *Wanderer*'s Convoy Escort Tasks, 1943
During this period, HMS *Wanderer* also sank *U-523* at 42N 18 02W on 25 August 1943 (*see* Map 7) and undertook a clandestine mission into the River Tagus to rendezvous with a civilian boat on 26 August 1943.

were placed, each under a white ensign, on a wooden slide and, at the appropriate moment, with the three wailing notes, were piped over the side. Then followed the usual three volleys.

Piping over the side was their entitlement. It was an honour then strictly limited and reserved before sunset for the Monarch and immediate members of the Royal Family in uniform, all Flag Officers of the Executive Branch, all officers in command of HM Ships and all those entitled to a formal naval burial at sea, and, at all times of the day or night, for all foreign naval officers. There it stopped. *No one else*, however high and mighty, could be piped over the side, though visiting generals and the like (on duty) might get bugles blown at them in big ships and the 'still' piped at them in ships which were smaller.

Perhaps it is appropriate here to say that, like other Commanding Officers, whenever it was reasonable to get down from the bridge at sea on a Sunday – which was seldom – I always took prayers. With no laughing allowed, we had hymns, to the ship's band of mouth organs! In reading the Naval Prayer and asking God to '... preserve us from the dangers of the sea and the violence of the enemy ...' I omitted the piece about the violence of the enemy. It seemed quite unreasonably presumptuous, even arrogant, to expect the Almighty to do what we were being paid for.

As another departure from the rules – an entirely unwitting one – I always read the Absolution. It really does make very fine reading! It was, too, a reminder to me of David Simson who, when he was on duty and had to take evening prayers at Dartmouth, always selected as fine reading the Collect 'Stir up, we beseech Thee, oh Lord, the hearts of thy faithful people …' no humble supplication but a cheerful, confident injunction the way he read it, but then his style was inimitable.

It was some months later that I learned that our recent victim had been *U-523*, one of the large Type IXC boats, capable of 18 knots on the surface and 7.3 knots submerged. Her Commanding Officer had been Kapitän Leutnant Pietzsch.

Light relief came the day after sinking *U-523*. There was a sealed envelope on board marked 'Secret' and personally addressed to me, to be opened when ordered by signal. The signal came. The ship was to enter Portuguese neutral waters under the cover of darkness, proceed up the River Tagus and go to a specified rendezvous off Lisbon. There we would meet an unspecified vessel at a specified time. The Orders said that identities would be established by this vessel flashing two signal letters by torch. We were given two letters to be flashed back. Thereafter, an RAF party, which we thought was taking passage to Gibraltar, was to be disembarked into the unspecified vessel.

The RAF party consisted of a squadron leader and about four other ranks. They had come from Londonderry and why they had not been put on board a more comfortable ship for passage had till then been a mystery. It was pleasant having the company of the squadron leader on the bridge – a man more like a young professor or a schoolmaster than an airman – though he volunteered nothing about himself or his men.

The prisoners of war were, of course, shut away below the waterline where they could neither see nor hear anything, the exception being the German Navigating Officer who was under guard in my day cabin aft with the deadlights screwed down.

'We'll have the navigation lights switched on,' I said to the First Lieutenant, 'and a few selected lights on the upper deck but not ones which will show up the guns. Also, we must go to Action Stations and be ready to open fire at once if the need arises. The men are not to be visible at the guns. No smoking and the ensign is to be a small one,' I added.

'Pity we can't go for a run ashore ourselves, Sir.'

'Caution is the watchword for the night, Number One. We might just possibly meet a German or an Iti playing funny buggers. Might even meet a Portuguese warship and I'm certainly not going to let the ship get interned by the Portuguese.'

Switching on navigation lights and then some upper deck lights had an unexpected effect of unreality – mildly intoxicating – in marked contrast to the very strict blackout we had observed for the four previous years at sea in HM Ships – and ashore too. The Ship's Company had to be brought back quite sharply to seriousness!

Straight out of the dark, we arrived at the exact time, at the exact place; so did our 'date'. The identification drill worked precisely and a largish white fishing boat with no lights came alongside us in a very seamanlike manner. We had the 20 mm Oerlikon guns trained on the boat and also, just in case of trickery, a small party armed with Sten guns, in charge of an officer ready and discreetly hidden on the upper deck; but all seemed well. In curiosity, I left the bridge to the First Lieutenant and came down to see what went on. The squadron leader and his braves were all on the upper deck in plain clothes, each with a hand-grip.

'What's all this stuff?' I asked the squadron leader, referring to the assorted gear on deck. He mumbled something about balloons, or words phonetically similar, but this was no time for pursuing trivialities. From the fishing boat onto our deck stepped a man dressed in a dinner jacket, an Anthony Eden black soft hat and a Sherlock Holmes type cape. Recovering from astonishment, I asked: 'Won't you come down for a quick cup of coffee or a drink?'

'No thanks, I'll just get these chaps and be off.'

It was a scene as remarkable as it was entertaining – especially the dress of the very capable man in charge. Dinner jackets were something we had not seen for four years, since the war started. I never heard another word about this little melodrama – never had any idea what it was all about. The Air Ministry never claimed back the RAF uniforms which were left behind – to be worn out at sea by the sailors!

From enquiries years later it looked as though *Wanderer* had on 26 August 1943 delivered an element of an advance party to implement the agreement, signed on 18 August 1943, with our 'oldest allies', the Portuguese, under which Britain was to supply a number of aircraft spitfires (and a few barrage balloons) and give a guarantee of armed help in the event of German aggression; in return, Portugal was to allow the use of air bases in the Azores Islands to British aircraft covering convoys. This became operative in October 1943, though, initially, the Portuguese firmly refused to let the Americans cash in!

The young Doc had an unusual thrill. Whenever the ship went to Action Stations as on this occasion, and he thought there might be a chance of business for him as a result, he would take the tools of his trade – scalpels, swabs and so on – and lay them all out in my day cabin aft. This was the operating theatre and my dining-room table was to be used for carving and stitching. That evening, however, the U-boat's Navigator was imprisoned in my day cabin. The Doc took no notice and got on with his usual preparations until it was apparent that the German was in a state bordering on violence. He was convinced that the moment had come: he thought he was about to have something cut off that he wanted to keep, and the Doc had to call the seaman guard in to restrain the man from violence.

On another occasion, a case of acute toothache on a rough day in mid-Atlantic was another medical drama. The Young Doc reported to the bridge that he would have to take the man's tooth out: could the ship, which was rolling heavily and zig-zagging with a convoy, heave-to on a steady course? Five minutes, subject to alarms, he was given. The doctor assembled the unhappy man, two of his messmates to hold him, a pair of boiled electrician's pliers and – being a Scot – two(?) half tumblers of neat whisky.

'Here,' said the Young Doctor to his patient when the ship was hove-to, 'You drink this one and I'll have the other and we're both going to need it.'

The operation was very swift and entirely successful!

From Lisbon, we proceeded without incident to Gibraltar to land the prisoners of war. For me, the action against the U-boat had satisfied two wishes held since early days at Dartmouth. One was, with or without authority, to order 'Splice the Main Brace'. The second was to give the order to hoist Flag Five, or whatever flag signal meant 'open fire at once'. There cannot have been many occasions during World War Two when the use of this flag was justified because it essentially meant it had to be a very close range encounter by day.

The nocturnal venture into neutral waters was the only time the prisoners were shut up. Otherwise, they were kept under the fairly theoretical guard of an Able Seaman with a Sten gun and they got on very friendly terms with our ratings. The U-boat's Navigator fed with our officers in the Ward Room. Since he spoke no English and none of our officers spoke any German and it was found that our Radar Mechanic did, the Radar Mechanic was lent an officer's uniform, was temporarily put in the Ward Room and told to converse with the German officer. The assumption was that the latter might be the more ready to talk immediately after the unpleasant experience of having his ship sunk – and also after the apparent fright given him by Surgeon Lieutenant Fuller, the young Doc laying out the tools of his trade.

Before we arrived, however, came a very fierce signal from Gibraltar saying that all prisoners of war were to be locked up below decks, with deadlights down so that they could not see which port they were in on arrival. The ship was berthed in a very privileged position alongside the Dockyard wall and some officious soldiers arrived to blindfold the eleven Germans who were taken ashore escorted by even more soldiers, this time with fixed bayonets. We never saw them again, of course. The Ship's Company did not altogether like seeing our prisoners treated like this. They had come to look on them as tame pets, rather as teenagers might look on a litter of, say leopard cubs.

For a few minutes, I met the Chief Security (MI5) official. He looked like my idea of a Spanish grandee. Stuffy fellow, I thought; he should be grateful we had brought him some interesting interrogation work to do. Years later, I worked with him; a kind, pleasant and entertaining chap he was. He never said so, but our attempts in *Wanderer* to get the Germans to talk may well have upset his professional approach. The only one piece of information that I remembered that the prisoners of war gave us was that they had heard the Hedgehog bombs! They described them as 'whistle bombs' – not inappropriate, as the U-boat had heard these wretched things whistling harmlessly by!

10. GIB AND BACK

Returning to 'Derry there was a welter of refitting and some shore training, work which mainly fell on Antrobus, the First Lieutenant. He did not look too fit but he sailed with us on another convoy to Gib. The trip out was not eventful – a few German aircraft appeared on the horizon, shadowing, but no attack developed. Infuriatingly, some defects had cropped up on arrival and there was some minor damage resulting in *Wanderer* being unable to sail with the homeward bound convoy. All was quickly put right and then the Flag Officer Gibraltar seized on the ship to join the local patrol in the Straits. Nothing promised to be more dull: U-boats on passage in and out of the Mediterranean would be using neutral waters, forbidden to us, and there were no other prospects whatsoever. I started to make a fuss.

An ENSA party was in Gib at the time entertaining the troops and one of the officers – possibly and surprisingly the First Lieutenant – invited Vivien Leigh, Leslie Henson and another comedian on board. My aims were to make them mildly tiddly and then to get them to make us laugh. Perhaps because the Staff College of that day allowed the planner to have only one aim, my second aim did not work. Fortunately, however, some other COs came to call and I retired with them to my day cabin. She was a very pretty, very thin and rather sad little girl, Vivien Leigh, with not much to say – no, no, a very beautiful, slim young lady of graceful poise.

For simple drama, Kidd had the edge on that little event. He, a most conscientious young man, was the officer in charge of the Confidential Books, that was to say, all books and certain important documents classified Secret and even Top Secret. He lost the key of one of the safes. He was quick in reporting it and I immediately put sentries to prevent anyone leaving the ship on any pretext whatever and reported the loss to the Flag Officer Gibraltar. The safe concerned was forced open and pairs of officers mustered the contents of all safes – each book and document and each page therein. There was nothing wrong. I never thought there would be; and yet it was just possible there might have been – or someone else might have thought so – and with Spain, which was pro-German, so close, secret and confidential cyphers and codes falling into enemy hands could be exceedingly serious. After the war, incidentally, I found a photograph of *Wanderer* in a book;[1] the caption said that the photograph had been taken by

1 *The Critical Convoy Battles of March 1943* Jürgen Röhwer Ian Allan. Shepperton Page 193.

German Intelligence Agents in Algeçiras to show the ship's special H/F D/F mast. So they were on the job locally.

After the quick, thorough mustering and checking of all our secret and confidential books and documents officially confirmed that nothing was missing, I ceased to worry. All the same, next came the ghastly prospect of dealing with the resulting paperwork and, luckily, this had to go to our administrative authority – still the Commodore(D) Western Approaches in Londonderry. The simple way out of this by no means serious situation seemed to be to confuse the correspondence – easy enough without trying too hard. To make sure of it, we decided to answer not the last letter received but the one before. In desperation, amid unfathomable cross-references, the Commodore told me to admonish Kidd and to pay for the new key myself. No sooner had I sent for Kidd and told him to consider himself admonished and given him a drink to celebrate this satisfactory solution than he returned in pallid anxiety to say the missing key had just come back from the Gib. laundry in the pocket of his white uniform shorts. I told him to throw it overboard at once and not to say another word to anyone.

Naval security, or rather the weakness of it, was a bee in my bonnet throughout my whole Service career. The Confidential Books, admittedly, were taken seriously. They had been for years and the rules for dealing with them were good and – most important – any officer breaking these rules by losing a book or even part of a book would invariably be tried by Court Martial. The consequences of conviction were such that they could seriously affect the officer's career and thus cost him indirectly a really painful amount of money. The security rules and precautions were feeble and ineffective when it came to other forms of physical security – if that is the right term – such as secret and confidential paperwork not formally categorised and listed as Confidential Books or 'Charge Documents'. They were almost non-existent. Especially in shore establishments, papers could lie in 'In' and 'Out' trays unguarded; when they were locked up at night, they would go into the standard pattern filing cabinet which I thought at the time gave the minimal degree of protection. The keys of these filing cabinets were like the thing that starts my mowing machine today.

'Spy' cases have been all too common in recent years. One angle on physical security is that it was, its intrinsic nature, dull: it was a nuisance and often distasteful, absolutely negative with no plus marks for good (normal) security and only bad marks for bad security when rumbled. On the whole, when bad marks were awarded they were seldom awarded to the top brass. On the other hand, special security of an operation when it was of direct consequence to the top brass was, with one notable exception, excellent. This, I think, proves the point that, too often, the buck stopped too quickly – too low down. Personal security, vetting, was another matter, and one with which I had little contact.

To all our ships at sea (as to the enemy), radio signal security was quite vital and we, in *Wanderer*, had the special High Frequency Direction Finding mast and equipment plus a very small team of a Lieutenant RNVR and three ratings to deal with the interception of enemy W/T traffic. They worked in a little dog's hole of a place aft glorying in the name of the High Frequency Direction Finding Office. Periodically members of the team could be seen, white faced, climbing in or out of the hatch on the iron deck. The situation was an odd one: this team was under my command but not under my operational control! They could, it seemed, make signals direct to the Admiralty if they intercepted an enemy transmission of value, without any reference to me. They told me nothing and their duty, so far as the ship was concerned, was limited to reporting bearings of any intercepted enemy transmission which could directly affect *Wanderer*.[2]

The H/F D/F party brought the numbers on board to 193 although the ship was only designed for a complement of 110. The eleven officers – twelve with me – were particularly badly placed. Some slept in the officers' bathroom and someone used to sleep in my day cabin at sea and sleep in my sea cabin when we were in harbour. There was at that time an allowance known officially as Hard Lying Money. The Admiralty, in their limited generosity, allowed us officers 'half-liers', while the ratings got the full allowance in that ship. I received one shilling and sixpence (7½p) per day while the ship was at sea.

Though not to be compared with Vivien Leigh coming on board or Kidd sending a confidential book safe key to the laundry, we did have one mildly unusual event at Gib. A merchant ship SS *Hallizones* was attacked somewhere out to the west in the Atlantic by a Focke-Wulf FW 200 aircraft; she was damaged, abandoned by her crew, but remained afloat. What happened to the crew was never related but *Wanderer* was told to search for this ship and take her in tow. At the same time, an aircraft was searching the area. Although both ship and aircraft were using radar, neither of us could find the ship. I asked permission to give up. No, said Flag Officer Gibraltar.

Somewhat surprisingly, we did find the damned ship! After doing a thorough asdic sweep against lurking U-boats, I put Midshipman Scott with a young engine room artificer and the ship's best Leading Seaman and three Able Seamen on board her. Another officer and the Chief ERA had assessed the damage to this 8,000-ton ship as one dicey bulkhead which they shored up. Then, taking the ship in tow, we set off, a whaler in tow of *Hallizones* so that Scott and party would not have to swim. The tow was going nicely, the weather was good but during the night the bulkhead went, the towing party called up on a signal lamp, they took to the whaler, slipped the tow and the ship disappeared gently below the waves. It was a negative and sad little operation; had we got the ship back to Gib we might have got some salvage money. It was disappointing both for *Wanderer* and

---

2 This little H/F D/F team was a minute part of the considerable Admiralty organisation which so effectively tracked U-boats Patrick Beesly's book *Very Special Intelligence* (Hamish Hamilton, London, 1977) covers the whole subject in most interesting detail. He includes a piece on the work done by a small team of clever, wholly inadequately rewarded Wrens who dealt with the captured German Enigma cypher machine My young cousin was one of these bright girls who did a job, perhaps laborious and dull, yet extremely secret and vitally important.

the tug *Prosperous* which had been sent out but did not arrive in time to get a line across.

Eventually, my series of complaining letters and signals from Gib worked. *Wanderer* was sent back to rejoin the Londonderry Escort Force. Perhaps it was the fact that we were fitted with H/F D/F that swayed the balance, wasted at Gibraltar where it was reasonable to assume they had similar, probably bigger and better equipment of their own. On arrival at 'Derry I heard we were to be put in another escort group and, learning the name of the Senior Officer of the group, I went to the Commodore saying I would like to be excused from serving under this officer. I knew him as a man who was a narky, sarcastic, by-the-book fellow and, most important, one of those Commanding Officers who was unlikely – as some were – to be involved in action. This, later, proved to be correct. In addition, I disliked and distrusted him! Not everyone likes everyone else. Having said my carefully prepared and paraphrased piece, there was a pause and then 'Shrimp', who always spoke from the back of his mouth as though it were full of spit, or his teeth did not fit, said: 'Do you really mean that, old boy?'

Yes, I did and was sure my serving under him would not work. Could I not go to Commander Gretton's Group or Captain Walker's?

'Have a drink, old boy. Would you like to go to one of the new 'Captain' class frigates?'

'No, thank you, Sir, not unless I can take my whole Ship's Company.'

Being not too sure of what would happen, it came as a relief a few days later to learn that the ship was to be put in a support group, the American synonym being, once more, hunter-killer group. I would not have liked the latter name with its implication that one was idling by not scoring one or so before breakfast.

'Shrimp', the Commodore Western Approaches, had both great character and ability. He was a leader and a driver with a practical outlook and yet he had charm, charisma – or whatever. He was an enormously broad man, not tall, but stocky, heavily built with a shock of curly hair and often a surprised and rather ingenuous expression. If he was at all scheming, he kept it to himself. He never waffled, never delayed a decision, never shouted. He would listen, preferably to anything he had not heard before; then came the answer straight back, nearly always cheerful – and final. The way the base was run showed he could make people work hard, well and willingly. It was said that he was not altogether a teetotaller; I think this was correct. It certainly was when I met him again after the war.

There were at Londonderry some one hundred escort vessels – destroyers, sloops, frigates and corvettes – to be administered. The Commodore, backed by his Chief of Staff, Captain (later Vice Admiral Sir Maxwell) Richmond and a very fine supporting cast, dealt with damage – mostly from the sea – equipment and its modification, discipline, personnel problems, endless written Reports of Proceedings and, above all, training for the conflict. The latter, of course, involved him and his staff in remaining very fully aware of the ever-changing U-boat tactics and technical developments and keeping abreast or even ahead of them. I think

'Shrimp' must have had one of the best trained and administered naval forces there had ever been in naval history. It was certainly a reflection of his training that our action against *U-523* had gone so well. Without the drilling – and grilling – our depth charge crews had had on the 'Derry shore trainer they would never have been able, in this fairly newly-commissioned ship, to put up the performance of firing a double pattern of charges in the time normally allowed for firing a single.

The standard of asdic operating during that U-boat hunt was also the highest I had ever encountered, even pre-war in the A/S School. That it was consistent over a period of around five hours was due partly, of course, to the natural skill of Kidd and Cocks. This was definitely enhanced because Kidd had taken the team so frequently to the attack teacher ashore that their reactions to 'operating procedure' were automatic and thus immediate and therefore less tiring over the hours of the hunt. When the U-boat was blowing tanks prior to surfacing, the operators at once recognised the sound because they had heard it so often on gramophone discs in their training ashore. The record range at which the target was first detected by radar, giving credit for the keenness and skill of the operators was also due to the shore tuning and the maintenance of the set by the Base Staff. It was due as well to the fact that Sub Lieutenant Foster, the ship's officer responsible, had arranged so much shore training that the operators were familiar with and entirely confident in the use of their equipment. The Sub also arranged that the radar had a 'red' crystal. What this meant was never revealed but the 271 always produced a first-class answer.

It was after the ship's return to 'Derry when, in a support group detailed for anti-blockade runner patrol, the sinking of *U-305* – outstanding asdic operating with which this book starts – took place. And it was the occasion when I was obliged to disobey the Senior Officer's orders. For whatever reason, after that episode, *Wanderer* was transferred to yet another support group. This was to bring a change of scenery.

In the meantime, we were delighted to be back in Londonderry among the many escort destroyers, frigates, sloops and corvettes all lying at berths alongside one another, all camouflaged, all at first sight so alike, differing only in length. It would not be true to say that no one relaxed on coming in to the Base from sea, yet I do not remember any serious drunkenness ashore nor fighting between Ships' Companies, not even between sailors and civilians.

Boiler-cleaning leave was the big thing when escorts came in from sea. After so many boiler-hours, the boilers had to be allowed to cool and then to be cleaned by civilian shore labour. There was thus no heating or lighting from ship's power; we were connected up to the electricity supply from ashore and, during the boiler-cleaning period, which was usually three weeks, leave was granted to one watch, half a Ship's Company at a time. The trip over from Belfast to Scotland, Belfast-Stranraer, by passenger boat was always crowded with vomiting soldiers and the long train journey afterwards to the south of England was never pleasant. Often, the train would be held up outside Euston station during a blitz with houses burning on either side of the track – horrible to see. Then there would be the walk across London, often during an air raid, with suitcase and gasmask haversack to Waterloo or Paddington station. Fire engines, ambulances and an occasional Government car on the streets – there were no taxis at night. My gas mask haversack was always·heavy, usually containing something like bananas from Gib. or tinned food, though never from the ship's official supplies.

What was so astonishing crossing London then, 1943-44, was the apparent indifference of the people to the bombing. I remember one morning calling in on my mother to have a bath and some breakfast in her flat, just off Lowndes Square. An air raid was in progress, my mother was knocking up a substantial fry; then there was a whistle of bombs which meant that the bomb would be a near miss, if not a hit. I was under the dining-room table in a flash. My mother brought in breakfast at that moment. She laughed; it was no good taking any notice of that sort of thing she said. The attitude of civilians who remained in London was one of fatalism born of courage and custom. It was not so much that I was frightened on that occasion (I like to think) but that fatalism would have been no good at sea where the requirement was for immediate reaction even if, as was occasionally the case, it meant no more than just mentally waiting, sweating and thinking what next.

There is earlier reference to the shortage of food for the civilian population and much the same applied to drink, to alcohol. Those serving afloat could not land alcohol. This was strictly forbidden as, by special privilege, drink on board HM Ships which were sea-going was, like cigarettes in bond, duty free. Attempts to smuggle from the ship, I, for one, dealt with severely. Whatever drink might or might not be available, people back in Dorset contrived to give the occasional party. They saved the small amounts they could legitimately get from their wine merchants and were helped by the occasional bottle of South African sherry which might be slipped from the Officers' Mess of some locally billeted battalion. It was always possible to add soda water, the CO_2 content making the alcohol take effect more quickly. For the enterprising, there was also draught raw cider – scrumpy – which, mixed with spirits, had a very envigorating result. Home wine-making had not then come into fashion but that did not preclude some ingenious and effective dispensing.

One such party attended by a Vice Admiral, retired, and his lady was memorable. The Admiral, a former gunnery officer, like many others of his calling was hard of hearing. A conversation was said to have been overheard:

Admiral's lady: 'Henry, dear, what are you drinking?'

Admiral: 'Why don't you wear your watch?'

Lady, more forcefully: 'No, dear, what are you drinking?'

'Don't be absurd. We've only just arrived.'

Lady, forcefully, straight down the old gentleman's ear: 'No, do listen. What are you drinking?'

In a bellow: 'What, this bloody stuff? Cat's piss I should think.'

A fast Atlantic convoy. With slower convoys there were often stragglers which could be in danger. (IWM)

Commodore (D) Western Approaches, 'Shrimp' Simpson, boss of some one hundred escorts at Londonderry. A great leader, and an outstanding, imaginative manager, he made no long speeches. Finally, he was Flag Officer Submarines. (IWM)

A destroyer escort's bridge. Bridges were open then and not always warm and dry. (IWM)

The writer on his bridge, breaking his own rules by being bareheaded!

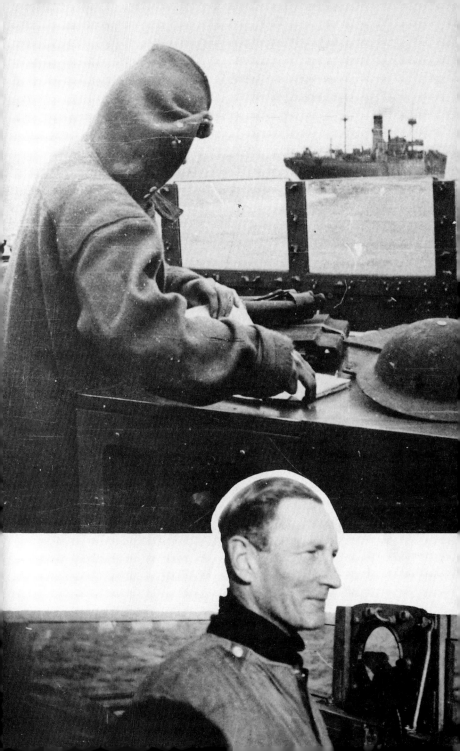

Type VIIC – the mass-produced U-boat. HMS *Wanderer* sank *U-305* in the Atlantic and, during the invasion of France, HMS *Wanderer* and *Tavy* sank *U-390* off Cherbourg – both were this type of U-boat, *U-307* being seen here.

U-306 refuelling at sea.

U-306. Type VII U-boats lying alongside.

A German Type IXC U-boat surrendering at the end of World War Two. (RN Museum, HMS *Dolphin*)

Depth charge crews at work. This was a job for strong men. A single pattern was three charges from the chute (shown here) and two from the throwers. A double pattern gave an extra layer in depth. (IWM)

Depth charge explosion. The depth setting varied from 50 ft to 500 ft. The deeper the setting the less the cascade – this looks like 100 ft. (IWM)

Hedgehog A/S Mortar – fall of bombs. Twenty-five bombs were ripple-fired ahead by the attacking ship. If one bomb hit the submarine target the remainder were supposed to countermine. (IWM)

U-523, Prisoners of War. *Wanderer's* Ship's Company grew quite fond of them, as teenagers might of a litter of leopard cubs.

Depth charge explosion. The setting here is shallow, about 50 ft. (IWM)

HMS *Wanderer* – fore super-structure. Seen from the forecastle the bridge super-structure looked like this.

HMS *Wanderer* – fore super-structure iced up. The bridge looked different under ice – it was not the same at all!

Russian convoy, ice forming. Unlike the more modern ships, *Wanderer* had no steam heating. Here the guard-rails are starting to form an ice wall.

Inspecting the ice. Everyone off watch had to turn-to with picks and hammers. It was the only time there was (temporary) grumbling.

HMS *Wanderer's* torpedo coxswain. The coxswain was the senior rating on board, a great leader especially when things were difficult.

The author takes a look at the icing-up.

An anti-submarine boom was substantial. It was very desirable that ships should go through the gate and not try to take on the boom itself! (Keystone Press Agency)

An anti-submarine and anti-torpedo boom. It was a very robust structure of baulks of wood and heavy wire mesh. (Popperfoto)

The corvette – an invaluable convoy escort. With good anti-submarine equipment and ultimately radar, the corvettes, mass produced to meet the lack of convoy escorts, fully proved their worth. This is HMS *Gentian*, of the 'Flower' class. (IWM)

The U-boat schnorkel mast allowed intake and exhaust from the diesel engine and recharging of batteries, thus obviating easy sighting, especially by aircraft.

Invasion of France – the beachheads. Behind the ships can be seen the artifical Mulberry harbours. (RN Museum, HM Naval Base, Portsmouth)

Part of a Mulberry harbour. In our pre-invasion briefing we were told to look out for seeing something in the Channel like Brighton Pier upside down under tow – but not told any more (security)! (IWM)

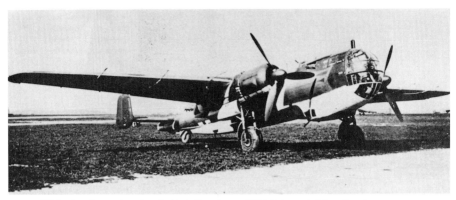

Glider-bomb carrying aircraft. Both Dorniers and Heinkels carried these bombs. Because they were quickly recognised as such, the first attack made on our convoys by such aircraft was successfully repelled, and the second then aborted. (RAF Museum)

The radio-controlled bomb. The battleship *Warspite* and cruiser *Uganda* were both very badly damaged by this type of bomb in the Mediterranean during the Salerno landings in 1943. (RAF Museum)

Lord Mountbatten's polo team, the 'Shrimps' in 1948. Left to right: David Dunbar-Naismith, Lord Mountbatten, 'Ruggy' Macintosh and Bob Whinney.

The author, as British Naval Attaché, Belgrade, and wife being welcomed by Admiral Anderson, USN (later Chief of the US Naval Staff), on board his US Sixth Fleet Flagship. (US Navy official photograph)

Official drinking – Belgrade, 1960. The author, the British Naval Attaché with General (sometimes Admiral) Manola, the Yugoslav Chief of Intelligence. Much intelligence business was done over booze.

Going on leave or going back to the ship, I nearly always popped in to the Admiralty to see what was new in the Anti-U-Boat Division and the Anti-Submarine Warfare Department. I did so in the first leave period after we returned from Gib. In the corridor of the Admiralty I passed Pegram, my last Admiral from Freetown days.

'Good morning, Sir,' I said, prepared to walk on.

'No, don't run away unless you are in a hurry,' and then, 'I see you got your U-boat and a good one too,' he said.

'Thank you, Sir!'

'I'm afraid there may be some disappointing news for you though.'

What, I wondered, had I done? Was I going to be taken out of my ship for some ghastly shore job?

'You won't get a DSO, I'm sorry to say. It seems that it's Winston's edict that only Commanders and Captains are to get DSOs for U-boats, irrespective of the circumstances, now that he says the tide of the Battle of the Atlantic has turned.'

I had been particularly keen to follow my father in getting this decoration and must have looked crestfallen.

'I expect you will get an OBE. That's quite a good decoration now, you know.'

'But, Sir, it's not an action award.'

'Well, perhaps it will be the DSC. Well, nice to see you old boy. Good luck.' It was typical of Pegram, now Vice-Admiral Sir Frank, a Sea Lord, a Lord Commissioner of the Admiralty, to stop to chat with a youngish lieutenant commander. Such news was the less disappointing, delivered by a man like him.

Back on board, there was a problem. It so happened that, immediately before this period of leave, Antrobus, the First Lieutenant, and, of course, the second-in-command, was forced to go sick. He had borne considerable weight seeing the ship through a major refit, and he had established the organisation which produced a most efficient ship. He was thus a great loss. A lieutenant RN arrived as his relief: plump, opulent-looking, with an air of over-confidence. I told him to get taped all the ship's anti-submarine, radar, depth charge and gunnery equipment, plus the watertight doors, the fire-fighting and life-saving arrangements, to visit every compartment and to read up all the very necessary bumph there was about our job as an escort destroyer. Then I left him to it.

Returning from leave at the pre-arranged time, I sent for this officer, acutely displeased. Why had he not met me formally on my return? Why were there the revolting remains of an oyster and champagne party in my day cabin? The answers were entirely unsatisfactory; discussion was pointless.

'Pack all your gear immediately and be out of the ship by eight in the morning,' I said. It was then about six pm. The Commodore's staff supported this precipitate act and by ten the next day, Lieutenant P. R. Michell, RN, arrived as the new First Lieutenant – a bright, imaginative officer. In no time, all was well.

11. NORTHERN WATERS

At one stage in the war, escort ships were sent from the Western Approaches to supplement the Home Fleet units escorting the merchant ship convoys Britain was running to Russia. The threat to these convoys was primarily from U-boats but there was a complementary threat from the enemy's heavy ships – battle-cruisers, battleships and cruisers.

It was with Russian Convoys that Captain Sherbrooke came to fame. His name comes up earlier as my Divisional Officer in *Rodney* and in training escorts in West Africa. Not one of the Navy's rugger-playing types, not even particularly forceful, he was even somewhat retiring, but positive and clear-headed with a very high sense of duty. At the conference before the convoy sailed, Sherbrooke had stated his policy to contend with attack by surface ships. Briefly, this was to get his destroyers between the enemy and the convoy and for the convoy to turn away and make smoke screens.

In a series of brush actions, whilst escorting Convoy JW 51B in bad visibility, Sherbrooke's destroyer, *Onslow* was hit on the bridge by the German heavy cruiser *Hipper*. Sherbrooke was seriously wounded but continued to conduct the action until physically unable to do so. The German forces, which included the pocket battleship *Lutzow*, were driven off, as already related, and Sherbrooke, who had lost an eye in the action, was awarded the Victoria Cross.

It was nearly a year later that *Wanderer*, by now transferred to the support group, EG 1, was detailed to supplement the escort of the Russian convoy JW 55B. On the way to join the convoy at sea, the Senior Officer of the Group, Commander Majendie, and the four of us Commanding Officers were bidden to lunch with the Commander-in-Chief, Home Fleet, Admiral Sir Bruce Fraser on board his Flagship, *Duke of York*. The Flag Captain, the Captain of the ship, the Hon. Guy Russell, my second Term Officer at Dartmouth, met us on arrival. What a sense of agoraphobia the vast open space of the battleship's quarterdeck gave – but what a lunch party! The Admiral talked music; none of us uttered a word; why on earth did he ask us? As we were leaving the ship, Captain Russell summoned Lieutenant Commander David Little, a Dartmouth mate of mine. We had a brief chat, not having met for so long and I thanked my stars not to be caught as one of the lieutenant commanders in a vast battleship. Good jobs, theoretically, they were said to be. They provided precious little chance for personal distinction in war.

The convoy JW 55B sailed from Loch Ewe on 20 December 1943 with the cruisers *Belfast*, *Norfolk* and *Sheffield* under Vice-Admiral R. L. Burnett in support while, as we knew, the C-in-C had a heavy force in more distant support against the possibility of attack by heavy German ships.

Unusually for that part of the world, it was a calm, sunny, even quite pleasant day and the Hands were cheerfully cleaning guns when a young Ordinary Seaman took a needless risk, slipped and fell over the side. Everything was quiet at the time and I had temporarily gone below. The Officer of the Watch, Sub Lieutenant Foster was extremely quick to react to the cry 'Man overboard'. He pressed the buzzer on the bridge to order the release of lifebuoys. The lifebuoy sentry aft was equally quick and the lifebuoys fell either side of and not more than ten yards from the man in the water. At the same time, the lifeboat's crew – always manned by those who got to the boat first, irrespective of who or what they were – got away very fast. They recovered the man and had him inboard in the doctor's hands within seven minutes of his going overboard. He was wearing a life belt and a lot of clothing, was known to be a strong swimmer and actually never went below the surface of the water at all! Despite this, the cold killed him at once. As with all such deaths, there had to be a Court of Enquiry when we eventually got back to Londonderry. No blame was attributed except to the poor boy himself. Foster, the Officer of the Watch, and the lifebuoy sentry were congratulated on their quick reaction. In fact, it could not have been quicker.

The weather on that trip soon deteriorated, becoming rough and foully cold and, of course, the more unpleasant with the very limited hours of winter daylight in those northern latitudes. One day, in the early afternoon just before dark, the Admiral ordered all ships in the escort to test armament. *Wanderer* opened fire first with Oerlikon 20 mm and 4.7-inch guns, followed by the other Western Approach ships and then came the Home Fleet ships! This sequence of opening fire was despite the fact that they, in the Home Fleet, had some steam heating to exposed mechanisms while we only had the minimum insulation. To me, there was never any doubt that we, in the Londonderry Command and probably in the whole Western Approach Command, were better trained and quicker (anyway among the smaller ships) than comparable ships in the Home Fleet.

As the ships in the convoy got further north, the tendency to ice up increased. Spray hit the guns, the superstructure and the life-saving rafts and froze on impact. It even froze on the wire guard rails until, if left alone, it would form a solid fence down to the deck. There was nothing for it, in our case, but to use pickaxes and hammers. I insisted that, at least in daylight hours, the men off watch – as well as those on watch – should be made to help. It was very strenuous work in that extreme cold, tough on the officers and men, and it was the only time I ever heard mild grumbling from the men, even though they came to appreciate that their lives could depend on it and that a top-weight of ice could, if bad enough, capsize the ship and slay the lot of us.

Dress was a consideration in those very cold northern waters. The 'pussers', that is Naval Stores, dished us out with some extraordinary thick 'long Johns' but there was no other special issue of clothing except perhaps gloves. However, there was our adopter town, Sutton Coldfield,[1] and an unknown lady – a Canadian? – known as 'Auntie May' who used to knit – lots and lots of socks and balaclava helmets and scarves – enough for everyone, we had. For myself, for the top half and working outwards, it was thick flannel pyjamas next to the skin; then a silk shirt, a Jaeger shirt and two thick woollen jerseys. For the bottom half, over the pyjamas were the pusser's long-Johns and flannel trousers; over the lot, a kapok-lined suit plus mittens, a woolly hat and fur-lined leather boots.

At sea in *Wanderer* there was no enforcement of dress regulations; anyone could wear anything he liked except that officers had to be recognisable as such. Everyone had to wear something on his head so as to be able to salute when coming on the bridge to make a report, if for no other reason. Khaki, the soldier's colour, was not allowed on principle and red was forbidden as being too easily seen from the air. All those who were clean-shaven had to shave every day, come what may; beards were not encouraged as too likely to contain yesterday's egg for breakfast.

Well up into the Arctic Circle we Western Approach ships broke off from the convoy. We were short of fuel. There had been no action up to then but, on the return journey south, we were delighted to hear the news about the sinking of *Scharnhorst*. In the early hours of 26 December 1943, not entirely unexpectedly, it had become known that this fast German battle-cruiser was at sea with escorting destroyers and was thus a threat to convoys. The weather at the time was bad and daylight in mid-winter in 72 degrees North was very limited. In the events which followed fairly quickly, the German destroyers got lost and returned harmlessly to harbour but our cruisers brought the enemy to battle and pursued *Scharnhorst* in the direction of the C-in-C in *Duke of York*. In the final stages, *Scharnhorst* came under particularly heavy and accurate gunfire from *Duke of York* and the cruisers as well as very close range torpedo attack from our destroyers. As was the case with *Bismarck*, the German ship fought bravely to the last, sinking about 8 pm. Convoy JW 55B escaped entirely to arrive safely.

Wanderer returned to 'Derry with a huge snowman on the quarter deck and, of course, with everyone back in proper uniform once again. Just before securing alongside the jetty, we noticed a ship of our own class, lying at anchor very badly down by the stern. What was the matter with her, I asked later. She had got into bad weather, I was told, and, instead of heaving to with the wind and sea on the bow, she had run before it. A large sea had washed over her quarter deck and she had got pooped – flooded aft – all too easy in that class of ship.

The ship's next Russian convoy was an epic which I could have done without. For some reason, *Wanderer* had left 'Derry after the rest of Escort

1 There was during the war years a practice for towns to offer to adopt one of HM ships. The adopting town would send its ship parcels including warm clothing and the ship would write back. (I was not very good at this, but some of the officers and ratings were.)

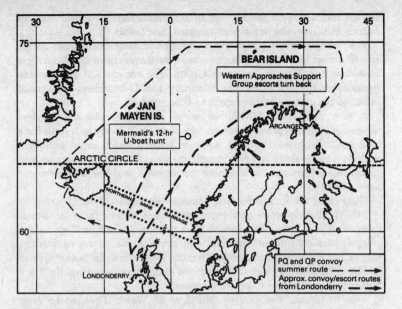

Map 6. Russian Convoys Winter 1943-44
In late December 1943 and in February 1944, *Wanderer* undertook part convoy
escorts of Russia-bound convoys to approximately 72N. A more westerly, and
safer, course could be followed when the ice edge permitted.

Group 1. The Hands were always fallen-in for leaving harbour. Now that
we were a support group specially intended to hunt submarines, 'D'ye ken
John Peel', the fox-hunting song, was played over the ship's intercom after
the fashion of a big ship's Royal Marine band in peace time playing on the
quarter deck when the ship left or entered harbour. In similar vein, the
gramophone would churn out when appropriate 'Little man you've had a
busy day' when we returned from sea.

Anyway, we were clear of 'Derry and were trailing down the seventeen
miles of channel in the River Foyle to the sea when large flights of duck
started to come over the bridge in a steady and, it seemed, non-stop
succession. I had no shotgun onboard and there were no other ships about
to be endangered so I sent for a rifle. We had been up and down this piece of
river countless times so I turned the ship over to the Officer of the Watch
while I swung the rifle and shot at duck. Quite suddenly there was a
shudder. At once I stopped engines and put them to full astern but it was no
good. We were aground on the mud. Many lieutenant commanders had
missed their promotion for much less. It remained to try the usual dodges to
get off: hauling off by kedge anchor; using the Ship's Company to roll the
ship by running from side to side and jumping in unison while the engines
went full astern. No good. I made a signal to say that we had hit a
submerged obstacle. 'You are aground' came the immediate reply. A tug

arrived and we were quickly off to sea, undamaged. Foolish? Yes, of course. But have you never been tempted, and fallen?

The Group joined Convoy JW 57 which had three cruisers and a light aircraft carrier in the escort plus, of course, destroyers from the Home Fleet as well as our Western Approach Group. The convoy had already been found by enemy aircraft and the Admiralty daily U-boat disposition signal indicated the convoy might expect U-boat attack.

In such operations, HM Ships were, of course, allocated wireless wavelengths (frequencies) on which they were to keep watch. It must have been on 24 February 1944 that we were keeping watch on an additional wireless wave to those ordered, namely the aircraft reporting wave, so as to get quicker information on anything the convoy's patrolling aircraft might have sighted.

There came the aircraft report, 'Attacking surfaced U-boat'.

'Plot,' I called down the voicepipe, 'get a range and bearing of the aircraft from the 271,' – the surface radar – 'plot the position and we'll go for it.'

Inside perhaps a minute the ship, which was within an inner protective ring of escorts, was off at 25 knots for the U-boat and the Senior Officer had been informed by signal that we had the position taped exactly. Back came a signal telling us to return to position.

'Take no notice,' I said to the Officer of the Watch. Then, to the Petty Officer Telegraphist: 'Have those signals been recorded in your Signal Log? If so, give the log to me at once.'

Then came a second signal, more imperative and apparently with the approval of the Admiral commanding the convoy escort telling us in firm terms to return to station. There was no way out; I was obliged to obey, speechless with fury. In fact, at about that time, one U-boat was destroyed by HMS *Keppel* and another by aircraft. All the same, I suspect the decision to recall *Wanderer* was not perhaps given much thought.

That same afternoon, before the early dark, the Admiral made a long signal giving the disposition of the ships in the escort which they were to keep during the hours of darkness.

'Put all the positions down on a plotting sheet,' I called down to the chart house, and added: 'Where are we tonight?'

'Same as in daylight, Sir.'

'U-boat's still in touch. Where do you think the attack'll come from?' I asked Frost, the Officer of the Watch, to see if he would confirm my thoughts.

'In this weather, the stern of the convoy is vulnerable, Sir', said Frost, not one to make long speeches.

'Yes,' chipped in Foster, who was responsible for the radar.

'There's a short sea astern and a stiff following breeze. Spray off the wave tops will cause clutter' – interference on the radar. A trimmed down U-boat could get in undetected – wouldn't need to snort.[2]

2. In mid-1943, U-boats were being fitted with air intake diesel exhaust masts permitting travel on diesels with only the *schnorkel* head, a very small radar target, above water This especially inhibited detection by Coastal Command aircraft. The *schnorkel* was often referred to by us as the 'snort'.

'Plot,' I called down, 'what does it look like on the plotting sheet?'

'Well, the Admiral seems to expect attack from ahead or on the beam. There are only two Home Fleet destroyers covering the whole back end of the convoy and, Sir,' added Bower, 'all the escorts have been allotted arcs of sweep for their radars.' This was unusual, even for those comparatively enlightened days.

I assumed that the two destroyers at the rear of the convoy would be using their radars to catch any surfaced U-boats that may try to overtake and attack from astern.

'It's been promulgated that U-boats have been making successful attacks undetected, down wind and sea. Can't you tell them, Sir?' said Kidd anxiously.

'No. We've got to assume the Admiral knows more than we do. I've already had one flea in the ear today and the air is already humming with signals.'

Later, it happened. The destroyer *Mahratta*, one of the two ships astern of the convoy, called up the Admiral on R/T. Up on the bridge I heard the educated and entirely calm voice – it could have been Drought, the Commanding Officer who had been at prep school and again at Dartmouth with me: 'Have been hit by torpedo aft and am stopped.' This was obviously a Gnat which had homed onto the destroyer's propeller noises.

This report was followed by a pause before the next. 'Have been hit amidships by second torpedo.'

Then there was another pause, probably Drought was trying to get all watertight doors shut and summing up the desperate situation. 'Life-saving equipment is being cleared away.' Still the same calm, unemotional tones.

Then, probably due to a fault in the R/T set, an unhappy warble developed in the voice. 'We are abandoning ship. We are sinking. We cannot last much longer.'

And that was it. It appeared that the Admiral sent two destroyers to rescue survivors. There were very few rescued. I believe at least some of the life-saving gear was frozen up. So far as we in *Wanderer* could make out, no ship was sent after the U-boat. Personally, from sheer impotence and rasping anguish, the *Mahratta* incident compared with the terrible moments when the straffing of the *Laconia*'s survivors was taking place near Ascension Island and with the staggering horror at the news of the sinking of the mighty *Hood*. But, it must be stressed, this was all just the impression from on destroyer escort's bridge.

Then, next day in Latitude 73 degrees North, the signal came telling our escort group, which was running short of fuel, to break off from the convoy and make for Hvaalfjord in the Faroe Islands to refuel. The convoy was barely out of sight to the northward when the other 'V' & 'W' class destroyer in the group reported an asdic contact, classified as a possible submarine. *Wanderer* was told to assist, the other two ships leaving us to it. In the admittedly difficult asdic conditions we investigated and even did an attack. I did not think there was any true evidence of a submarine there. Such false echoes – we called them 'non-sub', as you know – could be caused by patches of unusually aerated water, differences in water temperature and, more often, by fish shoals. Days later, for personal satisfaction, I visited and enquired at the Admiralty and found that there was no U-boat thought to be in the area at that time.

With the very limited fuel we had in hand, I told the other 'V' & 'W' to proceed to Hvaalfjord independently; we had even less oil fuel than she did and thus would have to be more careful.

Turning to the First Lieutenant, I asked: 'Number One, do the Hands know we are going south to refuel and are not rejoining the convoy?'

'Yes, sir, they know and' – more quietly – 'they are not sorry.'

To Bower: 'Plot, what's the weather report?'

'Bad, Sir. Admiralty forecast Gale Force Ten in this area and Number One and I have just done an independent synoptic which confirms it. The barometer is dropping like a stone. We could catch it any time now.'

'Number One, in a Force Ten we should heave-to. But we can't. Not enough fuel.'

'I'd better secure everything and batten down.'

'Yes, and send two good watchkeepers officers forward and the Chief ERA (Engine Room Artificer) and reliefs with food and bedding to the engine room.'

'Aye, aye sir. And I'll stop all traffic along the upper deck now. It's already washing down.'

In destroyers of all classes in those days, with weather approaching a gale, the upper deck would wash down, take over green seas which would throw a man straight over the side. And with our class of ship there was no way of getting from one end of the ship to the other without going along the upper deck.

Within the hour we had our full gale, Force Eight with nasty steep seas, typical of the Arctic sweeping over the upper deck, and the barometer was still falling fast. Our precautions were already justified and it was painfully clear that there was worse to come.

I summoned the Coxwain, the Senior rating onboard and, also, professionally the best helmsman. First, he was to remain in the wheel-house, awake or asleep until further orders, alternating at the wheel with the two next best helmsmen in the ship; secondly, he was to pass the word round the mess decks that if anyone were to go overboard I would make no attempt to pick him up. It was needless to add that he would die of cold within a couple of minutes anyway; also, in such weather I could not possibly risk the lives of others and even the loss of the ship in trying any life-saving. The Coxwain was a very sensible chap, a good strong influence on the Lower Deck – a man respected by everyone. I was lucky to have him.

With the onset of evening the situation looked grim. The wind was by then Force Ten. The precipitous seas were piling up on the beam and there was no indication of the weather moderating. In darkness, as always, the seas appeared more threatening, sheer mountains of black water broken by unpleasant advancing, toppling blue-white crests towering at the bridge height – or more it seemed – on the port beam. I had served in destroyers for some years, though never before in command and certainly never before had I seen weather approaching this ferocity. Provided we were not caught by a freak wave, provided there was no breakdown, particularly with the steering gear – a not unknown failure – we should make it. If the steering gear, on which there was much strain, were to fail there was no hope. There would be no chance whatever of a man getting along the upper deck to the vital spot, the tiller flat, right aft without him being swept overboard. No steering and we would lie stern to sea, getting pooped, flooded and sunk. There was no 'might be'. I saw it as a fact.

Steering was quite vital. Provided the wind and sea remained on the beam the helmsman could at least do his job and control the ship's course. But a relaxation, however brief, allowing the ship's head to veer to starboard, posed the threat of a sea on the quarter when the ship would be out of control. She would then swing stern to sea. And, once again, we should get pooped.

'Nothing to starboard,' I ordered the helmsman.

'Nothing to starboard, sir,' he repeated back.

Then down the voicepipe again: 'Cox'n, you're doing well in the Wheelhouse but the helmsmen must watch it like bloody hawks.'

'Aye, aye, sir,' cheerfully, 'like bloody hawks, sir. Nothing to starboard, sir.'

There was the story, I remembered, of the Mediterranean destroyer Flotilla, a few years back, caught in violent weather in the Gulf of Lyons, when one ship had a funnel washed overboard. While those ships had two funnels, we only had one: if that one went the boiler room would flood and we should have had it. With unbelievable horror, I found the wind was then freshening even further. Three ships in our Escort Group were, I later discovered, logging the wind as Force Twelve, the highest assessment of the Beaufort Scale, equivalent to hurricane – a wind force I had never before known as recorded by HM Ships.

At some time during the evening, snatches of song reached the bridge up the ventilator trunks from the messdecks. For God's sake not hymns! I thought but, hearteningly, no. Through the scream of the wind, the thump, shudder, swish and prolonged hissing each time a sea hit us, between the crashes of mess tables, mess lockers and other things breaking adrift, came the strains of 'Roll out the barrel'. As if there was not enough rolling, then came 'Roll me over in the clover, roll me over, roll me over, lay me down and do it again!' I found encouragement and consolation that the men were in good heart, cold, wet, being violently hurled about, their messdecks awash, damaged, ill-ventilated and stinking of the typical smell which was a mixture of wet corticene (a type of linoleum), cigarette smoke and oil fuel.

Little doubt the Almighty had many more requests to deal with in war than in peace; and when they felt the need arose, different people had different ideas on what to ask. Throughout that trip my prayer was that God should give me the physical strength and judgement to get the ship safely into Hvaalfjord. He did so, but without wasting any margin.

Nonetheless, at that stage things did not look at all good to me: there was a new threat. The bridge roll indicator could only register 45 degrees and we were going well beyond that; sometimes to 60 degrees, possibly more, and 70 degrees was the critical angle of roll for those ships; after that the ship's tendency to right itself decreased. Unless the weather moderated fairly quickly, we were not going to make it, even if nothing went wrong, and my fear was that with so little oil fuel as ballast we might roll under. We should have to try to list the ship to prevent her rolling too much to leeward. The Engineer Officer was, weatherbound, aft; his right hand man, the Chief ERA was also weatherbound, but in the engine room. All the ship's telephones were broken down so I sent to the messdecks for the Chief Stoker: very atypical – not the old-time, beefy, boozy buccaneer. He was a thin, rather shy man with a natty little beard.

'Can you list the ship? Pump over oil fuel and flood tanks with sea water so we don't roll too much to leeward?' I asked.

A pause, then: 'Yes. Sir, I am not quite sure ...'

'Get any records and bumph you can. Don't be too long and we'll work it out together in the charthouse.'

As Midshipmen, we were taught how to do sums involving flooding and counter-flooding and correcting a list on a ship but that had been some years before. However, apprehension sharpens the wits and by guess and essentially by God, the Chief Stoker and I managed to trim the ship to windward by twelve degrees, the amount we had aimed at. The alarming rolls to leeward were proportionally decreased and it seemed that, still provided there were no breakdowns and provided we did not have to alter course for any reason with that list on the ship, we would make it to the lee, the shelter of the Faroe Islands. We expected to reach the entrance to Hvaalfjord well after dark. It came almost as a shock when we got there – intense relief – suddenly we were in a lee, out of the violent wind and into calm water. At long last, we thought, our troubles would be at an end.

12. THE SEA IS HIS – SOUTH AGAIN

'Just had a muster,' reported the First Lieutenant, a voice in the dark, 'no one missing. No one badly hurt. But quite a lot of weather damage.'

'Pilot,' I called down to the chart house, 'where's the gate through the boom and how's it marked?' There was no information on this, he replied; and the anti–submarine–cum–anti–torpedo boom was a substantial affair of heavy wire mesh and large wooden baulks.

'Frost,' I said to the Officer of the Watch, 'with this snow and hail, the visibility is nil up·here. Nip down to the fo'c'sle and see if it's any better lower down.'

'Yes,' said Frost on return, 'it is better and the buoy jumper has volunteered to be lowered in a bos'n's chair in case he can see better still from just above the water.'

The bos'n's chair was a short plank on a rope and the buoy jumper was a coveted post given to a man who was accepted as a particularly nimble and good seaman. He, a young Leading Seaman, was told the ship would creep slowly along the boom till he saw the gate – the gap – through which we could enter the fjord. He was then to help con the ship through.

'Slow ahead, both engines,' I said. 'Frost, keep the asdic pinging on the shore. I don't want to get nearer to it than about 100 yards.'

'Gate green 45,' from the fo'c'sle.

'Starboard 20,' to Coxwain.

'Gate dead ahead now,' from the fo'c'sle. We could see it now. We were through!

'Half ahead both engines. Get the buoy jumper in quick and send him to the Doc for a slug of rum or whisky.' His legs had been hanging in the icy water and he was barely able to stand.

During the temporary calm lull the ship had been trimmed upright again. Then suddenly – bang – as a shock – we were out of the lee into the violent wind again, heading straight into it and making for the lights of the oiler at the top of the fjord – only to find that a frigate had baulked our approach. I was forced to turn back down wind. On the bridge we had choking funnel fumes and in the pitch darkness, with snow showers and painful hail, we could only just make out the high ground on either side. The shore we could not see and had to rely on the range the asdic gave us. It was very unpleasant and very irritating to find that we were not metaphorically home and dry after all that toil and misery.

After a few minutes – but too many for us – the frigate reported by R/T that she had at last berthed on the oiler and I tried to turn the ship back into the wind. Those old ships had a higher superstructure around the bridge with nothing to counter-balance it aft. Thus, even in moderate conditions, they behaved like a wind vane pointing backwards. That night, no use of the engines and the rudder would get the ship round, shaping up towards the oiler. I let go an anchor and used the engines at power, but still could not get her round.

'We're dragging fast,' said the Officer of the Watch, 'the beach is getting very close.' The wavelets breaking against the lee shore were both visible and audible on the starboard beam. We would be aground on a rocky lee shore before the anchor could possibly be weighed. 'Break the cable,' I ordered.

'Can't break the cable, Sir and the Senhouse Slip is jammed!' shouted back the fo'c'sle. The cable party's hands were anyway frozen and they could barely stand against the wind. I remember thinking, surprisingly, that I really did not care a row of beans; it looked as though we were going aground but there was just a small chance that we might get away with it.

'Clear the fo'c'sle,' I shouted, then, 'emergency full ahead both engines, hard-a-port.' The ship shot ahead, swung to port; there was a shuddering jerk, a report like a shot. We had snapped the cable – as I had hoped – and it flayed out through the hawse pipe with a harsh, noisy clatter. Up the fjord we went and alongside the oiler and, after a brief look at the damage, to bed. Not even a nightcap!

The whaler, our only seaboat – and lifeboat – was reduced to a few shreds of wood at each davit head; the motor boat had gone; the life-rafts were mostly smashed or missing altogether; there was much structural damage: plating stove in and buckled. The messdecks were flooded and there were leaks everywhere. A heavy armchair in the Ward Room had even taken off to make a hole in the bulkhead inner lining, just below the deck head! Surprisingly, there had been no serious injuries to anyone: just some burns, sprains, many bruises and exhaustion.

'Cor,' said one sailor, not knowing he was being oveheard, 'look at that f'ing awful mess,' – the damage, he meant.

'The sea is His,' observed his mate.

'And 'E can bloody 'ave it,' the first sailor replied.

In the meantime, *Watchman*, the other 'V & W' destroyer in the group, slightly ahead of us on passage, had ditched her depth charges to save top weight; we kept ours. Very unfortunately, when she came to the boom, she failed to find the gate and went straight into the heavy wire mesh to be unhappily stuck there, with oil expended and, if rumour were true, no lights or heating.

The wind had abated somewhat that next morning when we sailed south, leaving poor *Watchman* still firmly held in the boom. There was on passage a heavy sea still running, a sea on the quarter which no destroyer liked much, not even the bigger ones. We came down at a fair speed of 17 knots to be sure of not getting pooped – as well as getting to the other end quicker.

Steering was a bit tricky but not in any way like it was when *Cossack* and the other 'Tribal' were chasing *Bismarck*.

On arrival, there was the prospect of a Court-Martial for grounding my ship leaving harbour. Possibly, the Commodore Western Approaches had heard on the grape vine how it had happened; he was a keen wild-fowler and could have unofficially – if only slightly – sympathised? Possibly, the Senior Officer of the Group EG 1 thought his frigate had blundered in failing to get alongside the oiler in Hvaalfjord the first time and had thus nearly caused *Wanderer* to ground and become a wreck. More likely he thought it had been a mistake to recall *Wanderer* when we set off at high speed after the U-boat threatening the convoy had been reported by aircraft. For whatever reason, no rocket, no reproof, came my way. The Commanding Officers of two of the four ships in the Group were put ashore sick with breakdowns called 'operational fatigue' – and so, incidentally, was my Engineer Officer. That was a yardstick.

Without delay, the Commodore sent for me.

'You had an interesting trip?'

'Yes, sir.' The less said the better. He looked at me hard.

'How are you feeling?' I assured him I was feeling very well.

'You wouldn't like to be put ashore for a bit? I could put you back in another ship, a Captain class frigate, in command in a month or so.'

This was for the second time of asking and I definitely did not want it.

'You had a rough time. Congratulations on the way you handled your ship. That's all. Good luck, old boy.'

As for the ship's company, the spirit and discipline could not have been better. The officers and men were confident, they were capable and they knew it. In a way, it appeared that most of them thought life was almost entertaining, certainly not grim, and that the recent unpleasant trip from the Arctic Circle enhanced morale even further. The Quarterly Punishment Return was usually nil which certainly reflected the very high standard of discipline. Early in the commission, there had been a case of insubordination to a Petty Officer. I gave the culprit the choice of serving a cell sentence ashore or on board at sea in the tiller flat. This was the after compartment in the ship, not too well ventilated. In bad weather, the movement and vibration of the ship above the propellers was considerable. He chose the tiller flat. He later became one of our best Able Seamen, passing the exam for Leading Seaman. There was only one more serious case, right at the end of the commission.

Admiral of the Fleet Lord Cunningham of Hyndhope wrote,[1] 'I have always maintained there is more real discipline in destroyers than in big ships and, of course, we are always so much more in touch with our men. The skipper of a destroyer gets soaked to the skin on the bridge just the same as any sailor but his opposite number (in a battleship) walks dry-skinned from a luxurious cabin where he has been sitting aloof from all goings on, to an equally luxurious bridge.'

1 *Cunningham of Hyndhope* by Oliver Warner; John Murray.

Every Commanding Officer has his own recipe for running his ship. Perhaps mine was mildly unorthodox. In most, if not all other ships, smoking was then forbidden at work. We in *Wanderer* had no rule against smoking at any time, other than dictated by common sense and good manners. Men always smoked at their cruising stations at night, making sure that the flare of a match could never be seen. On the other hand, no man would come up on the bridge to make a report puffing a 'bine. Instead of the more usual lengthy Captain's Standing Orders, there was just one sentence: 'All officers and men are to conduct themselves in accordance with King's Regulations and Admiralty Instructions and my wishes.' Whether this was original I cannot remember but it was all-embracing and needed no amendment. The unwritten rules were, as in *Cossack*, that there was to be no shouting unless it was necessary and no whistling – as a personal idiosyncrasy, I hated it – near the bridge. One other rule was that anyone found not wearing his lifebelt would have a lifebuoy, the large circular object, hung round his neck until he found another sucker.

In airy-fairy discussion it was held in those days that a ship should be a benevolent autocracy. Agreed, but it was becoming ever-increasingly clear that the Captain was becoming more and more dependent on individual members of the Ship's Company. At least in escort destroyers, when on the job, the safety of the ship – and the convoy – could be in the hands of the radar operator on watch. He might perhaps be a young man of little over twenty or like the very efficient, conscientious and dignified gentleman of thirty-five of ours, Able Seaman Herbert, who had been a grocer only a few months before. Equally, a similar responsibility would be in the hands of the often young asdic operator on watch who would – or would not – detect the presence of a U-boat or an approaching torpedo in time. With the need for a very firm control in war, the prescription seemed to be more autocracy and more benevolence. The problem was to get the proportions right.

Returning to earth, or rather the sea, we did only one more ocean escort. It was in support of a convoy of which Captain Walker was the Senior Officer. John Walker was a man who had everything but the good fortune he had so richly deserved. He had an excellent academic and technical but also practical brain with great ability and had been, before the war, a Navy athlete. Also, before the war, as a Commander, he had a key job as Fleet A/S Officer in the Mediterranean and was thus the adviser to the C-in-C on A/S matters. He was always very smartly turned out, an impressive figure well over six foot, very well-mannered – and thoroughly likeable. He was not, however, a yes-man and the story was that he fell out with his C-in-C and was thus passed over for promotion to Captain.

Because of his practical ability and sound brain Johnny Walker, as a superannuated Commander, was invaluable in the Experimental Section of the A/S School at Portland at the outbreak of World War Two. After much effort, however, he got himself off to sea in command of an escort group of sloops where he developed with very great success his own ruthless, determined technique for the destruction of U-boats, with Lieutenant Impey as his A/S Officer. Walker had to accept, meanwhile, the death of his

126

son, killed in action in one of HM Submarines. Walker finally died having been specially promoted to Captain, very highly decorated and grossly overworked.

The particular convoy with Johnny Walker as Senior Officer was many miles west of the French coast when we joined it and was already being shadowed by U-boats. All Walker's escort vessels were streaming 'Foxers', that is to say they were towing noise-making paravanes, contraptions which produced a roaring noise in the water astern of the towing ship. The idea was that the German homing torpedo, the Gnat, which had been scoring some successes against escort vessels, would home onto the Foxer instead of the ships' propellers. Some weeks before, we in *Wanderer* had had a torpedo fired at us in northern waters. We detected and avoided it and I was confident we could do so again.

I had, however, been given a firm, direct order to use this wretched thing. We were unused to the permanent, distracting noise, the constant snarl in the asdic earphones. It put us off. One of Walker's ships did sink one U-boat despite the noise of the Foxers – and I missed an opportunity! About ten or twelve miles astern at night, a friendly aircraft was attacking a surfaced U-boat which was trying to catch the convoy up and refused to dive. Afterwards, I thought that, with such a strongly escorted convoy, I should immediately have gone in the dark for the U-boat at high speed. Johnny Walker, anyway, would probably not have recalled me.

The RAF – Coastal Command – had by then attained a high proficiency in detection and destruction of U-boats.

It was a day or so after our return to Londonderry, then in late March 1944, that the Staff Gunnery Officer (not a frequent caller) came onboard to see me. *Wanderer* was to have a two-pounder pom-pom fitted. Splendid, I said, make it a triple mounting and we will have it amidships. But, no, he said, it was to be a single mounting, mounted right in the eyes of the ship. There was something wrong somewhere, I replied; fitted on the forecastle it would be washed straight over the side in any Atlantic weather. It would leave a nasty hole where the mounting had been torn out and that would let the water in! No, I said, that seems crazy. He must produce the Commodore's authority before anything of that sort was put in hand. This came, together with a statement that *Wanderer*'s duties were to be altered: how was not specified.

On the strength of the general idea that close-range guns were to be needed, I wangled another Oerlikon 20 mm gun.

'You cannot have that,' said the Staff Gunnery Officer, 'there is no one trained to fire an extra gun.' There soon would be.

'Well, the deck would have to be strengthened to take the thrust when the gun was fired.' The gun was already in place so he had better get the Dockyard to take the work in hand.

We got our Oerlikon fitted on the quarter deck and our Mr Franklin was told that he and his depth charge crews could take it over. Later, both the extra Oerlikon and the pom-pom, fitted right forward were valuable.

This and additional training had kept us in and around our base longer than usual – over three weeks this time. By my reckoning in those days, if the ship was in harbour ten days, officers and men started to relax mentally and any time in harbour over a fortnight would mean their reactions would have slowed down. Incidentally, for those who were sea-sick, as I was, the same periods of time also applied. As a counter to this softening up, immediately on getting to sea, we would always drop a small buoy with a radar top-mark (in fact, a biscuit tin), make a smoke screen, retire to the far side of it and then, radar-guided, steam through the smoke at speed to give the buoy the works with all guns and even a depth charge. The general hassle, the banging and shaking of the ship at once brought it home that we were back on the job. Presumably, other COs had their own recipes.

On the next occasion of going to sea, *Wanderer* was on her own, having been told to go down to Plymouth to join a motley collection of destroyers employed against raiding and mine-laying German E-boats. The E-boats, capable of forty knots – and a genuine forty knots was a considerable speed then – were dashing over from their bases in occupied France in early spring 1944 to lay mines in our shipping lanes, mainly off Plymouth and to the eastward. Though we then knew nothing about the shape-to-come of Operation OVERLORD – the invasion of northern France – those who planned it did not want the proposed shipping routes to be fouled by minefields.

Going down Plymouth Sound to sea, with the Hands fallen in for leaving harbour and 'John Peel' being broadcast over the loud hailer system, was so pleasing, so peaceful on a warm sunny evening. Plymouth Hoe in a lovely green stretch lay to port, the woods of Mountedgecombe to starboard and Drake's Island squatting in the water ahead. Entirely incongruous, it seemed, that the four destroyers in line ahead should be setting out to spend the night trying to find and blast away at E-boats.

Once out in the area, our ships would spread about five miles apart and be left to patrol. One such night, a blank one when no E-boats came over, we could see the RAF making a very heavy raid on the French coast. Terrifying for those being bombed, this was awe-inspiring to us; with huge, semi-circular mauve flashes like solid sheet lightning going on and on and lighting up that part of the horizon.

The speed of events on E-boat operations could sometimes be considerable. Initial detection, of hydrophone effect (propeller noises) from the asdic, could be heard at surprisingly long range with these very fast moving craft; then, later came the echo from the radar; then perhaps, sighting the enemy in star shell illumination. The plot, doing it all by hand, had its work cut out. From the asdic, the radar, the plot, even visual sighting, we hoped to get *some* warning. I would head towards the target and increase speed and then Foster, the control officer, later Sub Lieutenant Sweeting, would take the loud-hailer, the quickest communication to the guns, and say something like, 'Alarm starboard, enemy approaching, open fire when seen.'

In one such close range encounter with the usual firework display, there was some swapping of fire, maybe some hits but nothing to show for it except some scoring in the ship's side plating where we had been hit – harmlessly at an acute angle, just as well as the plating was very thin. Then came a report from the plot of a small radar echo on a steady course and speed at a range of 8,000 yards.

'What do you think it is?' I asked.

'E-boat.'

'It's a bit far south. Should we get in range of the enemy shore guns if we go after it?'

'Might do, Sir.'

'Get the "bow and arrow" up and First Lieutenant on the bridge. We'll have a go at long range.'

When the ship had been converted to escort destroyer, the gunnery fire-control equipment was removed, so we made our own – of a sort. An obsolete aluminium fire-control disc, known as the Dumaresq, which solved relative triangle problems could, when used in conjunction with radar and the plot, give us the amount of aim-off to allow for the movement of the enemy during the shell time-off-flight. Then we needed to have the right fuse setting to explode the shrapnel shell over the target. This was where the 'bow and arrow' came in. It was a contrivance designed and made in the ship and consisted of a wooden board with carefully calculated curves marked on it and a sliding cursor; usually worked by Michell, the First Lieutenant, and perhaps Kidd or Allen, the New Zealander, it gave the fuse setting to be set on the shells so that one salvo of shrapnel from the 4.7-inch guns would burst just astern of the target, one would burst directly over it and a third would burst slightly ahead. The Gunnery Control Officer would pass the settings to the guns, give the order 'commence' and there would be three successive crashes, shaking the ship. The bow and arrow was produced on board in the first place to burst shrapnel over and frighten away 'Shads', German aircraft shadowing convoys from the horizon and homing the U-boat; furthermore, though it worked, it was not a very slick or serious weapon of war, as its nick-name implied, and could not be used if anything of consequence was going on. This time the team performed their act; the guns crashed and there was a pause.

Then: 'Target's on fire,' reported the Action Officer of the Watch. It was, and we were later credited (not too generously, I thought) with a 'probably damaged E-boat'.

Another night, Bower from the plot produced another target at even longer range.

'What's it like?' I asked.

'Speed eight knots, course steady, westerly. Might be a *Sperrbrecher*, heavily armed,' he reported, adding: 'Good fire control and radar. Guns trained to fire astern, adapted to cover the retreat of E-boats.'

'We'll leave it alone.' It was not worth risking missing the coming invasion by going after one of these; we would just get a bloody nose from such a ship with good fire-control, and also perhaps from the German shore guns as well. The information about these *Sperrbrecher*s came, incidentally, from the Admiralty *Weekly Intelligence Reports* (WIRs). Valuable, sometimes spicy little booklets, one edition had described how a lieutenant RNVR (or perhaps he was RNR) had escaped from a German prisoner of war camp with forged papers under the name of 'I. Buggeroff'.

Later that night there was an apparent lull and I called down to the plot: 'Anything happening?'

'Not much, Sir. Still the same *Sperrbrecher*. But now there's just another single new, distant contact. Been stopped for several minutes. We're bang in our right position and it shouldn't be our side. Radar thinks it might be a large E-boat.'

'We'll put some pom-pom star shell over it and see what it looks like.'

The pom-pom was fed by belted ammunition to fire, in succession, star shells, armour-piercing and shrapnel. I ordered a burst of six. Dead accurate it was, and showed our own Senior Officer's ship end-on to us and well out of position, as clear as daylight! Bull's Eye!

'How did you get on last night, Sir?' I asked the Senior Officer the next day in harbour.

'We destroyed one,' he said, 'but we were quite badly hit ourselves,' he replied.

'Many casualties, Sir?' I asked.

'No, fortunately none at all. Just a large hole in my sea cabin and some wine bottles broken. And they were insured.'

'These E-boats must be more heavily armed than we thought,' I said.

It seemed better to leave him thinking it was the work of the foe and not draw attention to his ship being well out of position. He was a nice chap but not at all easily amused.

The time at Plymouth was quite short. I had been told even then that I was to be Senior Officer of an escort group for the Invasion. There had already been some training for the event – of which more later – and then, in May, back we went to Londonderry for a final polish up; not that we knew at that stage when or where it was all to happen. It had been a pleasant break at Plymouth; there was always something so relaxing about the West Country air – not that it helped me much in the past days at the Royal Naval College, Dartmouth.

13. INVASION

Stalin, the Soviet dictator, had nagged aggressively for a 'Second front' since 1942, an all-out assault on Western Europe which would take the weight off his forces defending Russia and – though not said – would then allow his armies to advance into Europe. The Casablanca and the Teheran Conferences confirmed that the Allies' next assault would be on Sicily with that on France to follow. In London, initial planning for the inevitable invasion of France had been going on since 1942 but it was not until early 1944 that those like myself became unofficially aware that something big was going to happen. What, where or when we did not know and guessing was a waste of time. Again, like others no doubt, I could only hope that my ship would be in on it and ready.

By the beginning of spring 1944, the vast assemblies of troops and vehicles in the south of England and the restrictions on access in some coastal areas made it plain that the event was likely to be in the first months of summer.

Soon after returning from Plymouth to Londonderry, I had been told that, still in command of *Wanderer* and still a lieutenant commander, I was to be the Senior Officer of an international escort group of about half a dozen escort vessels. As a prelude to this, I was sent to do another course at the Tactical School at Liverpool but this was to be a special one, a one-off. Captain Gilbert Roberts was again the Director of the School and he certainly had retained his knack of making the classroom both very usefully informative and also entertaining. About the invasion, he revealed to the dozen or so of us attending nothing about the place, the date or time of the day. Some thought it would be the Straits of Dover and some even thought it would be the south of France. We were, however, given an idea of the friendly forces and the tactics likely to be used and how the operation might go. All seaborne traffic, for example, would have to go round an imaginary point in the ocean which he said we might think of as Piccadilly Circus. This we later found was a point a few miles south of the Isle of Wight. Then, he said, we might well see something that looked like Brighton Pier under way – but upside down. This was later identifiable as a section of a Mulberry artificial harbour; but at the time it was only evident that we were in for a novel seaborne operation.

In addition to the Tactical School briefings, we had special, unprecedented battle training in our ships at sea off Belfast. It was a very lively and imaginative affair, the staff aspects being organised by Commander John

Grant on behalf of the Western Approaches Command. Effectively, this high-pressure training taxed the whole of each vessel's fighting ability and for us in *Wanderer* was enjoyable in that everyone, officers and men, individually and collectively, knew their stuff. A peak moment was when, escorting a notional convoy, the ship's 4.7-inch guns were firing at a high-speed target with practice shells and the pom-pom and the Oerlikon 20 mm guns were engaging a close-range aerial-towed target, the asdic team were in contact with and attacking a tame submarine while (friendly) aircraft were firing live ammunition just ahead and astern of the ship. In addition, I was acting as Senior Officer of the escort, ably assisted by Bower on the plot. This training inevitably involved some risk and, very sadly, there were fatal casualties in a Norwegian MTB when it was hit by a practice shell from a frigate, while it was towing the high-speed target.

Immediately the battle training was over, I went round the group informally to meet some of the ships' officers and to see what they looked like. In one ship there was an RNVR officer, quite pleasant looking, though seemingly rather shy. His name, his Commanding Officer said, was Callaghan and he was interested in politics! I never saw him again, however, as his ship was transferred out of my group before D-Day.

More was the pity. For some unknown reason the ships in my group, some of which were foreign, were changed at the last minute; thus I had no chance, before the operation started, to meet the COs of the other ships with whom I would be working. It is always a help to know roughly what to expect from those on your own side! This was (almost) the only retrospective criticism I had of the truly wonderful prior arrangements for that herculean maritime assault – the biggest ever staged!

It was, I recollect, a day or so before the Convoy Conference that we arrived in the Bristol Channel and I was summoned to the office of the Flag Officer Milford Haven and given a small sealed sack.

'What is it?' I asked the authoritative Wren Officer – a very serious young lady.

'A book, and you may not break the seal until ordered by signal.'

It was obviously a set of instructions for the invasion and was so voluminous that there was no chance of absorbing quickly whatever might be in it. The day before I thought we might sail I broke the seal and told four officers each to read a section of the book, putting them on their honour not to discuss with one another or anyone else anything that they had read. When the signal authorising the breaking of the seal came, we all conferred. This had been, of course, a precaution against getting caught out not knowing the orders when perhaps trying, at sea, to deal with some urgent operational matter. Later, I myself looked at the book – *Operation Neptune* – the nautical component of Operation Overlord, which was the code name for the whole invasion. The book was a masterpiece, the product of some very high-powered brain work. It must have had a wide distribution yet, to the best of my belief, there was not one leak in security.

When we eventually did finally all assemble, convoy and escort, it was in Cardiff Roads, with some three dozen merchant ships carrying primarily a

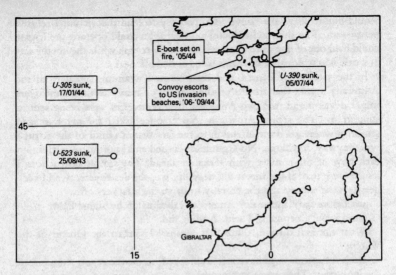

Map 7. HMS *Wanderer*: victories and D-Day duties, 1943–44
On 4 June 1944. *Wanderer* sailed as senior officer escort to a convoy bound for the
US UTAH and OMAHA beaches.

United States build-up Division. The escort consisted of seven warships: *Wanderer* as the Senior Officer of the Escort, with a British frigate, a French frigate (not recorded in Ministry of Defence papers), a Belgian corvette and three Canadian corvettes. There would also be some coastal forces, which were to join later, so we were told.

In retrospect, I was glad not to have guessed in advance at the non-stop events and problems – nearly all unconnected – which were to arise in the next few days. There was to be no even, easy flow in the constant and rapidly changing situation. Small problems some may have been, but with little margin of error.

The Convoy Conference prior to our sailing was held ashore at Cardiff and was so particularly dull and uninformative that the Flag Officer Cardiff fell sound asleep. The Conference certainly had the merit that it could not possibly have alarmed the Masters of the merchant ships who were being briefed for the venture. The Commodore of the Convoy, Captain H. T. England, RN, a retired officer who had been at my prep school some years earlier, was a large, stalwart man who inspired confidence. Thus, I felt there should be no misgivings in the merchant ships when we, Convoy EBM 2, finally sailed on D-Day Minus One for the 'American' beaches of Normandy.

Personally, I was less easy in my mind. There had been no real briefing on the enemy forces we might meet: heavy forces? E-boats? – and the Admiralty did not *always* have U-boats taped, as we well knew. It was thus that, when a frigate reported that she had a serious case of appendicitis and

133

would like to leave the convoy temporarily to land the victim, I refused permission. The ship had a doctor on board; he could operate; the frigate could haul out of line onto a reasonably steady course while the doctor was at work. Miraculously, the man's pains passed off.

In the vicinity of Land's End there came a warning signal from the Admiralty saying that attacks on the convoy by heavy German destroyers might develop and that two American fleet destroyers were being sent to support us. The senior American ship at once asked for my rank and seniority whereat I drew attention to the fact that as senior of the escort I was, anyway, in charge. No arguments ensued and I put one American on each bow of the convoy with *Wanderer* ahead. The simple instructions I issued were that, if the threat did develop, we, the destroyers, would keep between the enemy and the convoy to drive the attackers off.

Just before dark the senior American called us up by signal light:

'Read it out, Yeoman,' I said. And he did.

'What the hell do you think that means?' I said to the Officer of the Watch.

'Both American ships have increased speed,' came the report from one of the look-outs. They were leaving us.

'Their signal must be the English equivalent of "proceeding in execution of previous orders",' commented the OOW.

'Can't think of any appropriate reply. Just make back "Goodbye Yeoman".'

Presumably the American ships knew more than I did because the threatened attack never developed: had it done so it could have made a nasty mess of our convoy – and perhaps a vital mess in that the convoy carried a United States Division. This was the first of several occasions when it would have greatly helped to have been given the temporary rank and authority of Commander.

All was then quiet until we approached 'Piccadilly Circus', by then more formally known as Point zz, and the convoy at that point abandoned its broad front, forming into long lines. The need was to keep within the channels which had been swept clear of mines. This meant that the escort ships had a great length of merchant ships to guard, a task made the more difficult by the strong cross tide in the English Channel. This tended to displace ships sideways out of their proper stations in the convoy. In fact, one ship did get mined on passage though I did not hear about it at the time, but, fortunately, no lives were lost.

A most unhappy event occurred after we had rounded Point zz. In pitch darkness, in the very early hours, several small vessels were detected by radar and plotted approaching from ahead. They were plugging along slowly on a steady course back to England and could only be friendly; friendly and tired, small landing craft, not keeping a look-out. Being ahead of the convoy, we in *Wanderer* did everything possible to alert them with signal lamps and even loud-hailer. It was no good, they headed straight on and some, with some unpleasant clashes, went into ships of the convoy. I made warning signals, telling the escort to look out for survivors, but under the circumstances, when we really did not know what to expect next, I did not prejudice the convoy's safety by any organised search for them.

'Contact bearing 205 degrees, range 10,000 yards, Sir,' from the radar, quite suddenly.

'What does it look like?' I asked.

'Could be an E-boat.'

'Action Stations!'

'Target seems to be stopping,' reported the plot.

'Fire star shell, Sir?' from Sweeting.

'No. We'll get closer. Be ready to open fire at once.'

'Asdics, let me know at once if the target moves its engines.'

'We're very close now, Sir. Make the challenge?' from the Officer of the Watch.

'Yes.'

'Challenge made Sir,' from the Yeoman of Signals who had flashed the two appropriate letters on a small box lamp, and then: 'No reply to challenge, Sir.'

'We can't miss now. Keep all guns on target. Perhaps it's broken down.'

'We'll go alongside. Put the ten-inch signal lamp on the target and see what it is.'

Through a megaphone I then established that it was a large American patrol boat, not broken down but completely lost. I gave it a harsh verbal blast through a megaphone on the dangers of not keeping a proper look-out and of not replying to the challenge – and then the course to steer to get back to its base. The sailors had a word for it: lucky for some.

We arrived off the American beach early in the morning of D Plus One; another of my merchant ships immediately struck a mine. I told her to anchor because she could no longer move under her own steam but I did no more; she was not sinking or on fire.

It seemed that the Senior American Naval Officer dealing with shipping and convoys was in an old British cruiser lying at anchor and so I signalled him asking for instructions. There was no reply. I tried again; there was no reply; so I went over in *Wanderer*'s motor boat. Only the Commodore could give instructions, they said. Surely, I remonstrated, there must be someone on duty to act on the Commodore's behalf on routine matters. No, only the Commodore could give instructions. It was then 7.30 am.

'Wake him up,' I said in exasperation.

But no, not for a lieutenant commander; it was evident that would not do. Such a situation could not arise in the Royal Navy. In high dudgeon I left a message – be it hoped, reasonably polite – that I would arrange a return convoy with escort myself, did so and set off back across the Channel. There was no point in hanging about. Any action against enemy ships would be in mid-Channel.[1]

1 The writer's liaison with the United States Navy during the Invasion was not one of easy understanding. He had the indeterminate feeling that they did not regard it as *their* war – as opposed to the Pacific where the American Navy fought with such outstanding courage and skill This is a reluctant comment observing the kindness and hospitality of the US 6th Fleet under Admiral Anderson some years later in the Yugoslav ports.

On the way back to Falmouth, which was to be our turn-round point in the UK, a profoundly awesome – almost solid – mass of friendly raiding aircraft passed overhead. Liberators, we thought, certainly five hundred, even one thousand of them. It was hard to estimate the number. How utterly terrifying to be at the receiving end of that heavy, droning holocaust!

At Falmouth, we, as an escort group, and the convoy were dealt with promptly – just, of course, as we expected. We were turned round and sent back to France with what was fortunately a small convoy.

Just after we had passed 'Piccadilly Circus' in the dark, the OOW called down the voicepipe to me: '*Tavy* has opened fire.' (She was a frigate.)

'What the hell at?' I asked as I dashed up to the bridge.

'Looks like radio-controlled bombs.'

'Press the alarm!'

Full marks to the OOW for his quick, accurate recognition – we could see the pilot lights of the bombs glowing red, planing down on the escorts and merchantmen. Every ship – warships and merchantmen with any guns – opened up.

Five enemy aircraft were making the attack and it was soon plain that they were using the moon to silhouette our ships. I put *Wanderer* straight into the line of the aircraft approach so that each one would fly directly over us on its run-in. Just before it was overhead, *Wanderer*'s engines were reduced to slow speed so as to show minimum wake from the air. We withheld fire until the aircraft was nearly overhead. Then we opened up at point blank range.

After the third or fourth time and we had at least one aircraft already down, I popped down to the plot to see where all our ships were (it was virtually all hand-plotting then). Unexpectedly, another attack had started and Frost, the Action Officer of the Watch, had, quite rightly, given the order to open fire, but marginally too early, thus giving the aircraft the chance to return our fire, though fortunately without success. Provided we withheld fire till the last second there was absolutely no question but that we were hitting each aircraft hard with pom-pom and 20 mm Oerlikon guns each time. We could see the tracer hitting and some of it bouncing off the aircraft's belly armour.

The fireworks that night were spectacular with the glow of the bombs, the tracer from all the escorts and the merchantmen as well. It was exciting, very satisfactory and, for a night action, in no way confused.

The score, when we had driven the enemy off, was certainly one and probably two or more aircraft and about six radio-controlled bombs shot down while none of our ships was hit. It was a pleasing little operation.

Radio-controlled bombs were not among the potential hazards of which Captain Roberts had warned us. Good old WIRs – not only did they advise us on the love-life ambitions of Italian charioteers and the pseudonyms for escaping POWs but they had warned us, some months ago, of these bombs which, be it noted, had hit and so very seriously damaged the battleship HMS *Warspite* and the cruiser HMS *Uganda* off the Salerno beaches.

136

This, to me, showed that skill above average had been displayed by those concerned in this action and that this had saved damage to the convoy. I put in a brief report recommending one member of *Wanderer*'s gun crews, determined by drawing lots, for a Distinguished Service Medal. The Commanding Officer of *Tavy* plus one or two others were recommended for Mentions in Despatches – including 'Duke', the man thus nicknamed by the sailors because of his so-called BBC accent.

On another night not long after, when we were escorting a cross-Channel convoy, this time a big one, Duke excelled himself. He was a German Jewish music student from Leipzig who had fled the Hitler regime pre-war and had been recruited by Lord Reading's organisation for international Jewry in this country. His job in the ship was to man a special R/T receiving set and monitor German communications to aircraft and ships. It was not a simple matter of translation from German to English but demanded rapidly turning the technical language of one country into the technical language of another.

Not an imposing military figure: Duke was short, plump, bespectacled and red-faced. He wore the unbecoming uniform of a ship's writer with peaked cap and a black-buttoned coat. He was a young man of great guts and personality and was highly popular and, as the result of his work, greatly respected throughout the ship.

His day, or rather night, came when, for the second time, he was able to warn us when German bombers were being scrambled and being instructed to attack a nearby British convoy.

'Assume they're coming from the nearest German airfield in France and that they're coming for us and give me their ETA here,' I called down to Bower on the plot. He was very quick, and a signal, priority 'Most Immediate' went out from *Wanderer* telling escorts to be prepared to make smoke in three minutes' time. The aircraft were detected by radar and the smoke screen was ordered in almost exactly the three minutes. The new Gunner, Mr Franklin, a very good officer, reported from aft by telephone that he could not make our smoke canister ignite. This was often a snag but it was a snag we had never had in serious circumstances.

'Tell him to stuff a red-hot poker from the Ward Room galley into it and bloody well hurry up!' I remember saying.

The wind was on the convoy's port bow, in exactly the right direction, and the smoke screen was spectacularly perfect – far better than anything in peace-time practice! The convoy was completely covered by dense, low-lying smoke. The enemy aircraft flew round the convoy several times and then went back harmlessly to where they came from.

There was one paragraph in the Operation NEPTUNE orders which said that during the Invasion, Senior Officers and Commanding Officers were not obliged to send in written Reports of Proceedings, as was the usual custom. Foolishly, I never reported this event – foolishly, because the very quick, imaginative and accurate work of Bower assisted by Allen, and of Duke had without doubt saved a convoy of about thirty ships from attack and damage. Such work should have been recognised, at least by Mentions in Despatches. My reasons for making no report at that time were, first, the Operation NEPTUNE orders, and secondly, because I had just sent in a report with recommendations for awards for the previous similar action. Days later, enquiring unofficially at the Admiralty, I was told that, for the only time on record, all my recommendations had been turned down by the Second Sea Lord and Chief of Naval Personnel, Admiral Sir Algernon Willis. I should have appealed but did not know till some years afterwards that appeals about awards were permitted. Duke, my apologies.

Thereafter, *Wanderer* continued, as the Senior Officer of escort groups, to plug backwards and forwards between the American beaches and Falmouth where Vice Admiral Sir G. F. Edward-Collins (serving as a Rear Admiral) was the boss. He was, for obvious reasons, known as the 'Giant Panda' and was not a light-hearted gentleman. Probably overestimating the resilience of us all in *Wanderer*, I never spent a night off the American beaches but, rather, turned round straight away with a return convoy. Maybe this was driving too hard. The first one to keel over was a young Ordinary Seaman who deserted. It did not seem to matter: he was a pleasant, harmless, wet mum's boy; we could get along without him. Infuriatingly, he was picked up by the police and sent back to the ship for me to deal with him.

'Where have you been?' I asked him when he was brought before me as a defaulter.

'In a hostel in Portsmouth, Sir,' he said. 'I didn't know where else to go because my home's in Ireland and I'd not got enough money for the ticket.'

'Why did you stay away without leave?' I asked.

'I was frightened, Sir,' he replied.

'This is ridiculous,' I said. 'No one in the ship has been killed, no one has even been wounded.' Then, to the Doc, the Surgeon Lieutenant: 'This man must be medically examined.'

Later, I told the young Doc to hawk the youth round the local hospitals until there was one which would accept him as a nut case. There was no vice in him; the Detention Barracks would do him no good. Wrong, perhaps? In war, a man who deserts his ship should be severely dealt with. Yes, by the book perhaps it was wrong, but on the *pro bono publico* basis, the padded, rather than the unpadded cell seemed the best answer.

Back to the job, there came the day when (for the first time!) the American Commodore did organise a convoy and *Wanderer* was told to join the escort after the convoy had sailed. The Commanding Officer of the senior ship and, thus, the Senior Officer of the escort, was a Reserve officer marginally junior to me so I took over from him and, to avoid disruption of escort positions which had already been allocated, I stationed *Wanderer* in the convoy's rear. This was a lucky decision which fitted in well with events to come.

We had just taken up our position; Bower had plotted the positions of the other escorts round the convoy and gone below to lunch, when a frigate ahead, in the van of the escort, made a signal which was very puzzling. It was to the effect that she had just attacked an asdic contact and was subsequently being pursued by a Gnat homing torpedo which was running on the surface. There was plainly something up with the frigate, *Tavy*.

We were fortunate in *Wanderer* in that, just before the Invasion, we had acquired a Loran-type piece of navigational equipment. It could give us an immediate and precise fix; the ship's exact position could be put on the chart within a few seconds.

I spoke to Kidd, the OOW: 'Tell *Tavy* to switch on 1FF. 'Increase to twenty-five knots, then nip down to the plot and put the ship on the chart. Also put *Tavy*'s position down and give me a course to get to her – also an ETA.'

To the Type 271 radar: 'Give the plot *Tavy*'s range and bearing.'

To the helmsman: 'Steer 320 degrees' – a guessed course.

Within a couple of minutes, Kidd was back on the bridge and, steering an adjusted course, we were going straight through the middle of the convoy – rear to van – from the back to the leading ships. There was no knowing what we might find had been the cause of the frigate's asdic echo; perhaps an old wreck on the bottom. For safety's sake, however, I decided to treat it initially as an enemy submarine and order Action Stations – achieved, as ever, at speed.

'Object in the water ahead, Sir,' reported the starboard look-out.

'What is it?'

'Looks like a minesweeping float,' said Frost, the action OOW – then: 'It's snagged to one of the clear-channel buoys.'

There it was: with the fast tide running past it, the stationary minesweeping float looked, at first glance, to be travelling through the water. That was the so-called Gnat all right.

'Contact confirmed submarine,' came the report from the asdic cabinet. I still was not sure.

'Man in the water 200 yards ahead,' reported the port look-out. The man was not too far from the reported asdic contact, which was a nuisance – some airman who had inconveniently fallen from the skies, I thought. He might be friendly; he might be enemy. What the hell next?

'Kidd, your contact will have to wait a couple of minutes, I am going to drop the man a life-saving float first or we'll slay him with our depth charges.'

We shouted to the man to pull himself onto the float – English, French and German, we tried. Finally, he understood.

'What's the target doing?' to the asdic cabinet.

'Stopped; lying on the bottom.'

'Attacking at fifteen knots – all charges to be set deep.'

The target was not, in fact, in deep water but, with the charges set deep, there would be a longer interval before they exploded and thus *Wanderer* would have more time to get clear of the heavy detonations which always shook and could damage the ship. Then from about a thousand yards, in we went. Ten charges were dropped. Gushes of diesel oil resulted from the attack. It was a U-boat all right.

'Signal from the frigate, Sir, requesting permission to recover a souvenir.'

'Reply "no". Keep clear till I have finished.' Then, having established with the echo-sounder and the asdic which way the submarine was lying on the bottom, attacks were made along the target's length twice more with depth charges until there can have been almost nothing left. After that, the man in the water was recovered, unharmed, from his life-saving float. He was German and said he was the Engineer Officer of the U-boat – rather a sour, bad-mannered man, very much a Nazi. He did not even thank us for helping him. There were no other survivors and, having been told to land our prisoner at Portland, I proceeded there at speed. After the arrival, I gave the order to splice the main brace. After we had sunk U-523 in August 1943, I had done this illegally but, since that time, an Admiralty Fleet Order had been issued authorising Commanding Officers to do this whenever they were satisfied their ships had destroyed a U-boat. It was comforting to be on the right side of the law – like being certain that one's socks were laid out in the right way when turning in at night in Dartmouth.

Some weeks later it transpired that the enemy submarine was U-390, a Type VIIC, commanded by Oberleutnant Heinz Geissler, which had sunk one of our merchant ships earlier during the Invasion, though not a ship from one of my convoys. It had been a slick little operation, dealing with U-390, but it very much emphasised, once more, how officers and ratings could work as a team so calmly and so easily to sort out what might otherwise have been a confused and unsatisfactory muddle. Nevertheless, put in perspective, the circumstances were in no way hazardous as compared with those, for instance, faced by my old course-mate Gordon Luther when he found himself as Senior Officer of an Atlantic convoy inadequately escorted and under heavy attack in rough weather. Those were harsh days, as they were in the Mediterranean when Cunningham, the C-in-C was said to have pronounced destroyers as expendable.

'How is everything down below?' I asked Lieutenant (E) Short, the Engineer Officer, chattily next morning, meaning by that, how was everything in the engine room, the boiler room and all the compartments below the waterline.

'Well, Sir,' he said, 'rather serious. We've just been round to check and there are one hundred leaks from the sea and two hundred and fifty internal.' By the latter part of his statement, he meant leaks between adjacent compartments.

'Come off it, Chief, we always do have leaks.'

'No, Sir, not like this. Now they can't even see the gauge glasses in the boiler rooms for steam, nor can they see their way round the engine room properly when the ship is at sea.'

'We shall have to have a detailed, written report. In the meantime the question is whether it is safe to go to sea. I can't have men's lives risked unless there is a bloody good reason.' We talked it over further and I decided that, in the event of likely enemy action, it would be justified to go to sea; otherwise it would not be. The ship was twenty-five years old, she had really been built for quite a different purpose and she had taken some really very heavy bashing from both bad weather and from the ship's own depth charges. Her condition was plainly very bad.

Thus, I made a signal to the Flag Officer Portland spelling it all out and saying unequivocally that I regretted I would not take the ship to sea, except for action against the enemy, until something was done about the damage to the ship's hull. Then I waited, but nothing happened. No one sent for me. No one came on board to see me. I was left guessing. Surely, it could not be that the whole shore staff felt unable to make some sort of personal contact and find out what it was all about? But, yes, it could, and the Admiralty was finally informed by signal. By telephone from the Admiralty, I was told to report there for a new job – very annoying but not altogether surprising as my appointment in command was only for eighteen months and the time was about up. As in the days when I was appointed to a shore job from *Cossack*, I tried to get out of it. It was no good; I had to go.

Leaving any ship for the last time was always sad and somewhat emotional. Leaving *Wanderer*, my command for eighteen very eventful months, was a trauma. The successes – and the failures – of that ship and all the officers and ratings in the ship had been my responsibility and so had their safety. It was the same for all Captains of all ships, from coastal forces to aircraft carriers, but was perhaps accentuated in the smaller ships which were much closer communities. The Ship's Company in *Wanderer* had been a fine, loyal, very efficient and cheerful supporting crew to whom I felt great gratitude. The fact that I, personally, might be in trouble for my signal refusing to take the ship to sea, was, at the time of my leaving, of little consequence to me compared with the anger at being hurried out of the ship to serve ashore.

'No cheering, no fuss,' I said to the First Lieutenant. 'Order a taxi on the jetty and make sure there is no one more than usual to see me leave.' Cartwright, keen to be in on the act to the end, followed me to the taxi at what he considered an appropriate distance with the final suitcase.

Whatever happened to Cartwright? When he was demobbed, he might have done anything; I am sure that he would not have done nothing. The Chief Gunner's Mate I heard of again: he kept a pub in Chatham, though regrettably I never discovered which one. Then Able Seaman Herbert, peacetime grocer, wartime genius radar operator: back to the shop? Peter Michell, the First Lieutenant with his excellent technical brain, finished up with an electronic firm of high repute. John Frost I met again, quite unchanged in civilian life. Mr Franklin, the Gunner, ultimately was very deservedly promoted to Lieutenant Commander. Kidd became a doctor. I tried unsuccessfully to get him to volunteer for a permanent commission in the Royal Navy. When he had finished his medical training and I was serving at the Admiralty again, he came to supper in my little London flat. We had a lot of gin and a haggis that I had bought by mistake. Sidney Fuller, the young Doc, is slowly retiring from medical practice ashore but we meet periodically.

And what of Duke? It was only while writing the final draft that I learnt with astonishment and pleasure from my cousin Michael, the Bishop of Southwell, that this ex-naval rating had divulged to him that he had served in HMS *Wanderer* in 1944, that his name was actually Langford and that he was currently Rector of Winthorpe. It transpired that, as an alien, Langford was ineligible for the commission for which he had been recommended from *Wanderer* and that after the war his life took no less remarkable turns than before and during the war, as the following narrative recounts:

In the autumn of 1985, we, the clergy and people of the diocese of Southwell, welcomed a new bishop. When I first heard his name, Michael Whinney, I immediately thought that he must be a relative of Lieutenant-Commander Whinney, who had been the captain of the second destroyer, HMS *Wanderer*, in which I served during the war. I told the bishop so when I met him. He wrote to his cousin Captain R. F. Whinney, and to my great delight it transpired that Captain Whinney was indeed my old 'skipper'. I had a most interesting letter from him, in which among other things he invited me to write a short autobiography.

I was born Werner Lampel on 20 February 1919, only son of Samuel Lampel, cantor (junior minister) of the Liberal Synagogue at Leipzig (then central, now East Germany). My mother belonged to the well-known Grüneberg family, business and financial people at Hanover. There was a story that one of her ancestors had been financial adviser to one of the kings of Hanover. I do not know whether that story is true, but I do know that when my mother married my father they had practically no money betwen them.

We called ourselves liberal Jews, as distinct from our orthodox co-religionists. In modern English usage one might read 'conservative' for 'liberal' and 'fundamentalist-talmudic' for the others. It was more of a cultural than a theological distinction: we treasured things German and European in literature, music, art and philosophy. My father was an accomplished oratorio singer and I was taught the piano and the organ from an early age.

After Jewish primary school I went to the then famous König Albert Gymnasium, a prestigious grammar school with a leaning toward the humanities and a particular stress on Latin and Greek. The first foreign language we were taught was English, and French, the second.

My last three years at school coincided with the rise of Nazism to its full and evil extent. I was isolated, segregated in class and, when a sufficient number of fellow-pupils was around, mercilessly bullied. I remember my headmaster (a devout Roman Catholic who secretly detested everything connected with the Nazis) calling me privately into his study to apologise that he could not make me 'primus omnium' (head prefect) because of the political situation generally and because of the particular fact that his deputy was an active SS officer, who wore his uniform more often than an ordinary suit. Despite all this, I managed to obtain my 'Abiturium' (higher school certificate) in eleven subjects with four distinctions (I was lucky). I applied to Berlin university for immatriculation in 1937, only to be told by the secretary of the Nazi student union on a grubby postcard that they did not want any Jews there.

My parents began to realise that there was no future for us in Germany, certainly not for me. In any case, we were classed as 'stateless', i.e. having no nationality. Through the generosity of a number of distinguished English people, the British Home Office allowed a number of young Jewish men, myself included, to come to Britain on a refugees' work permit. The tail end of official Nazism for me was literally the sight of the tail of a German aeroplane displaying the swastika, when, just twenty years old, I stepped on to the tarmac at Croydon airport on 20 March 1939.

Efforts to get my parents out were numerous but totally unsuccessful. At one time I had secured for my father a verger's job in a synagogue in Toronto, but the Canadian government demanded a security deposit (in cash) of five thousand Canadian dollars. All I possessed were two suitcases containing clothes and other personal items, the clothes I was wearing and seventeen shillings and one penny. I had no friends nor any connections with people who might have been able to produce that kind of money. As a result, my parents were murdered by the Nazis in one of their notorious extermination camps.

I was completely alone in a new country, itself under the severe strain of preparation for war, but I was free as never before. What struck me most forcibly was the kindness of everyone I met. I still remember the words of the immigration officer at the check point at Croydon: 'I wish you the very best of luck in my country.' And I began to hope that soon it would be my country as well.

Posters were going up all over London, 'We've got to be prepared – think of doing National Service'. I went into an office and volunteered for just that. I said to the young woman at the counter: 'May I join? You see, I am not a British subject.' She answered: 'Yes, by all means. Does your offer include combatant service?' I said: 'Of course, anything I can do.'

Eventually, with six hundred other refugees, I enlisted in the Auxiliary Military Pioneer Corps (now the Royal Pioneer Corps). It was not easy – a good thing it wasn't; security in that situation was a new and untried thing, particularly as for Nazi bureaucratic reasons we held German passports flamboyantly marked with a red rubber-stamped 'J' (for Jew). The Crown lawyers came up with a magnificent description of us: 'technically enemy alien, of loyal disposition to HM the King'. I remember taking my first oath of allegiance before the adjutant in German, because that was my mother tongue.

Now I had a British army private's pay book and was very proud of it, a sign of my liberation and the hope of a new life. Our Colonel was the late Rufus Isaacs, Marquess of Reading, a flamboyant personality, more of a lawyer (he was a KC) than a soldier, a 'dandy' in an amusing, old-fashioned way, but a shrewd judge of men and situations. The officers under him were veterans from World War One, some with distinguished service. They are all dead now. Some of the later Pioneer Corps officers I have no wish to see again for obvious and quite different reasons.

As soon as I joined the Pioneers – staying in the Corps for four years and rising to Orderly Room Sergeant – I wanted to get out and transfer to something better and more active, and was eventually selected to become one of the fifty or so 'Writers Special' in the Royal Navy. This term and the very unbecoming uniform with it described a rating who carried out very junior but also very responsible work in intelligence – interpreting enemy radio traffic, essentially at sea, though between the end of the European and the end of the Japanese war it included a number of tasks in translating, publishing and interpreting captured German 'classified' operational material.

My first ship was HMS *Westminster*, which at that time had the duty of guarding East coast convoys between Rosyth and Sheerness. Just before D-Day, June 1944, I was transferred to HMS *Wanderer*, a very similar destroyer dating from the 1914–18 war. I found myself in the communications mess, comprising signalmen, telegraphists, code operators and similar people. I remember them as a splendid lot, practical, sensible on the whole, not the wisest when it came to relations with women or the consumption of alcohol (most of them were very young). They were very kind and straightforward. I liked them immensely, and I think I was accepted by them, even if I did not speak Cockney dialect, as most of them did. Because of this difference, I was landed with the affectionate nickname of 'Duke'. There was an intriguing piece of division of labour: they sewed on my buttons and helped me with other bits of domesticity; I wrote their love letters for them, impressing on them that they must copy in their own hand what I had written; there might have been complications otherwise!

I remember them with affection. Life on the lower deck proved an invaluable training for my later work among Durham and Northumberland miners. We were all very sorry when HMS *Wanderer* had to be taken out of commission and the ship's company paid off. I liked the old 'sardine tin', uncomfortable and overcrowded as she was. My next ship, the frigate HMS *Curzon*, modern, smart, efficient, does not evoke the same fond memories.

In that work, now ashore in the peaceful setting of a well-appointed businessman's house in London suburbia, we were joined by a number of Wrens, university graduates in modern languages, who, being British, were officers, of course. As president of the Petty Officers' mess in that place, I took it upon myself to invite these WRNS officers to our coffee and tea breaks, known in the Service as 'stand easy'. This was, strictly speaking, against protocol, but it appeared that the RN and RNVR officers there – a very able but very shy lieutenant-commander RNVR, a somewhat embittered lieutenant RN and a paymaster lieutenant RNVR who hated his job – were quite glad for me to take these girls off their hands. I loved the Navy, 'warts and all'; even today the sight of the White Ensign makes my heart beat faster.

During those six years, I changed my name, properly and legally, as suggested by the Army authorities, to Herbert Langford, and, toward the end of the war I was converted to the Christian faith and became a member of the Church of England. After the war, in the summer of 1946, I became a British subject, then being twenty-seven years old, taking the oath of allegiance in English this time! Just after Christmas 1946, I married Molly Hughes, an Ulsterwoman, and a keen, practical and practising Anglican Churchwoman, who literally changed me from a kind of 'zombie' into a human being. Sadly, she died two and a half years ago. We had over thirty-seven years of unimaginable marital happiness. On a generous ex-serviceman's grant I went to London university and took a first class honours degree in History in 1950, then found a vocation to the Church's ministry, and went to Wells Theological College. After I worked in Northern parishes, mining villages and towns for twelve years, I was Vice-Principal of St Chad's College in the University of Durham for six years and then registrar of theological examinations at Church House, Westminster for two years. I came to where I am now nearly fifteen years ago, a small parish, no longer village, not yet commuter suburb, in the East Midlands. Some of my colleagues have become bishops, some canons. I have opted for the life of a parish priest. I love my work and my people (and my home, even if now I am on my own). I can retire, but I do not want to do so yet. It's a long way from Werner Lampel, a refugee on the tarmac at Croydon, to Herbert Langford, rector of Winthorpe.

What about the rest? That is where the Army have the edge on us: they can meet those with whom they served through The Regiment. The Navy had no such precise, friendly focus for those who served together.

14. ON TO VE DAY

In October 1944, having had almost no leave – not that I wanted any – I joined DAUD, the Anti-U-boat Division of the Admiralty. More or less on arrival at the Admiralty, I heard on the grapevine, with some considerable relief, that the Admiralty Division concerned had approved the line that I had taken at Portland over *Wanderer*'s damage. Then the news came that Michell, the First Lieutenant, had taken over Command and sailed the ship to Chatham where it was announced that Short, the Engineer Officer, 'The Chief' and I had got it right and that the damage was too great for the ship to be considered fit for operation – even far too great for it to be repaired. My father said that his friend, Admiral of the Fleet Lord Tovey, by then C-in-C the Nore, had met the ship on arrival at Chatham wishing to congratulate me on keeping the old vessel going for so long. He added that Lord Tovey was sorry to find that I had left. So, the weight lifted, I was in the clear again.

The actual job in the Admiralty was to be the Analyst on the U-boat Assessment Committee. If it had to be a shore job, there could not have been one more interesting. Every report by every ship claiming to have attacked a U-boat had to be analysed – the narrative of the action, the ship's plot of our own ships' and U-boats' movements, together with the chemical range recorder traces had to be gone over thoroughly. The Analyst then had to produce a suggested verdict – sunk, damaged, probably damaged, undamaged or no U-boat present at all. The Chairman of the Committee, Captain Howard-Johnston, the Director of the Division would then take the separate opinions of the Intelligence gentry and give his final ruling. So far as I know, at that stage of the war, Howard-Johnston's ruling was never wrong.

The autumn of 1944 was a time of innovation for many asdic-fitted vessels. For reasons already described, accurate attacks on U-boats which had dived deep were proving particularly difficult because the asdic beam would go over the top of them in the latter stages. By the time I had reached my new Admiralty desk, many ships were being fitted with a device which would enable them to maintain contact with deep U-boats to close range and would also give the target's depth and thus overcome the difficulty. Furthermore, a number of escorts had a mortar fitted to them known as the 'Squid'. While the Hedgehog – an unreliable weapon, I thought – would fire bombs ahead of the ship, the Squid would lob small depth charges ahead and they *would* explode. For many escorts, the dice were thus far better loaded in their favour.

The dice were, however, not favourably loaded when the frigate HMS *Mermaid* sank *U-394* on 24 August 1944 by attacks with the well-tried 300-lb depth charges. The action took place in 72 degrees North, well inside the Arctic Circle and well north of the north coast of Norway. *Mermaid* was one of a group of ships supporting a convoy bound for North Russia when, at 3.30 am on 24 August 1944, the ship detected a U-boat by asdic. In all, *Mermaid* made nine separate attacks and then directed an unorthodox depth charge barrage together with two other ships which were unable to pick up the asdic contact. The asdic conditions were very difficult, as they so often were in those northern waters, and, though fitted with an anti-submarine depth-finding device, the variations in the temperature of the water made it unreliable.

There were three particular points of special interest. First, a personal one, the ship was commanded by John Mosse, a member of the triumvirate with Gordon Luther and myself, who had lived in a caravan on Portland when we were qualifying for A/S officers. A second point was that the action against the skilfully handled U-boat lasted for just on twelve hours – a very long time, possibly a record. The third point of interest is that the skill, tenacity and confidence of Mosse, a trained A/S specialist, emphasised the fact that anti-submarine training had never had its fair share compared with, say, gunnery, in earlier years, essentially including those pre-war. No *animus* here: I admired the confident, very skilled part Gunnery Officers played as the *soi-disant* and powerful elite of the Royal Navy – and this is not patronage to make the old sweats' teeth grind!

It was thumbing through the back-numbers, so to speak – the reports of U-boats recently sunk – that I came across the report of *U-377*, sunk by unknown cause in January 1944. It fitted exactly with a contact attacked by *Wanderer*. This contact had been a firm one, estimated to be at 300 feet. We attacked with one pattern of depth charges, regained contact temporarily and the contact then slowly faded. There was no visible evidence on the surface: no oil slick we could see, no wreckage, no appreciable bubbles. With nothing to show but the range recorder trace, I never reported anything about it.

Retrospectively, at my Admiralty desk and later, I had thought it probable that the single, ten depth charge attack had been accurate and that a U-boat had gone to the bottom out of control. The ocean was extremely deep there. However, having failed, against the extant orders, to report attacking a good asdic contact, I had no evidence except the ship's Deck Log. Reasonably enough, Captain Howard-Johnston said that the log was not good enough for reassessment. Failing to report the attack on that contact, unexciting as it was at the time, had been a mistake. It had also been a mistake failing to report our second action in repelling attack against our convoy by aircraft with radio-controlled bombs in the Channel. Bloody-mindedness – whatever the cause and however illogical – can affect anyone's attitude and even one's judgement.

The job in the Anti-U-boat Division was hard work, as are all jobs of great interest, and with the analysis, went several other fascinating commitments. Thus it was all the more disappointing, after a few weeks, to keel over and go sick with what the Navy called 'operational fatigue': that was to say, a nervous breakdown without the attendant histrionics. The timing was especially unfortunate as the Half Yearly Promotions were due in a few days, on 31 December 1944, and no officer was ever promoted when on the sick list. On top of that, Admiral Willis was Second Sea Lord and it was certainly no help to be in disfavour with *any* Member of the Board of Admiralty when they were making the selections for promotion. Perhaps cynically, it was said to be even worse for the candidate if no Member of the Board had ever heard of his name at all! But I was not too filled with hope.

My 'brass hat' – promotion to Commander – at that time came as a surprise with hearty sighs of satisfaction. It was a somewhat hazardous hurdle, this step in rank: sixty per cent of us Executive Branch officers were being superannuated, passed over for promotion at that time. The rate of promotion had been little better than in peace. To fill the gaps for the extra Commanders and Captains needed, the Admiralty gave what was known as War Service rank mainly to a number of those on the Retired List, promoted them in some cases and employed them mainly in administrative jobs ashore. This policy had its shortcomings but it did mean that, unlike the Army, none of us in the Royal Navy, as opposed to the Reserves, had to step down in rank when the war ended. Let it be quite clear though that War Service rank did not refer to gallant Commodores of convoys, who were all senior officers no longer so young and all bearing a full and vital responsibility at sea with little staff to help them – and normally living in both danger and discomfort.

Soon after promotion, I attended an Investiture at Buckingham Palace, to receive the Distinguished Service Cross and Two Bars, accompanied by Jimmy and the small Christopher, born in 1940 – Rosalind was only an infant. His Majesty the King very graciously said a few words to me about the importance of the anti-U-boat war. Afterwards, with my mother, we had a drink at the Ritz. 'What, no champagne?' said my mother.

It was a few days after this that I met my friend, 'Egg' Burnett (later Rear Admiral) in the street.

'How are you?' he asked, knowing that I was on the sick list.

'Well, not quite fit yet,' I replied.

'What you want is some hard work,' he said, unsympathetically.

He was entirely wrong; what a ludicrous comment! He did not know what the bloody hell he was talking about! But, next morning, I knew he was absolutely right. I went straight to the Second Sea Lord's Office to ask for a job and was told to go to Fort Blockhouse, HMS *Dolphin*, the Navy's submarine headquarters, as the Executive Commander – an excellent job.

'They wanted a Gunnery Officer as a disciplinarian but I can't find one, so you'll have to do,' said Captain 'Pinky' Holland-Martin (later Admiral Sir Derek), whom I had known of old.

'What, me a disciplinarian, Sir? My punishment returns are always very low.' Whenever possible, I made it a warning the first time; the next time it was the works – no irritating minor punishments.

'Well, I can only go by your confidential reports, old boy, and I think you'll do.'

This was a splendid job for a recently promoted Commander, much better than I could have hoped for. Professionally, anyway, things were going well. The stigma from the *Rodney* days was at last entirely gone.

EPILOGUE

After the first boozy acclaim, which lasted several months in Blockhouse, peace came as a weighty anticlimax. Agreed, there were no more blackout, no more conscription; conversely, there was no immediate de-mobbing, no lifting of rationing of food, clothes or allocation of drink. Then, for the submariners and others, who might be well decorated, the excitement and responsibility was replaced by a vacuous discontent. Readjustment after five-and-a-half years of war was not at all happy for those in the regular Royal Navy. There were the trials by Court Martial of those deserters and saboteurs – not from the Submarine Service – rounded up for imprisonment. And there were innumerable trials caused by wives. Also, of course, it was a permanent open season for big scale ingenious rackets in many naval establishments.

One September Sunday morning the newspapers were brought into my office: headlines of an air crash in West Africa – no survivors. I knew Joan was flying out to Buenos Aires; I scanned the list anxiously. Her name – not full names – came last. The shock and loss were intense.

Fortunately, the days were overfull with readjustments to peace, discipline, progressive de-mobbing, Parliamentary visits, unravelling rackets and the normal, not inconsiderable, admin. As a brief break, I was summoned to explain asdics to the Shah of Persia. Remarkably clued-up he was.

It was sad to leave Blockhouse, especially for the Admiralty in the Underwater Weapons Department, where they were *inter alia* fighting the anti-U-boat war again – without any experience. I left, prematurely made redundant, mildly ashamed of having been so crudely outspoken.

Executive Commander of *Euryalus* in the 1st Cruiser Squadron in the Mediterranean was a surprisingly good job. Rear Admiral Mountbatten, in command of the squadron, was playing himself back into the Royal Navy after being Viceroy of India and the Supremo in the Far East before that.

Everything clicked well professionally for me. Furthermore, the Admiral detailed me to play two of his ponies for his polo team, the 'Shrimps'. A very different entertainment bonus was Calvi. She was given me as a (suckling) booby prize for failing to kill a wild boar when shooting in Corsica. She lived on board in the Ward Room vegetable locker; she went to football matches with the sailors and had too much beer; and she came to the Captain's dinner parties and had chocolates from Lady Mountbatten.

When Calvi got too big, I found a good home for her with the Naval Ophthalmic Specialist, Jan Steele-Perkins, and, having arranged for the ship to be berthed near the RN Hospital jetty, made a signal: 'Female patient requiring stye treatment will be at hospital steps at 1530.' And she lived happily ever after and had many children.

The day came when the Admiral sent for me to say that I had been kicked out of his polo team – I had just been keeping the seat warm for someone else. I was very much honoured to learn that this was Prince Philip, and soon after I was playing for an Army (!) team against the 'Shimps' when I had a fall.

'Someone's come off, Uncle Dickie,' I heard Prince Philip shout.

'It's only Bob Whinney. He won't hurt himself,' was the reply. But as the result of that fall I was invalided home, soon to recover from back injuries.

A shore job with gloomy prospects followed, in charge of the Seaward Defence School. Providence intervened: there was a national panic (1950). We had to train, as an emergency, all the men and ships to lay the underwater defences for all the ports in the United Kingdom. For this, thanks to the hard work of others, including some overzone lieutenant commanders, I was promoted to captain.

'Where would you like to go, old boy?' asked the Naval Secretary when I went to apply for a new job.

'Preferably in command of a destroyer flotilla in Korea, Sir,' I said, 'but if I can't have that, almost anywhere except the Underwater Weapons Department.'

'That's odd, old boy,' he replied, 'because that's exactly where you're going as Deputy Director, in charge of the Department in Bath.'

At least I learned the power of the Civil Servant to influence and to distort and delay policies affecting ships at sea. But Jock Anderson, a senior Civil Servant of the Royal Naval Scientific Service, was a splendid, modest man grossly under-recognised (with a CB but no 'K') for the quite outstandingly valuable lead that he gave to the development of asdics, especially before and during the war. And it was Jock, among others, with whom I then had to deal.

For personal reasons (culminating in divorce), I asked not to serve my full two years in the job and the Naval Secretary offered me the choice of four good appointments. Though too far from the sea and ships for my liking, I had to opt for the job of Chief Staff Officer Intelligence Mediterranean and Middle East.

This double-hatted job was the idea of Lord Mountbatten, then the C-in-C Mediterranean, and was intensely interesting with the whole of North Africa and the Eastern Mediterranean on the boil – fighting – arms smuggling – violence – political plotting. For the British, there was, in particular, the *Enosis* trouble in Cyprus – and Egypt.

The 1956 Suez operation was a misbegotten affair. A year before, I had concluded – and said – that Israel would, in self-defence, be forced to attack Egypt. America, followed by Britain, then withdrew help promised with the building of the Aswân Dam which triggered Nasser's seizure of the Suez

Canal. Instead of immediate and limited military action, Sir Anthony Eden, the British Prime Minister, vacillated. Much of the miserable rest is history.

My two year Intelligence appointment dragged on to three years; then I was invalided home, exhausted, relieved by two captains. Mountbatten, my first boss, was very easy and pleasant to work for, interested and very well informed and – usually – very entertaining. Not unnaturally, the Navy saw him as a Naval officer and one with a brilliant technical, imaginative brain and an immense grasp of detail, but there was divided Naval opinion about this glamorous world famous figure.

The Lower Deck thought him wonderful. Among the officers there were those whom he had not favoured who could be sharply critical of him. Then there were those of us who were in the war and knew that as a captain in command he was consistently unfortunate, with one glorious defeat after another. That he was courageous and dashing with very outstanding charm was beyond question; ambitious – yes, most certainly and with powerful driving force; conceited – well, yes no ducking it; scheming – yes, and ruthless too, but then every very senior officer must be within limits; successful showman – *par excellence*; ambisextrous – no, rubbish, despite a few queer friends, it seemed. As a man who was royally connected and a friend of the King's, extremely wealthy, widely backed by high influence, he was the most powerful senior officer in the British Armed Forces since Alfred the Great.[1]

After a short stint in a theoretical sea command in the Reserve Fleet at Chatham, I asked the Director of Naval Intelligence for a job abroad as a Naval Attache. Professional suicide, I was told, but, hard to believe now, whatever the prospects, I truly did not want to be promoted.

Before leaving to take up my appointment in Yugoslavia, Bridget Coote and I married. We spent two mainly very pleasant years based on Belgrade and touring the very lovely Dalmatian coast. It was an easy way out of the Navy.

'You were too much of a rebel,' a friend of mine said in retirement. This was not entirely so. It was more than that; particularly when younger, I had been inspired by a sharp but kindly comment some years ago by the Commander of *Iron Duke*: 'For God's sake, use your bloody swede.'

And that – on the whole – was what I had tried to do – but perhaps sometimes faster than the speed of thought.

1 Lord Mountbatten obviously had a particularly great influence on his own Service To the writer, one broad and interesting outcome of this has been that the Executive (Seaman) Branch has lost its place as the privileged elite of the Navy It is novel for a disciplined organisation – Communist state to cricket club – to lack a privileged elite

APPENDIX

The following information about the U-boats sunk by HMS *Wanderer* was kindly supplied by Gordon Williamson.

U-305   Type VIIC U-boat, built by Flender-Werft, Lübeck.

Service: 8. Unterseebootsflotille, September 1942 – February 1943
                  1. Unterseebootsflotille, March 1943 – January 1944

War Voyages: 27 February 1943 – 12 April 1943
                  12 May 1943 – 1 June 1943
                  23 August 1943 – 16 October 1943
                  8 December 1943 – sunk 17 January 1944, last reported position 49.39′N–20.10′W.

Commander: Kapitänleutnant Rudolf Bahr. Born 1 April 1916. He served on *Prinz Eugen* from August 1940 to June 1941, then followed U-boat training. He served as First Officer on *U-69* from October 1941 to June 1942. After more training, he was given command of *U-305*. He held the Iron Cross 1st and 2nd Class and was awarded the Deutsche Kreuz in Gold two days before his death.

Insignia of U-305.

U-390	Type VIIC U-boat, built by Howaldts-Werke, Kiel.
Service	5. Unterseebootsflotille, March 1943 – November 1943
	7. Unterseebootsflotille, December 1943 – July 1944
War Voyages	2 December 1943 – 13 February 1944
	21 June 1944 – 24 June 1944
	27 June 1944 – sunk 5 July 1944, last reported position Seine Bay.
Commander:	Oberleutnant Heinz Geissler. Born 29 August 1917. After U-boat training, he served on *U-376* as First Officer. After further training, he was given command of *U-390*. No decorations are recorded but he probably held Iron Cross 1st and 2nd Class.

U-523	Type IXC U-boat, built by Deutsche-Werft, Hamburg.
Service:	4. Unterseebootsflotille June 1942 – January 1943
	10. Unterseebootsflotille February 1943 – August 1943
War Voyages:	9 February 1943 – 16 April 1943
	22 May 1943 – 26 May 1943
	16 August 1943 – sunk 25 August 1943
Commander:	Kapitänleutnant Werner Pietzsch. Served on *U-123* as First Officer from May 1941 to March 1942. He served with U-boat 'Ace' Reinhard Hardegen. Pietzsch survived the sinking of *U-523* and was captured along with thirty-seven of the crew.

BIBLIOGRAPHY

Eira, Alan. *Invergordon Mutiny*. Routledge and Kegan Paul. London.

Macintyre, Donald. *Battle of the Atlantic*. Batsford Press. London.

Peillard, Leonce. *U-boats to the Rescue*. Jonathan Cape. London.

Röhwer, Jürgen. *The Critical Convoy Battles of March 1943*. Ian Allan. Shepperton.

Roskill, DSC, RN, Captain Stephen. *The War at Sea* Vols I, II and III. HM Stationery Office. London.

Shirer, William L. *The Rise and Fall of the Third Reich*. Secker and Warburg. London, 1959; The Reprint Society, 1962.

Vian, P.L. *Action This Day*. Frederick Muller. London.

Warner, Oliver. *Cunningham of Hyndhope*. John Murray. London.

Wheeler-Bennet, John. *King George VI*. MacMillan. London, 1958; The Reprint Society, 1959.

Wincott, Len. *Invergordon Mutineer*. Weidenfeld. London.

ACKNOWLEDGEMENTS

The Naval Historical Branch of the Ministry of Defence, under the direction of Mr David Brown and his Assistant, Lieutenant Commander Wilson, have been most helpful in supplying me with information and verification of dates. I am also very grateful to the Imperial War Museum and to Commander J.P. Mosse, DSC, RN, for their assistance. Other sources of information have been acknowledged in the bibliography. All accounts of events and opinions expressed are, however, entirely my own. I am grateful to John Murray (Publishers) Ltd for permission to quote a short passage from *Cunningham of Hyndhope* by Oliver Warner.

I am greatly indebted to Ria Bennett for all the hard, effective work and useful suggestions in getting the manuscript typed up – and to her husband Eric for his background support. Dr Sidney Fuller has been most generous in allowing me to use his photographs and, in general, Alec Lumsden has given valuable help over photographs, while Commander Richard Compton-Hall, MBE, has helped greatly with the nuts-and-bolts of presentation.

To my elderly mates in the motor boat *Melion* syndicate, four of us aggregating over three hundred years (not to mention the lad of just over sixty), I owe apologies for sometimes being absent, while scribbling, from place of duty, namely fishing boat's crew.

Particularly to my wife, Bridget, I owe much – especially for her tolerance while the manuscript had occupied too much time and space around the house.

INDEX

Numbers in *italics* refer to the black and white plates.
Ranks of titles in parentheses are those ultimately attained.